Rail Network Design and Planning

Steven Boldeman

© Dolans Publishing

Copyright Notice
All rights reserved. This work is copyright. No part of this work may be reproduced, stored in a retrieval system, or transmitted in any form or by any means with the prior written permission of the publisher. Except as permitted under the Copyright Act 1968, for example, any fair dealing for the purposes of private study, research, criticism, or review, subject to certain limitations. These limitations include restricting the copying to a maximum of one chapter or 10% of this book, whichever is greater.

National Library of Australia Cataloguing-in-Publication Data
Creator: Boldeman, Steven Author
Title: Rail Network Design and Planning
ISBN: 978-0-6483093-3-8

Subjects – Railroads – Planning
Transportation – Planning
Transportation - Australia

Dolans Publishing

For Vivian

Table of Contents

Chapter 1 Introduction 1
Chapter 2 Describing a Rail System 2
    Number of passengers per day 2
    Route Length 2
    Number of Stations 5
    Traffic Type 5
    Power Supply 6
    Gauge 7
    Number of Lines 8
Chapter 3 Types of Passenger Rail Systems 11
    Light Rail Systems 14
    Heavy Rail 29
    Other Rail Systems 46
Chapter 4 Overview of Rail Infrastructure 57
    Track 57
    Signalling 66
    Electrical (Traction systems) 75
    Tunnels 81
    Bridges 87
    Road and Pedestrian Level Crossings 89
    Control Systems 92
Chapter 5 Rail System Drawing and Configuration 97
    Passenger Orientated Rail Drawings 98
    Geographically Correct Maps 103
    Detailed Drawing of Rail Systems 104
Chapter 6 Stations 117
    Styles and Configurations of Stations 118
    Straight and Curved Platforms 125
    Terminal Stations 128
    Interchange Stations 129
    Components of a Station 131
    Access in and out of Stations 140
    Light Rail Stations 143
    Network Design around Stations 146
Chapter 7 Structure/Loading Gauge, Geometry, Heights and Grades 151
    Loading and Structure Gauge 151

Superelevation (Cant) *158*
Platform Heights *158*
Grades *161*

Chapter 8 Network Design 166

Introduction *166*
Avoiding Mistakes with Network Design *168*
A Standard Rail System for Large Cities *169*
Some Examples of Network Design – Multiple Lines *183*
Rail Systems and Connections to HSR *196*

Chapter 9 The Kinematics of Train Movement and other useful equations 199

Chapter 10 Stabling 213

The Tidal Nature of Commuter Services *219*
Well designed stabling *220*
Different Configurations of Stabling *221*
Stabling of Freight *224*

Chapter 11 Types of Transport Projects 228

Chapter 12 The Process of Designing a Rail Network 240

Chapter 13 Measuring Success and KPIs for Rail Systems 253

Chapter 14 Keeping Costs Down 270

Introduction *270*
Strategies to Reduce Costs *270*

Chapter 1 Introduction

Rail systems have seen a tremendous upsurge in interest and construction in the last 10 to 20 years. Across the world many counties are in the process of building many new rail lines. Rail is considered to be something that industrialised nations need, and modern rail systems are seen as a strong indicator of the health and well being of the economy in a country.

Rail systems are composed of simple elements, and yet combined can become very complex. The choice of the right elements for the right situation is the focus of this book.

This book is no more than a basic introduction to a very large area of rail network design. A number of different scenarios are discussed for what makes a good and bad rail system.

This book explains the equations of movement that can be used to describe the movement of trains. These equations can be used to understand and estimate how long trains take to travel specific distances under certain conditions.

Structure and loading gauge is very important for the design of any rail system. These parameters play a powerful role in the design and management of any rail system.

And of course no book on rail would be complete without a discussion of rail stations. For any passenger rail system, stations are a very central part of the system, and is the place where passengers board and alight. Stations are the focus for a variety of different engineering systems, such as ticketing, passenger information, and fire and safety systems. Stations are discussed in detail.

Chapter 2 Describing a Rail System

The type of rail infrastructure used for any rail system depends on the nature of the rail system. Rail systems come in a variety of different forms, and the rail mode determines the type of infrastructure installed, and how much of it is installed. We cannot sensibly discuss rail transport without first identifying, broadly, the different types of rail systems and how they are described. This is the purpose of this chapter.

There are several commonly used parameters that can be used to almost completely describe a rail system and many of these are described below. Some of them are related to the size of the network, the number of people that use the system, how the system is used by its passengers, and some other useful information.

Number of passengers per day

The size of any rail system is often judged in terms of the number of trips per day. A rail system that moves 10,000 per day is dramatically different to one that moves 1 million per day. Small rail systems can have a lot less infrastructure, compared to a large system that might move 3 million per day.

An alternative name for trips is boardings.

Below is a general guide as to the size of a rail system, and whether it is large or small.

Sizes of rail systems – Number of Passengers		
Trips per day	**Description**	**Comments**
<10,000	Very small	Tourist trains, some tram systems, a small light rail system, an APM in an airport
10,000 to 100,000	Small	High speed rail, most commuter rail systems, small to medium light rail systems
100,000 to 1,000,000	Medium sized	Metros with 2 or 3 lines, large light rail systems, large

Sizes of rail systems – Number of Passengers		
Trips per day	**Description**	**Comments**
		commuter systems
> 1,000,000	Large	Very large commuter systems, some metros in big cities. No light rail or high speed rail systems move this number of people, nor monorails

Rail as a transport system is capable of moving very large numbers of people. Buses may only move small numbers in comparison, as a reasonable sized bus may move 60 to 100 people, and a commuter train may move a thousand. One of the great advantages or rail systems is the ability to move large numbers of people. A BRT (Bus Rapid Transit) system that has 20 buses per hour, will only move between 1200 to 2000 people per hour for one line in any one direction, and for rail transport this would be considered a very low number. Even the largest BRT systems are small in comparison to a moderately sized rail system.

Route Length

The route length of a rail system is an important metric. Rail systems can be very small, but can also be very effective. A short length system can move very large numbers of people, especially if it is a metro, even it is quite small. Tram and light rail systems often have a very low number of kilometres of route length, whereas a regional rail system can be extremely large.

Route length is normally measured in kilometres, unless it's in North America or the UK. Care needs to be taken in not confusing route length with track length. The route is the rail corridor where the tracks pass through, and there can be more than one track in any rail corridor. Some rail corridors have many tracks, and up to six is quite common, and some places there are more. There are also some places where trains are stored, and this is called stabling. When counting track length, stabling and marshalling yards can add a lot of kilometres, but for route length add very little.

Describing a Rail System Page 4

The table below shows how many route kilometres constitute a large or small system. Again, these numbers are just a guide, and are included to give the reader some sense of what a large or small system looks like.

Route kilometres		
Length	**Size**	**Comments**
< 10 kms	Tiny	One metro line, tourist railway, monorail, airport system
10 – 30 kms	Very small	One or two metro lines, mostly removed legacy tram systems
30 – 100 kms	Small	Many metro systems, many light rail systems, small commuter rail systems, no high speed rail
100 – 500 kms	Medium	Very large tram or light rail systems, commuter rail systems, smaller high speed rail systems
500 – 5000 kms	Large	Large commuter or high speed rail systems, no metros, light rail, monorails nor trams in this category
> 5000 kms	Extremely large	National rail systems, extensive regional train system

What is large for one system can be small for another. High speed rail systems tend to be large, hundreds of kilometres at least, whereas metros are far smaller.

Number of Stations

The number of stations is a key measure for any rail system. The number can vary enormously, as high speed rail systems may have only a tiny number of stations, for example the high speed rail system in Taiwan only has 8 stations. On the other hand, even small tram or light rail systems can have very large numbers of stations, as every street corner can serve as a station. Tram stops are often only 500 metres apart, and a stop on one side in one direction does not mean that there is a matching tram stop on the other side/direction. A tram system of 10 kilometres may have 20 stations. In a tram system there can be large number of stops.

Even for heavy rail, it is not always clear what constitutes a station for counting purposes. Some stations are only opened at certain times of the year, or for special events. Others, especially ones for horse racing or stadia, are only opened when an event is on. There are also small stations where trains do not ordinarily stop, and sometimes these are called halts. A halt is a stop where passengers need to ask rail staff for the train to stop, otherwise the train does not stop. Passengers who need to board a train from a halt need to signal to the driver to stop, and with some luck, this will happen.

Despite the problems with counting the number of stations in a rail system, most of the time it is a very good measure of the size of a system. In most situations a station can be clearly identified from the surrounding track.

Traffic Type

Many, or maybe most, rail systems move only one type of rail traffic. For example, a tram system moves only trams, and does not move commuter or high speed rail traffic. There are always exceptions to this, and some tram systems used to move freight, and there are still a very small number that still do. The different categories of rail traffic types are:

- Light rail
- Trams
- Freight
- Metros (heavy rail)
- Commuter (heavy rail)
- High speed rail
- Others

Describing a Rail System Page 6

It should be noted that a rail system that has both passenger and freight traffic is often described as a "mixed" system.

Power Supply

The source of power for any rail system is a very important parameter for any railway. The choice of power source has a large influence on the type of infrastructure that needs to be built to support rail operations. As a rough guide, electricity is provided for rail services where there are large numbers of train movements per day, or for high speed rail. Freight, regional, overnight and commuter systems often use diesel power.

Many rail systems are powered through electricity. Steam power was once extremely common as a source of power, but has fallen out of favour with its high maintenance and running costs. The trend away from steam and to diesel and electric power took decades, and by the mid 70s most of the steam locomotives had been removed, although in some parts of the world continued to be used for another 10 years or so. Steam locomotives now are only used on tourist lines.

There are other methods of propulsion other than steam, electricity and diesel power. An extremely small number of rail systems still use cables, where the rail vehicle grabs onto the cable and is pulled along. This type of system was once common, and cables run underneath city streets, pulled from a central point called a powerhouse. One of the last remaining cable car systems is in San Francisco, and this system is still manual, so a tram employee (called the gripman) needs to apply a clamp to the cable to get the street car to move.

Most trains are diesel or electric, although there are some tourist trains that are steam powered. Diesel systems use diesel fuel to move trains, and electric systems use power generated far away at a power generator to move. Electric systems can be divided into a number of smaller categories, and these are based on the type of electrical power provided. Each rail system can be identified as using one or more power systems that are typically used in a rail system. Power systems are either AC (alternating current) or DC (direct current). AC is now the standard for new rail systems, although the voltages need to be higher, and in some cases this can present a safety risk, so for light rail and trams DC is still preferred. DC is the older power system that previously was commonly used, but now is being slowly replaced with more cost efficient AC power.

Also with the power system almost always a voltage is specified. Common voltages are:
- 750 volts
- 1500 volts
- 3000 volts
- 25,000 volts

The first three voltages are used for DC, and the last one for AC. There are other more unusual ones, but these are the more commonly used voltages. Specifying the power supply for an electric railway requires stating the voltage, followed by whether the power is AC or DC. So specifying a power system would be something like; 1500 Volts DC, or 25,000 Volts AC. The type of power system in use will further influence the choice of trains that are used on the system, and also may increase or decrease the costs and structure of any tunnels constructed.

Where a system has no electricity supply for traction, and there are many of these, then often the system is described as unwired. Power is needed for stations and lighting, but this may be unconnected to traction power.

Many rail systems deliver power through wires suspended over the train, and power is delivered through to the train through a structure on top of the train called a pantograph. However, another structure is also possible called a "third rail", and for this system power is delivered near the ground. This information is also included in any description of a rail system.

Gauge

The gauge of a railway is the distance between the insides of each rail. Most railways have only one gauge, although there are exceptions, such the Tokyo metro. The most common gauge, the one used in the US and for almost all high speed rail, is standard gauge, which is 1435 mm. This corresponds to 4 foot 8.5 inches. Gauges wider than this are normally described as broad gauge, and narrower than this are described as narrow gauge. Common sizes are 1067 mm (cape gauge), and 1520 mm (Russian gauge).

Gauge Distance

The gauge distance is measured from the inside of each rail to the other. This measure can change a little when the rail is worn, but for reference purposes the gauge is set for one railway (or line as the case may be).

Almost all high speed rail systems use standard gauge. Most modern installations, except where interoperability with older systems is needed, use standard gauge. Standard gauge is the most commonly used gauge, and more than 50 % of the world's railways, in terms of track length, use standard gauge. The use of non-standard gauges will impact upon rollingstock purchases and decisions.

Number of Lines

The number of lines is a useful measure for any railway. A line is a continuous length of track along which passengers can travel without alighting from a train or breaking their journey. In a metro system or a light rail system it mostly very clear how many lines exist, and where lines start and end.

Typically a system with over 6 lines would be considered large, and one with 1 or 2 lines is a small system. Some systems have over a dozen lines.

A commuter system may or may not be described in terms of the number of lines. Commuter lines can converge to a single large station, and there is often shared track where trains from different destinations share the one track. In this situation it can be very difficult to determine how many unique lines there are. In Sydney it is almost impossible to determine how many lines there are as many of the lines meet each other a large distance from the city. Alternatively, in the Go Transit system in Toronto Canada it is very clear how many lines there are because each is mostly separate from each other, and can be easily counted. Again, for a commuter system, more than 6 or 7 lines would be considered a large system.

REFERENCES

1. Zhang, Y & Yan, X & Comtois, C *Some Measures of Increasing Rail Transit Riderships: Case Studies*, Chinese Geographical Science, Volume 10, Number 1, pp 80 – 88, 2000

2. CFL, *Rapport Annuel*, 2011 (In French)

3. Metro de Porto, *Annual Report*, 2009

4. Jernbaneverket, *On Track 2010*

5. State of Florida Department of Transportation, *Central Florida Commuter Rail Transit Design Criteria*, October 2008

6. DB Netze *AG Network Statement 2014*, April 2013

7. Cheng, HY. *High Speed Rail in Taiwan: New experience and issues for future development*, Transport Policy 17 (2010) 51-63, Nov 2009

8. Chun-Hwan, K. *Transportation Revolution: The Korean High-speed Railway*, Japan Railway & Transport Review 40, March 2005

9. Texas Department of Transportation *Austin San Antonio Commuter Rail Study*, 1999

10. Metro de Porto *Annual Report 2011*, http://www.metrodoporto.pt/en/

11. Burge, P. et al Modelling Demand for Long-Distance Travel in Great Britain, www.rand.org, 2011

12. Cataldi, O. & Alexander, R. *Train control for light rail systems on shared tracks*, Railroad Conference 2001

13. Transport for London *Rail and Underground Annual Benchmarking Report* June 2012

14. Prescott, T. *A Practical Scheme for Light Rail Extensions in Inner Sydney*, Transit Australia, vol 63 no 11, 323 – 330 Nov 2008

Chapter 3 Types of Passenger Rail Systems

There are many different types of rail systems, and each has advantages and disadvantages. When one thinks of rail images come to mind maybe of high speed trains or of metros running underneath major cities. The range of different types of rail systems is actually quite large, and the reader might be surprised as to the variety and large differences between them all.

The distinctions between the different types of rail systems is not always clear. Whilst it is easy to distinguish between a freight system, and a commuter one, things are not always so easy. For example, the distinction between a light rail system and a tram system is particularly difficult, as the different types of systems in many cases are quite different, but in others extremely similar. Whilst some tram systems, especially historical ones, appear different to light rail, more modern trams are almost indistinguishable. As such separating out the different types is not an easy task, and an attempt is made here to classify the different rail systems, and it is not possible to consider all the different variations, but nonetheless an attempt must be made.

Rail systems fall under larger headings, and one of those is light rail. This is particularly problematic, as light rail is both a heading and a rail type. This makes things extremely confusing, as the term can refer to either a whole group of different systems, or one particular type of system. The convention that has been adopted to manage this crazy and almost impossible situation in this book is to describe the group of rail systems that fall under the heading of light rail as "light rail systems" and the specific system referred to as light rail as just "light rail".

The choice has been made in this book to separate all the smaller rail systems into the heading of "light rail system". There is no real definition of what this means, especially as a heading, but it is a term commonly used in Australia. It seems clear when looking at the different systems which is a light one, and which heavy, but it is difficult to provide a clear definition. Some of the characteristics of a light rail system include:
- Trains are narrower
- Trains are shorter
- Trains move at slower speeds
- The capacity of any rail lines is lower
- They are physically lighter, and the maximum axle loads can be quite low

- Stations are smaller
- They tend not to have large complex junctions
- They are often much cheaper to construct
- Each individual rail line is quite short, and a maximum line length would be about 30 to 40 kilometres. In contrast high speed rail lines can be hundreds or even thousands of kilometres long.

Alternatively, some light rail systems can be quite expensive to build, especially where the frequency of trains is very high, and the system is driverless. Light rail systems with high capacities can resemble much larger rail systems, and the number of people moved can be reasonably large, ie, one hundred or two hundred thousand per day. The platform heights for light rail systems can also be very low, but in some systems platform height is the same as a heavy rail system.

It is also possible to operate two separate rail systems over the same tracks. Freight trains often share their tracks with regional or commuter trains, and more rarely light rail. Light rail trains can share tracks with heavy rail, so that the infrastructure supports two or potentially more rail systems at the same time. This situation would typically be described as a "mixed system", with at least two different rail systems.

Freight systems can be described as either light rail system or heavy rail classification, and particularly serious rail freight systems, with high axle loads are called "heavy haul".

To the casual observer the type of rollingstock is often the best way to determine which type of rail system is which. Rollingstock has been designed for each different system, and they look different, so this is quite a good way to start. There are however lots of other system parameters that are also relevant, and the top speed is one, and the number of passengers moved is another.

One of the key distinctions between railways is whether they are "at grade" or "grade separated". Grade separation refers to putting different types of transport modes, or even the same ones, at different heights so that traffic on each can pass one another easily, without having to wait for the traffic to clear an intersection before proceeding. The development of light rail, where trains are often at the same grade as road traffic, has changed the perception that grade separation is always necessary for a rail system.

The photo below shows two grade separated metro lines. This design allows one train to pass over another. For high frequency rail services grade separation is the key to ensuring that trains move smoothly. Where one of the lines crosses another at a junction, the junction may be described as a "flying junction" (as it is in this case in Singapore).

Elevated Metros

Another important distinction between rail systems is the ability of some rail vehicles to have articulation. Articulation is the presence of a joint in a vehicle, so that the vehicle can "bend" around corners and curves. Trucks and buses can be articulated, and rail vehicles also. Light rail vehicles may be articulated, to allow them to turn around very sharp curves. Whilst in the past the lack of articulation in trams was an easy way to separate these vehicles from light rail vehicles, some modern trams are articulated as well.

It is sometimes possible to blend two different types of system together. There is no rule that dictates that a rail system must have characteristics from only one type of system, and hybrid systems have been created. Possibly the best known hybrid is the tram-train system that was pioneered in Karlsruhe city in Germany, where trams were re-designed to operate with higher speeds on main line tracks.

Light Rail Systems

Trams

Trams are a very old form of rail transportation. They evolved from the horse drawn carriages that were common in large cities in the mid nineteenth centuries, and were initially steam powered (or pulled by cables). Almost all remaining tram systems in the world are now powered through overhead power lines, where power is supplied from a remote generator to the tram.

Trams are called streetcars in the US and Canada. They are still used in parts of North America, including San Francisco, and Toronto. Trams can be used as simple tourist railways, as they are slow, but a good way of seeing different parts of the centre of a city. Trams may be free in some parts of the centre of large cities, and can be a very pleasing experience to travel on.

Trams were an extremely common system in the Western world until the 1950's, when governments started to remove them. Before their removal they were a central part of the transport for the public for many cities, and some of the tram systems removed were extremely large. The tram system in London was particularly large, and was dismantled with surprising haste in the late 40's and early 50's. Now tram systems are something of a rarity, and very few cities have any kind of remaining tram system. This was particularly the case in the US and Canada, where almost all the old tram systems were removed. Only Toronto and New Orleans operate trams systems that resemble what they were 70 years ago.

In Australia, and the Asia Pacific, the only significant remaining tram system is the one in Melbourne, although there is a much smaller system in Hong Kong that continues to operate for over 100 years. By route kilometres it is the largest remaining tram system in the world, although in the past there were systems that were much larger. The now dismantled system in Sydney was much larger than the one in Melbourne, but has been entirely removed.

Tram systems are rarely double decker (or bi-level) Trams are usually quite narrow, and it is challenging to construct a double decker tram that is both stable and comfortable to use. The trams in Hong Kong are a very rare example of bi-level tram, and offer a quite rough ride.

It is important to distinguish between light rail and tram systems. This distinction is often very difficult to make, but there are significant differences. Light rail is often seen as the logical evolution of tram systems, as light rail is capable of moving more people faster than tram systems. In this book light rail and tram systems are treated as being quite different. Light rail is often contained in separate rights-of way from road traffic, but can have grade separation as well. Light rail vehicles are also longer than trams, wider, and capable of higher speeds and carrying more passengers. Perhaps the most significant difference between trams and light rail vehicles is that trams are have hard chassis with no articulation, and light rail vehicles are longer and can have many articulated sections. Having said that, many trams are now also articulated.

Trams owe their popularity, and demise, to where they operate. They operate down the centre of streets in the middle of major cities, in what in Australia we would call the CBD, but in the US would be described as downtown. They are very slow, but are often filled to capacity. This should be contrasted to the situation with light rail, where trains often run on grade separated tracks, or in the middle or roads where road traffic cannot intrude with their separate right of way.

Loading and unloading times on trams can be very long. As there are only a small number of entrances and exists, overcrowded trams can be very slow in moving off from one stop to the next. Trams are not a very effective mass transit system, for moving large numbers of passengers. They are really too small to move millions of people per day, and are better suited for applications where the number of people moved is modest.

Trams are at the same grade as road traffic, and so collisions between trams and cars are possible, and even common. In one year in Melbourne there were over 1000 collisions between trams and road vehicles. Trams need to be strong enough to withstand a collision with a road vehicle from almost any direction. Whilst the collision between any train and road vehicle is serious, the collision of a heavy rail train and a road vehicle can be catastrophic.

The main differences between light rail and trams are:
- Trams are much shorter than light rail vehicles
- Trams travel down the middle of roads in the centre of cities, something that is often described as being "at-grade", and do not have a separate right of way
- Trams are not connected together

- Trams make a large number of very frequent stops
- Trams are often 2.45 metres wide, whereas light rail is often 2.65 metres wide

Very old trams often look like this one below. This is a W class heritage tram from Melbourne. Note the shape and structure, and that passengers need to step up from the ground to get into the tram. It is also very short, and is only 14 metres in length. It is also rigid, so that there is no articulated section where the tram can bend around corners.

Melbourne W Class tram

Notice that the tram stop has protection for passengers. Passengers wait alongside the fencing, protecting them from road traffic. The gap between the tram and the fence is quite narrow, but this situation is far preferable than having people wait on the side of the road and cross in front of traffic to reach the tram.

The tram shown below is also in Melbourne and was built in the 80's and 90's. It is not single body like the W class, and is articulated to allow it to pass through tight curves. This tram still has high floors, but looks more like a conventional light rail vehicle than older trams. In Melbourne this type of tram is known as a B class tram.

Melbourne B Class Tram

This is a tram stopped on Brunswick St in Melbourne. Notice that there is no dedicated tram stop in the middle of the road, and passengers must cross the road from the kerb to reach the tram. Cars are expected to stop before the end of the tram to allow people to board the tram. This situation, very common in a large legacy tram system like Melbourne, is probably mostly unacceptable in any modern tram system.

It was a common feature of trams that passengers had to step up into the tram and this was a major problem for people with disabilities. There has been a major design effort since the 90's to reduce the height of the floor on trams to make them more accessible for wheelchair bound passengers and others who might struggle to climb the stairs. Trams, and light rail, can be classified as ultra low floor, low floor, or high floor. Whilst the low floor design is popular with passengers, maintenance costs are higher. Ultra-low floor trams and light rail vehicles have been plagued with numerous engineering problems, cracked structures and shells, although things do seem to be getting better for this technology.

High Floor Tram

Passengers boarding this tram will need to climb from the lowest step to the highest. The tram above is considered to be high floor, as for the purposes of determining if this vehicle is low or high floor, it's high floor because this calculation is made from the ground to the floor of the tram where people are sitting, not to the first step.

Low floor trams and light rail vehicles are typically 300 to 350 mm from the ground to the floor of the tram. Ultra low floor trams that distance can be even lower, even as low as 180 mm. High floor trams the distance is often 550 mm or even more. This distance can be reduced by elevating the surface of the road or sidewalk.

It should be noted that many trams and light rail vehicles which are low floor are not consistent height throughout the entire vehicle. The floor above the bogies may be raised, so that passengers moving through the tram will need to walk up and down steps to get from one end to another. This is undesirable from the perspective of passengers with disabilities, but better than having a high floor where disabled passengers can't get on at all. Where the tram is only partly low floor, passengers with limited mobility will need to stay near the doors, as they can't move up and down throughout the steps that are in the vehicle.

The percentage of floor area that is low floor is an important percentage for any tram or light rail vehicle. A typical number seems to be about 70%, although the number can be lower than 50% or up to 100%. This figure is important in purchasing any tram or light rail vehicle.

Given the obvious convenience of low floor trams, why was anything built with a higher floor? Surely it made more sense to design all the trams and light rail vehicles with a low floor? The answer to this is that it was only recently that the technology was available to build a successful a low floor tram. High floor rail vehicles structurally stronger, and trains with higher floors are stronger than those with lower floors. So very long trains, and definitely those over 100 metres in length, will need to have high floors. Even comparatively short trains, such as the DLR or the Bangkok Skytrain, which are only 60 to 80 metres in length have quite high platforms, as it is easier to design trains with higher floors. Rollingstock manufacturers are designing stronger and stronger vehicles, which can combine low floors with longer trains, but there are still limits on the length of these trains.

Note the significant differences between this tram, and the ones above, it has a much lower floor, is articulated in several places, and looks a bit "space age". This particular tram had very few seats, and most of the space inside was for standing passengers. It is also 100% low floor, and there were no steps other than the one into the tram.

Low Floor Tram

The vehicle in the photo above is a good example of rail vehicles that can lie between light rail and trams. Given where the vehicle operates, and its width, and the average speed, its probably best to consider this vehicle operating as a tram, even though there are signs and advertisements throughout Melbourne describing this vehicle as light rail.

The photo below shows tram tracks running down Bridge St in Melbourne. Notice that the street is very wide and that trams and road vehicles have a separated right of way. Trams are free of interference from road traffic, and most of the system in Melbourne is like this. This good design is a key reason why the tram system in Melbourne was able to survive, and it's crucially important for any new tram system to be separated from road traffic as much as possible.

Separate Right of Way for Trams

Most trams are only one level, but there are a small number of systems with double decker trams. Trams in Hong Kong are double deckers. This system is a very old system, and operates wooden double decker trams with two sets of stairs at either end of the tram. There is not much suspension, and it's a very bumpy ride. The cost of a ride is very low, somewhere around 40 US cents (as of 2012), and it's extremely heavily used. These trams operate at amazingly frequent intervals, and there are hundreds of trams in use at any one time.

Double Decker Tram in Hong Kong

The tram system in Hong Kong seems a bit neglected, and there were and still are a lot of ways to improve it. One very significant problem was that tram stops were often not located at traffic lights, but 10 to 30 metres before an intersection. One result of this is that trams stop to let people out, then travel a short distance to the traffic lights, and then stop again. Tram stops should be located at traffic lights, so that when stopped at the lights people can still board the tram, and the tram does not need to accelerate and then stop at the traffic lights.

A modern trend has been to install computer control over traffic lights so that trams get priority. Infrastructure is installed to detect the presence of any tram, and then change the lights to allow the tram to proceed sooner than the normal sequencing of the lights would allow. This situation is particularly common for light rail, where the number of road crossings is much lower than for trams, and the intention is to get the train moving as fast as possible. So doing can substantially increase the average speed of trams, and this is a good way to improve the quality of the system.

An interesting feature of tram systems, and this is especially true for Melbourne, is that often tram stops are marked only with sign, and nothing more. Tram stops are not really stations, and are very low key, and those new to an area with trams may not even notice that the tram stop is there. Stations for other types of rail systems, even light rail, are much larger and more expensive to build.

As a guide for the design of new tram systems, it's best if:
- Trams operate on separate right of ways from road traffic
- Critical intersections are identified and equipment installed to give the tram priority over other road traffic
- Tram stops are located at traffic lights, where there are traffic lights along the tram route
- Passengers are provided with a place to stand next to where the tram will stop
- Trams should be located in central areas of cities or in places where the population density is very high.

(Classic) Light rail

Light rail is seen by many as the next evolutionary step in the development of tram systems. Light rail vehicles are usually larger and longer than trams, and several vehicles can be combined into one longer train, something that is unusual for trams. Whilst there does not seem to be any formal definition anywhere that supports this rule, it seems that light rail vehicles are normally 2.65 metres in width, which is larger than the 2.4 metres common for trams.

Light rail vehicles are designed to travel along city streets. They can climb steep grades, and turn through very tight curves, much like trams. They are a very versatile train type, and can go almost anywhere. Light rail vehicles can climb grades of 10%, and almost unthinkable grade, and far more than any other rail system other than a ratchet and pinion rail line. Light rail vehicles can also negotiate around very tight curves, and curve radii of as low as 20 or 30 metres is possible. Heavy rail is often limited in the size of the curve, and a typical lower value for the tightest curve is 200 metres.

The picture below shows the light rail vehicle moving through central Sydney. Notice that it is a larger and wider vehicle than the trams pictured above. Whilst trams are often only 25 to 40 metres in length, light rail vehicles can be much longer than that, up to 60 metres, and can be coupled together to form even longer trains. This particular light rail vehicle is not designed to be coupled with other light rail vehicles.

Light Rail in Sydney

Once again we note that light rail vehicles can operate on city streets, and building a rail line with a shared right of way with road traffic can be a very effective way to save money on construction costs. As always it is better if the rail line is separated from road traffic as this allows average speeds to be higher, as there is no need for light rail trains to stop for road traffic, although achieving this is sometimes very expensive and not economic.

It is important to distinguish between classic light rail, and an intermediate capacity metro. The DLR (Docklands Light Rail) is often classified as light rail, and it is a light rail system, but it is much more like an intermediate capacity metro, and has many of the features of one. It is not considered to be classic light rail within this book. The DLR is fully automated and there are no drivers, and it does not operate down city streets, but is fully grade separated. The DLR is a very good system, re-classifying it as an intermediate capacity metro is no insult. This type of system will be discussed further below, under the correct heading.

Light rail vehicles traditionally have drivers, important because light rail vehicles need to avoid street traffic, and collisions. At the time of writing it is not possible to design a light rail system that is able to avoid street traffic and pedestrians in all situations, so drivers are needed. Light rail vehicles are designed to be able to withstand an impact from a road vehicle, and are toughened up to resist collisions and not allow any injury to the passengers inside. This toughening can add a lot of weight to the vehicle.

Light Rail in Hong Kong

Light rail has become very popular in the US, and in Germany, although it exists in many different countries. The pictures above and below show a light rail system in Hong Kong. Note that the system used there has high platforms and vehicles are not joined (amalgamated) together to make longer trains.

One of the main attractions of light rail systems is the relatively low construction cost. Costs are lower because the light rail trains travel along city streets, and expensive tunnelling can be avoided. Light rail is also a solution where the number of passengers is not that high, and there is a need or desire to install a rail system. Heavy rail systems are excessive in many situations, and a light rail system can be a more appropriate solution. Aside from the lower construction cost, light rail is seen as a sexy and attractive looking system, and this type of rail system has proved very popular with passengers throughout the world.

An added advantage of the light rail system is its simplicity. Unlike heavy rail, which is technically very complicated, light rail is a lot simpler and easier to install and manage. Lower speeds, and the lower loads associated with smaller trains, means that the system is relatively simple to install, and the complexity associated with speed calculations and vertical curves for example is avoided.

Automated People Mover

Automated people movers (APMs) are automatic trains that are driverless, and operate on separate right of way with grade separation. They are often very small and often installed in airports, theme parks, and other large facilities. These vehicles fall within the family of light rail systems, and are common in airports in Asia. Also sometimes included in this category are larger automatic trains such as the Docklands Light Rail (DLR), which is driverless, and technically speaking an automated people mover. Larger APMs are very similar to light metros, or intermediate capacity systems, and are also discussed under that category.

The picture below shows an APM in Singapore. The vehicle is very short, and it runs on rubber tyres. It is also driverless, and moves around the small network by itself picking up and dropping off passengers. This particular system is a contained within an airport. The capacity of this system is not large, and the distances travelled are short.

An APM Vehicle in Singapore Airport (Changi)

Airports often have trains that move travellers from one terminal to another. A particular large airport may need such a system, as the distances between terminals are so large that transport is needed. These rail systems can be quite significant, and the system in Hong Kong Airport contains two short lines. The APM in Changi airport has several lines, all of them quite short. APM systems in airports are provided as a convenience for passengers, and add to the value of the airport. APMs also exist in theme parks, particular large ones such as the different Disneyland parks.

Intermediate Capacity Metros

Intermediate capacity metros are a system that is designed much like a metro system, with few seats, low headways, and many doors to allow fast and easy boarding and alighting, but much lower capacity and smaller trains. Some intermediate capacity metros are also Automated People Movers, some are not. As a group these rail lines are sometimes described as a "light metro".

What distinguishes an intermediate capacity system from a full metro is:
- Trains are less than 60-70 metres in length
- The trains narrower than full metros
- Stations are much shorter in length, therefore cheaper to build
- In some cases built with rubber tyres rather than metal wheels, although there are some full sized metros with this technology too

Intermediate capacity metros seem to be increasing in popularity, and their numbers are slowly increasing. There are a few rail systems of this type of system in Asia, and the Bangkok Skytrain is probably the best example. The picture below shows a train in the Bangkok Skytrain.

Bangkok Skytrain

There is much to recommend these systems. They are often extremely cheap to build, and well below the cost of a metro system. The Bangkok Skytrain was constructed at a cost of only $20 million per route kilometre, and amazingly low price, and this cost was achieved 2009 to 2011, relatively recently. Trains in an intermediate capacity metro are also very short, 50 to 60 metres is common, and costs are kept down so purchasing rollingstock is very cheap. Stations in an intermediate capacity metro are also short, and an 80 metre station would be considered large. As such it is easy to place stations in convenient places, as they are so short. Stations are also cheap to build.

Intermediate capacity metros would normally be classified as light rail systems. Recall with light rail systems, the lower capacity of this type of system means that the total capacity in people per hour is lower than a metro. A medium capacity system will usually have less than half the capacity of a metro, maybe even a third, and so there is a significant risk of severe overcrowding. Intermediate capacity metros often operate full, even late at night and on weekends. This type of system is attractive to use because of its cost and versatility, but is frequently overcrowded, a trade-off that is sometimes worth making.

Intermediate capacity metros are commonly installed on concrete viaducts, which makes them cheaper than tunnelled full size metros or at least in South East Asia that seems to be the case. It seems common to install this type of system in elevated viaducts, and this also reduces the cost compared to tunnelling. Intermediate capacity systems can operate at very low headways, similar to metros.

Freight Systems (Light Rail)

Freight trains are rarely small enough to be considered light rail, but in a small number of cases they do exist. Sugarcane railways are where sugarcane is transported from the farm to a sugar mill, and these freight systems are often, but not always, operated on 2 foot gauge (61 cm). This is the smallest gauge in operation in a rail system in any significant way at the time of writing of this book. The locomotives and freight wagons are much smaller than traditional freight trains, and their signalling systems are very simple indeed.

The photo below shows some wagons transporting sugar cane in Northern Queensland. Notice that the wagons are very small, and maybe only 3 to 4 metres in length. The ones in the photo below are fully loaded and on their way to the mill.

Sugar Cane Wagons

Small rail freight trains in some mines were also common, but the author is not aware of any that have continued in operation, although they were once common in Australia.

Heavy Rail

Heavy rail systems have much longer trains, move more people faster, and longer distances. It would be very surprising for a light rail system to move passengers one hundred kilometres from one large city to another. Heavy rail systems are more expensive to build, and ordinarily require a larger space (structure and loading gauge).

Metros

Metros are the mainstay of many transport systems. There are hundreds of metro systems installed around the world, and they have been installed in places such as Algiers and San Juan in Puerto Rico. Many more systems are currently being built.

The metro has become the standard for transport around large cities. The metro system forms the backbone of any transport system in many large cities, and bus lines and other forms of public transportation integrate into the rail system. The key to the success of the metro is its ability to move large numbers of people quickly and efficiently from one place to another, as well as its engineering simplicity, and relatively low cost of operation.

Metros almost always have very few seats. People need to stand most of the trip, and consequently many people can be packed into a metro. More people stand than sit, as seating takes up a lot of space. The number of people that can be moved by a large metro is extremely large, over 70 thousand pph (people per hour) in one direction, and this can be done at relatively low cost. The ability of a metro system to move such large numbers of people quickly is one of the key reasons why this system has become so successful. The cost of operating a metro system can also be low when compared to the number of people moved, and in very busy cities it may be possible to operate a passenger service at a profit, without any kind of government subsidy.

Metro trains also have a large number of doors. Metro rail carriages are never double decker (bi-level) and so can have large numbers of doors. Dwell time is an important parameter for many rail systems, and it is defined as the time a train spends at any one station waiting for passengers to alight and board. The minimisation of dwell time is critical to getting trains through a rail system quickly, and on many different types of system, especially commuter systems, the dwell time can be very long. Metros have very low dwell times because doors are numerous and people can move into the train quickly as most people stand. The low dwell time of metros is another contributor to their success.

Inside a Metro

The picture above shows a metro train in Hong Kong. As with many metro trains, there are seats along the side of the train, and none in the middle. This allows a very high concentration of people in the train.

Metro trains mostly move along a single line, starting at one end, finishing at another, and then returning along the same path. More unusually, the metro line may bifurcate, and split into two, with maybe half the trains going to one terminus, and the other half to the other. This is different from a commuter system, or a light rail system, which often has a main station where many of the services converge, and passengers can make their way from one service to another quickly and easily. Metro lines do not converge to a central terminus, and so passengers that need to use more than one line must change trains at a large interchange station. These interchange stations usually have the metro lines passing over and under one another, so that passengers need to use stairs or escalators to move up and down to get to the right platform. This is one of the main disadvantages of metro systems, but can be managed quite effectively with good station design.

Metros have high service reliabilities. Metro trains are almost always on time, mostly due to the simplicity of the system, and that metros operate grade separated from other road and rail traffic. As metros run backwards and forwards all day, from point A to B and then back again, there is very little track infrastructure needed and so there are very few engineering failures. A metro can be compared extremely favourably with commuter rail systems which are often plagued with problems and are frequently late. An on-time-running (OTR) figure of over 99% is the minimum for a properly maintained and operated metro.

Metro trains are not physically very high. Commonly 3.5 metres in height from the bottom of the wheels to the top of the roof would be considered normal for a metro train. This allows tunnelling costs to be significantly reduced, as the size of the tunnel that needs to be excavated is smaller than for commuter trains, especially double decker commuter trains.

Metros can move immense numbers of people. Most rail systems can only move 10 to 15 thousand people per hour (pph) in one direction, but metros can move 60 to 80 thousand in an hour. Some metro lines in Asia and other countries can move over 1 million passengers per day, a truly enormous figure.

Metro systems can have a powerful effect on transport within a city. A good quality metro can clear the roads and allow cars to move through cities very effectively. Even a small number of metro lines can have this effect, and 3 or 4 metro lines is usually enough for cities with even 5 to 6 million people. Hong Kong, which has 4 metro lines (as of 2017) and some other lines that are basically commuter lines, is well served. The same can be said for Taipei, where the city has effectively 3 metro lines and one medium capacity line (although they claim there are many more lines than that, essentially there are three main ones). The utility of metro lines is often very high, and even a small number can transform transport within a city.

Metros are not as suited for long distance travel. As most passengers stand, a journey that takes hours would require passengers to stand for hours, and many people can't or won't do this. High speed and regional trains are never metro trains. So the question arises as to how far passengers will be able to stand when travelling on a metro line, and whilst no one seems to have written or researched this topic, perhaps the answer should be about 1 hour.

Metro lines seem to be getting longer and longer. Traditionally metro lines where quite short in length, and lengths of 10 to 15 kilometres were common. For example, the longest line in the Paris metro is only 24 kilometres long. The author used to believe that one of the lines in Shenzhen was far too long , at 41 kilometres in length, and then another line was constructed in New Delhi that was 49 kilometres long, and another line is under construction in Malaysia that is 51 kilometres long. There is even a line being extended in Shanghai, which was completed in 2010, which is over 61 kilometres long.

The reader should remember at this point that metros typically average 35 kms/hr as an average travel speed, which can be higher or lower depending on the spacing of stations. A metro line that is 60 kilometres in length may require someone to stand for 2 hours to get from one end of the other, and even more if they need to change trains and use another rail line. Older people and those with disabilities will have difficulty in completing this type of journey, as standing for hours may be difficult or even impossible.

The picture below is of a metro station in Taipei. This type of open layout for a metro station is a little unusual. Note the platform screen doors.

A Busy Metro Station in Taiwan

Metro systems may or may not have drivers. Older systems will have drivers, but a more modern approach has been to build systems that are entirely automatic and require no drivers. As metro trains are usually captive along one line, and underground, it is relatively easy to program a computer to drive the train. Often rail staff are on board the train, and may control some aspects of the train operation such as opening and closing doors and making announcements. In this case rail staff are described as "operators" rather than drivers.

The design of stations in a metro system is very important. The large number of people present in the system, and on each train, means that it is very important to get people on and off trains quickly. The key to designing a good metro station is to allow people to move freely in both direction, and this often involves separating passengers walking through the station in different directions. The correct design of stations is very important for metro systems, as most stations are underground, and so there is a rick of fire. Also the large number of people using the system means that dwell times can be very large is the station is not designed with care.

Metros can operate at very short headways, 2 ½ minutes is common. Another common headway between successive trains is 5 minutes. This extremely high frequency of trains contributes much to the popularity and convenience of metro systems.

Commuter/Suburban rail

Commuter rail is a rail system where passengers are moved from an outlying area into the centre of a city, and then back out again. Commuter rail is often considered a rail system for working people, as most trips occur on weekdays. Commuter trips are often from suburban stations far from the centre of the city, to the business centre, and then back out again at the end of the working business day.

Commuter trips are often 1 hour or more in length. Commuter trains have lots of seats, and are not metros, so most people are not expected to stand. It is often the case that people stand on a commuter train, but often this is only for the last few stops before the train reaches the centre of the city.

Commuter trains differ significantly from metros. Commuter trains often travel at higher speeds than metros, a common maximum speed for a metro is 90 kms/hr, whereas commuter trains often reach speeds of 130 kms/hr or even faster. Commuter trains are larger, heavier, and longer and often longer than metro trains. The additional speed requires a heavier and more powerful train. Commuter trains also have extensive seating.

The train below is a commuter train in Brisbane (in Australia). This one is on an elevated concrete viaduct, and at Brisbane airport.

Commuter Train on a Viaduct in Brisbane

Commuter trains can be either single or double deck. Double deck trains are common for commuter trains, especially in Europe, and also the US and Canada. Double deck trains can be an effective way of increasing the capacity of a rail line, as more passengers can be seated for one carriage. Double deck trains are used extensively in the Sydney rail system as well.

The photo below is of a double decker train in Paris.

Parisian Double Decker Train

Commuter trains may operate on a large number of different stopping patterns. The stations that a service stops at is called the stopping pattern, and there are many different possible combinations of stopping patterns even on quite simple lines. A metro system, and light rail, trains almost always stop at every station. With any commuter line there are sometimes stations where very few people board and alight from, and so not every train needs to stop there. Commuter trains, because of the large distances they travel, will need to travel as quickly as possible, and not stopping at smaller stations can reduce the travel time. This is common with commuter systems.

The need for up to date information on a commuter line is very important. Again, as commuter services may not stop at every station, passenger information systems need to display where the train will stop, and when it will arrive at the station. As commuter systems can be very complex, and therefore difficult to understand for passenger, and trains can move in many different directions, providing prompt and accurate passenger information is very important in a commuter system, as it is in any rail system.

The photo below shows the inside of a commuter train in Brisbane. This configuration is 2 x 2, and most of the space inside the train is taken up by seating.

Inside a Single Deck Commuter Train

Commuter systems often have a large central station where all the commuter rail services converge. Easily the most famous of these is Grand Central Station in New York, which has the largest number of platforms of any station in the world (but not the largest number of passengers). Metro systems do not converge to a single station, and this is a good way of distinguishing the difference between the two different types of rail system.

Commuter rail systems often have much more rail infrastructure than metros and light rail. At the commuter main station there are many tracks that carry trains to the station, and many points to move trains to the right platforms. The infrastructure at a main station can often be very expensive to install and costly to maintain.

In a small number of commuter systems, trains carriages are split between 1st and 2nd class. Different fares are charged for each, and more comfortable seating is provided in 1st class. Hong Kong has such a commuter rail line (it's not really a commuter line, as it goes to the border with mainland China, but close enough) with two classes. Passengers in 2nd class get metro style seating, which is very limited and not comfortable at all, and in 1st there are quite "standard" fabric seating in a 2 x 2 arrangement. The fare for 1st class is double that for 2nd class.

Again, comparing commuter systems to metros, most commuter rail systems operate above ground. In the centre of the city, there are sometimes some commuter stations below ground, but most stations away from the centre of town are above ground. Commuter systems are longer and larger compared to metros, and can be over 500 routes kilometres in length. The commuter system in Sydney is over 800 route kilometres in length.

Commuter systems almost always have drivers. The long distances commuter trains travel makes automation difficult, and drivers are almost always used. There may be other staff on the train as well, for example a guard who opens and closes doors, or a ticket conductor that goes through the train and sells tickets of checks passengers have paid for tickets. Commuter trains are more difficult to drive than metros, within the rail corridor many things can happen that require intervention by a driver. There can be landslips, or animals on the track, or trespassers. Trees may fall over onto the track when winds are high.

Commuter systems may share rail tracks with freight, commuter trains operate at low frequencies and over long distances, and so it is often not economical to separate commuter lines from freight ones. Commuter lines that share tracks with freight trains as well typically have a lower capacity.

Commuter trains mostly do not have toilets, unlike regional services. Commuter trips are typically about 1 to 1.5 hours and this is considered short enough that toilets do not need to be provided.

Commuter systems can have a very low service frequency, and one train every 20 or 30 minutes or is quite common. In some systems one train every hour is considered acceptable. Passenger information becomes very important in this environment, as passengers need to plan to meet the train they need.

Regional rail

Regional rail services are those that move from a large city or town to remote or rural towns or villages. They can be, but often are not, commuter services, and regional services can have travel time of up to 3 or 4 hours. Regional services can be very infrequent, from one every half an hour to one per day. Regional services always have a driver, and maybe other staff on the train. Some regional services may have toilets, or even a buffet car where light refreshments can be ordered.

In Australia regional services often pass through areas of national park and wilderness, where there are large numbers of animals and very few people. Collisions with animals are frequent. There is often no mobile phone reception for large parts of the trip for regional services.

Sydney Regional Train

The photo above is a regional train. Note the clear differences with the other doubler decker trains displayed earlier, the much smaller doors, and the greater overall length of the carriage. Loading and unloading of passengers can be very slow for a regional train, but that doesn't necessarily matter because regional services move only moderate numbers of passengers, and the trip length is commonly 3 to 4 hours. It is preferable to design small doors because this increases the structural strength of the train. Carriages in a train designed for regional services can be very long because this reduces the overall cost of procuring the train.

Regional services can be powered by either electric power, or propelled by diesel motors. Many regional services are diesel powered, as there is relatively little rail traffic on many regional lines, and the cost of installing overhead power cannot be justified. Where trains are powered by diesel, then a refuelling depot is needed to top up trains when they run low on fuel.

The photo below was taken at Southern Cross station in Melbourne. This regional train was destined for Albury. Non-driven carriages, drawn behind a locomotive, are referred to as coaches. This configuration is often used for regional services as it is cheaper then electric multiple units (EMUs), or diesel multiple units (DMUs)

Melbourne Diesel Hauled Regional Train

Regional services may operate with very few passengers, and as such don't generate a lot of revenue. Many regional services are provided as a community service, and so are not profitable, and need government subsidies to continue to operate. The regional services that the author has seen in Asia, such as in Thailand, Taiwan China and Malaysia, and in Australia are often dirty and not really very pleasant at all, but provide a basic service to those living in remote places with small numbers of people.

High Speed rail

High speed rail (HSR) is a flashy, sleek and sexy system that is the glamorous side of rail transport. High speed rail is often defined as being any rail system where the train reaches 200 kms/hr, or 125 miles per hour.

High speed rail can be divided into two broad categories; trains/systems where trains travel at less than 250 kms/hr but over 200 kms/hr, and those that travel above that. Below 250 kms/hr, HSR trains are sometimes diesel powered, and do not have the extreme aerodynamic streamlining that gives high speed trains their futuristic look. The more sophisticated high speed rail systems all have top speeds in excess of 250 kms/hr, alternatively HSR rail vehicles that use existing lines have top speeds mostly below 250 kms/hr. Some high speed trains are designed to tilt, although most are not. At high speeds tilting as a strategy is not effective for high speed trains.

Below is a high speed train in Taiwan. High speed trains in Taiwan are based upon a Japanese design (as of 2012) and based on the 700 series Shinkansen.

Taiwan High Speed Train

High speed rail is offer a very high level of service. Its speed and convenience often contribute to this perception. The installation of high speed rail often refreshes and renews the rail system in a country or region. High speed rail sometimes codeshares with airlines, so that passengers can buy a ticket that combined flights and rail trips.

While most high speed trains are single deck, there are a small number of double deck high speed trains. The Japanese have the E4 Shinkansen, and the French have the TGV duplex, but other than those specific trains, all other high speed trains are single deck. Double deck trains have higher capacity, which can be important where route capacity is limited.

High speed trains are almost always powered through overhead power, at 25 kV AC. DC power cannot propel trains at high speeds, as high voltages are needed, and diesel trains can only reach about 250 kms/hr, with difficulty. The higher voltages are needed to drive trains to higher speeds.

High speed trains can be very comfortable. The rail infrastructure that supports the train, such as the track, sleepers and ballast, needs to be very strong and in very good condition so that trains can operate smoothly. This results in a very smooth ride quality that provides very little sensation of movement to passengers. Walking around the train is easy, because the ride is so smooth, and some high speed trains have buffet or dining cars where passengers can get meals.

It is a great achievement for a country to install a high speed rail system. Despite the volume of discussion in Australia and other countries concerning high speed rail, very few systems have been installed. There is only one small high speed line in the US, and it operates at around the 200 kms/hr mark, and so does not have the glamour of the French or Japanese systems. Even in the UK there is only one dedicated high speed rail line, which links the Chunnel to London.

Countries where there are significant high speed rail systems, in 2012, include:
- France
- Germany
- Spain
- China
- Japan
- South Korea
- Taiwan

Other countries have smaller parts of a high speed rail system, one such country is Sweden, where a lot of research has been conducted into high speed rail, despite the small size of their high speed system. The line between Moscow and St Petersburg also has some high speed trains, but the line is shared with freight, and this reduces the average speed and the route capacity.

High speed rail systems face many technical challenges. High speed trains are moving too quickly to move through curves quickly, and can only move through very high radius curves. This often means that high speed rail systems cannot move around mountains and other obstacles, so the rail line often passes through mountains and over other natural obstructions. The alignment of a high speed rail line is very inflexible, and the line can only be designed around any kind of natural barrier with great difficulty.

Tunnels present all sorts of problems for high speed trains. Tunnel design requires the consideration of air movement caused by the train as it moves through the tunnel. The pressure of the air in front of the train is higher than behind the train, and the faster the train moves the worse this problem gets. The pressure drop can cause discomfort to passengers, as the pressure inside the train will equalise with the pressure alongside the train. Rapid changes in air pressures will cause passengers to experience pain in their ears. What is commonly done is to seal the train as much as possible, but even so the seals are not perfect, so the pressure will drop in the train as it passes through a tunnel. Sealing the train can reduce the impact of pressure changes to passengers, but in particularly long tunnels the pressure drop will be significant, even in a well designed train.

High speed trains moving through tunnels can cause an effect often described as similar to sonic boom, and the boom is generated at the exit of the rail tunnel. A high speed train entering the tunnel will generate a pressure wave, which creates the sonic boom. A number of design features can be installed into tunnels to attempt to mitigate this problem, but the most effective strategy is to reduce the speed or the increase the cross-sectional area of the tunnel through which the train is moving. In many cases neither of the strategies will be available.

High speed trains in Taiwan and Japan have very interesting ticketing systems. One feature of these systems is that passengers can buy either first or second class tickets, and first class is more comfortable than second class. But the major difference with "normal" ticketing is the difference between a reserved seat and a non-reserved seat. Reserved seats are those where a seat number is allocated, and these are more expensive that non-reserved. The risk with a non-reserved ticket is that a seat is not available, and it is possible that a passenger may have to stand for part or all of their trip.

High speed rail systems may have services with different stopping patterns. All stops trains alternate with express services, and passengers will want to take the service that takes the minimum time to get to their destination. Prices can be different between HSR services with different stopping patterns, those trains with more stops are cheaper.

Given the appeal and popularity of high speed rail, it is surprising that more of these systems have not been installed. High speed rail competes effectively where the total travel time between one major city and another is 3 hours or less. High speed rail is particularly effective where the travel time is 2 hours or less. When this is so, high speed rail can be so dominant that air services between the two cities is discontinued, for example, Paris and Brussels. Where the travel time is less than 3 hours but more than 2 between cities, then air services will continue but will have a small percentage of the overall market.

Where the travel time is over 4 hours, high speed rail is no longer competitive with air travel. The trip time is simply too long. Many (or most, depending on the type of engine) planes travel at approx 850 kms/hr, less for turboprop planes, and at that speed a trip of 1000 kms is slightly over an hour. For a high speed train, for a top speed of 300 kms/hr, longer journey distances can. High speed rail will only have a small percentage of the market for trips of this length.

Long Distance Rail

One type of rail system that is often forgotten is the long distance rail system. This book uses this title for this type of rail system, but in truth there is no universally accepted definition for this type of system. This category applies for trains that travel over 5 or 6 hours to get to their destination, or even longer. In Australia the train trip from Sydney to Perth takes 3.5 days.

Long distance services are often overnight, and passengers sleep on them. More expensive tickets offer passengers a sleeper berth, and they may sleep in comfort on the train. In some cases a full bed is provided. The experience in Australia has been that sleeper berths are easily the most popular option for long distance rail, despite their additional cost, and are always booked out before other ticket classes.

Below is a photo of a travel compartment in a sleeper carriage in the long distance train that travels from Kuala Lumpur to Singapore. Long distance travel is still somewhat common in Malaysia, and sleepers are available on many night time trains. In a private room there are two bunk beds, as well as a toilet and shower.

Sleeper Compartment in Malaysia

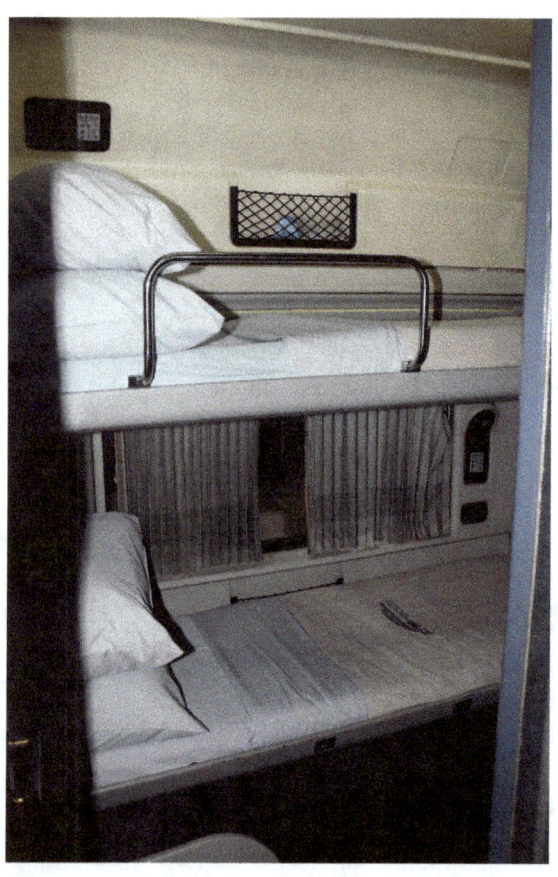

Long distance services are common in Australia, as the distances are so large. There are a number of train services where travel takes well over a day, and these trips can get very boring. The author's experience of this trips is that many of them are rather dull.

Where a rail line has not been upgraded to HSR, or even to a reasonable speed, then overnight distance trains are common. For passengers sleeping on the train makes the trip appear to pass faster, even though it is still a long trip. To justify having sleeper berths on trains, the travel time needs to be at least 7 hours, but preferably 9. Otherwise passengers will have an interrupted sleep, and arrive at their destination at an early time in the morning. For example, a train that leaves at 9pm, and takes 6 hours to reach its destination, will arrive at 3am in the morning. Unless passengers are allowed to stay and sleep in their beds then many will be unwilling to wake at this time in the morning.

Where the train trip is especially long, and the rail operator has made an attempt to upgrade the service, then sometimes the long distance trip is referred to as a rail cruise. A rail cruise can be extremely expensive, thousands of US dollars, and can be over 10 thousand US dollars for 2 people. A rail cruise is often slower than a normal long distance service, and may stop for a time in different cities, and provide tours to places of interest in the city. This kind of service is rare in Australia, but the small number of services provided are profitable, and it's a rare example of a rail company operator generating a healthy profit. In Australia a company called Great Southern Railways provides rail cruises that are very long, in some cases 21 days, and their trains travel all over Australia. These cruises are very expensive, and are more similar to ocean cruises than rail a service.

Long distance overnight trains that offer sleeper berths seem to be disappearing, especially from Europe. Only a very small number of people can be moved in a sleeper carriage, in one sleeper carriage in Malaysia, the capacity of the carriage was 12 people, a very small number. Sleeper carriages are rarely economical to operate, and the cost to passengers to have a separate cabin with beds can be very high. The role and significance of overnight travel seems to be shrinking.

Other Rail Systems

Monorails

Monorails are normally classified as a type of rail system even though monorails systems are significantly different to almost all other rail systems. Monorails were a popular transport system in the 80's but have since fallen out of favour. There are many monorail systems installed in the world, and possibly the most significant is the commuter monorail system in Tokyo, which connects Haneda airport with the rest of Tokyo city. This monorail moves more people than any other monorail in the world per day. Kuala Lumpur also has a monorail line, which is very heavily used.

Maglev systems are a type of monorail, but are discussed separately below. Maglevs differ from monorails in the way the rail vehicle is propelled.

Mumbai in India has constructed a new monorail line, although their enthusiasm for monorails seems to have waned.. Whilst monorail systems are still being built, they are mostly installed in airports, theme parks and other entertainment related venues, such as casinos and hotels. Serious commuter monorails are rare, and there may be only 20 in the entire world. Overall the experience with monorails has not been a happy one, and several monorails have been installed, only to be removed later. Bankruptcies and failed companies are common with monorail systems.

Monorails can perform very similarly to any other rail system. Rubber tyred monorails can climb grades of up to 6% and top speeds of 80 to 90 kms/hr seem common. Monorails are most comparable to intermediate capacity metros, as they travel at about the same speeds, and carry similar number of people. They also cost about the same amount of money per route kilometre. The system under construction in Mumbai has an estimated cost of only US $22 million per kilometre (2012 dollars), which is a good price, but similar to what was paid for the Skytrain in Bangkok.

The picture below is of the Kuala Lumpur monorail. The vehicle length is rather low, but it is a very effective rail system and moves large numbers of people, despite its short length.

A Monorail in Kuala Lumpur

One criticism of monorails is that the monorail itself, what the monorail vehicle runs on, is unsightly. Another way of saying the same thing is to describe the monorail as visually intrusive. This is true, although not as visually intrusive as an intermediate capacity metro, built on an elevated system.

Monorails are for all practical purposes intermediate capacity systems. The capacity of a single monorail is unlikely to be more than 500 people, which is about the limit for light rail and intermediate capacity metros. A small number of monorails are able to carry thousands of people in one train, as a full metro can.

The high frequency of failure of monorails as a system is somewhat baffling. As a transport system they are safe, and cheap to build, and operate at reasonable speeds. It is surprisingly that monorails have been so unsuccessful in so many cases. Perhaps some reasons for the many failures of monorails are:
- Monorails compete with light rail and intermediate capacity metros, such as the DLR, or the Bangkok Skytrain, and do not quite perform as well
- Monorails cannot be expanded to have the same capacity as full metros
- Monorails cannot travel large distances, as most passengers stand when travelling on a monorail
- The ride quality in a monorail is not quite as good as light rail or metros
- Many monorail systems suffered from excessive political interference, especially during the planning stage
- Many monorails had a very low design capacity, and so were unlikely to ever generate a profit
- Transport orientated development is more difficult with elevated monorail stations, as they are smaller, reducing revenue
- Monorails have no real cost advantage compared to intermediate capacity metros
- Most importantly, a power failure for a monorail can have terrible consequences, as cranes need to be employed to remove trapped passengers, unlike intermediate capacity metros, where passengers can walk to the next station

On the other hand, some of the advantages of monorails are:
- Quick to build
- Cheap
- Monorails can accept sharp curves, down to as low as 50 metres (that said, light rail vehicles can accept 15 to 25 metre curves)
- The airspace needed for monorails is smaller than for light metros

Overall, one could easily say that monorails offer no real advantages over a light metro system, and have only disadvantages, the most important of which is the inability to get passengers off a train that breaks down. It would seem reasonable to recommend that monorail systems should only be used where light rail or an intermediate capacity metro is impossible, and this would generally be rare.

Maglevs

Perhaps one of the most interesting rail systems is a technology called the "Maglev". This has been in existence since the 80's and there is constant talk of the installation of new maglev systems. At the time of writing of this book only one commercial Maglev system is in operation, and this connects Pudong airport to the Shanghai metro system. A picture of this system is below:

Shanghai Maglev

Maglev is a contraction for magnetic levitation, and the train itself does not have any wheels and does not even contact the monorail. The train floats above the monorail and, as it has no contact with any surface, can reach speeds of over 400 kms/hr.

Despite the promise of Maglev technology, in practise only one commercial system has ever been installed. There also exists a low speed Maglev system in Japan, but its top speed is very low, so the full potential of the technology has not been achieved.

The author is not convinced by the arguments for a maglev train. The major problem to be overcome is economics, and central to this is the cost of accelerating trains to speeds over 400 kms/hr. A number of high speed trains have been developped, using conventional tracks, where speeds of over 350 kms/hr have been achieved. These trains rarely operate over 300 kms/hr as the power consumption required to drive trains at any speed faster than that is very high. Power consumption seems to increase exponentially with speed, and at 400 kms/hr power consumption must be very large indeed. This problem cannot really be resolved, other than constructing a vacuum tunnel for the maglev, something that seems rather improbable.

Tilt Trains

Tilt trains are an interesting type of technology used on intercity and regional services. The train tilts so that it can go around sharp curves at a higher speed. The speed increase can be considerable, and this technology, and the equations to calculate maximum speeds.

The greater the degree of tilt, the better the train can accept sharp curves. Tilt trains have revolutionised rail travel between many different centres, and can dramatically increase higher average speeds on existing rail lines, especially where those lines contain a lot of curves.

Tilt trains are normally only single deck, and passengers must be seated. The tilting action makes standing on a tilt train a little difficult.

The photo below is of a tilt train in Taiwan and from the outside it does not really appear any different to any other trains, although the outer shape is slightly different from other trains.

A Tilt Train in Taiwan

Tilting trains are usually regional or intercity trains, that travel from one city to another. It would be strange to use a tilt train within one large city, as a substitute for a metro or commuter system.

Tourist Trains

A tourist train is a train which provides an enjoyable experience to passengers, and may or may not connect important destinations that passengers may want to go. Most tourist railways go nowhere important, and the experience is the reason why the service is popular. Alternatively, a tourist railway may connect tourist destinations to the main rail system.

Tourist railways often use old rollingstock, which is custom made for that particular application. The structure of the rollingstock may be very unusual, and may not even afford protection from rain or wind. Some tourist railways connect hard to reach places, and the rollingstock required to achieve this can be very distinctive.

The picture below shows two different types of tourist tram in the town of Christchurch in New Zealand. On the left is the tourist tram that runs around the city, which is an old style tram that is rigid and very short. On the right is a tram that has been converted to be used as a restaurant.

Tourist Trams in Christchurch

Tourist railways can be divided into several categories:
- Railways through parklands, mountains, and other areas which are very scenic and the entire trip might last 1 to 2 hours. The Kuranda railway form Cairns in Australia up into the nearby mountains is probably the best known example of this type of train in Australia, but there are several others.
- Rail cruises, where the rail trip might take weeks, or in some cases, months. The cost of the ticket is extremely high, potentially thousands or tens of thousands of US dollars, for one ticket. Food is provided, and the quality can be very high. Passengers will sleep on the train. The Indian Pacific in Australia is an example of this type of rail service.
- Trains that are mostly "normal", but are richly decorated, and connect the rail system to an area which tourists commonly visit. The commuter train in Paris to the palace at Versailles is a good example of this kind of train, other examples include the Disneyland train in Hong Kong, or the Xinbeitou train in Taipei to the hots springs resorts. These trains are often visually impressive and richly appointed. There are no trains like this in Australia

- Old heritage trams that move throughout cities. These trams are often 100 years old, and have a lot of charm. The distance moved might be quite small. The best known example of this type of tram is the San Francisco heritage tram.
- Trains, that are more like trolleys, that climb steep inclines, and connect major destinations to carparks or other access points to a high value destination. This type of tourist railway is relatively common, and Perhaps the best known of these is the Peak Tram in Hong Kong, which connects the Peak on Hong Kong Island with the rest of the island. This type of tourist railway is sometimes used to connect mountains and ski fields to access points.
- Small railways, sometimes monorails, contained entirely in amusement parks, and are paid for an operated by the amusement park owner.

As can be seen from the list above, tourist railways are actually quite common and varied.

Tourist trains have high ticket prices, and so can operate at a profit. Passengers rarely would use a tourist railway for daily transportation.

REFERENCES

1. Zhang, Y & Yan, X & Comtois, C *Some Measures of Increasing Rail Transit Riderships: Case Studies*, Chinese Geographical Science, Volume 10, Number 1, pp 80 – 88, 2000

2. Smith K. *Alstom puts weight behind Citadis Dualis*, International Railway Journal, Feb 2010

3. ALSTOM, *AGV Full Speed Ahead into the 21st Century*, 2009, www.transport.alstom.com

4. BTS Group, *Annual Report 2009/2010* (the Bangkok Skytrain)

5. Kemp, R. *T618 – Traction Energy Metrics*, Rail Safety and Standards Board, Interfleet Technology, Dec 2007

6. Taipei Rapid Transit Corporation *2013 Annual Report*, http://english.metro.taipei/ct.asp?xItem=1056448&ctNode=70219&mp=122036

7. Dearien, J. *Ultralight Rail and Energy Use*, Encyclopaedia of Energy, Elsevier Publishing, March 2004

8. Siemens, *Siemens Velaro datasheet*, www.siemens.com/mobility

9. Fabian, J. *The Exceptional Service of Driverless Metros*, Journal of Advanced Transportation, Vol 33, No 1, pp 5-16

10. Kimijima, N. et al *New Urban Transport for Middle East Monorail System for Dubai Palm Jumeirah Transit System*, Hitachi Review Vol 59, (2010), No 1

11. IBI Group, E&N Railway Corridor Study: Analysis of Tourist Train Potential, (Date Unknown)

12. Hassan A The Role of Light Railway in Sugarcane Transport in Egypt, Infrastructure Design, Signalling and Security in Railway, Chapter 1

13. Parsons Brinkerhoff *High Speed Rail*, Network, Issue No 73, Sept 2011, http://www.pbworld.com/news/publications.aspx

14. Chun-Hwan, K. Transportation Revolution: The Korean High-speed Railway, Japan Railway & Transport Review 40, March 2005

15. Alstom Metropolis 21 st Century Metro Train Technology, http://www.alstom.com/turkey/products-and-services/-alstom-transport-turkey/rolling-stock/

16. Scomi Rail, *Monorail The Revolution of Urban Transit*, http://www.scomirail.com.my/

17. Duncan, B *The Hunter Rail Car: A versatile design solution for regional rail transport*, Australian Journal of Multi-disciplinary Engineering, Vol 7, No 2

18. Burge, P. et al Modelling Demand for Long-Distance Travel in Great Britain, www.rand.org, 2011

19. Railway Gazette *Commissioning the world's heaviest automated metro*, Metro Report 2003

20. Stadler *Electric Double-Deck train KISS*, www.stadlerrail.com

21. Transportation Research Board *Integration of Light Rail Transit into City Streets*, 1996

22. Turnbull, G. *The development and retention of Melbourne's trams and the influence of Sir Robert Risson*, ISSN 1038-7448, Working Paper No. 01/2002, Aug 2002

23. Transportation Research Board *Track Design Handbook for Light Rail Transit*, Second Edition, TCRP Report 155, 2012

24. Mora, J. *A Streetcar named Light Rail*, IEEE Spectrum Feb 1991

25. Sarunac, R. & Zeolla, N. *Structural and Crashworthiness Requirements of Light Rail Vehicles with Low-Floor Extension*, Transportation Research Circular E-C058: 9th National Light Rail Conference

26. Schroeder, M. *Developing CEM Design Standards to Improve Light Rail Vehicle Crashworthiness*, Proceedings of JRC2006 Joint Rail Conference April 2006 Atlanta

27. Daniel, L. *Light Rail Systems – Assessing Technical Feasibility*, Conference on Railway Engineering Melbourne May 2006

28. Swanson, J. & Thomes, C. *Light-Rail Transit Systems*, IEEE Vehicular Technology Magazine, June 2010

29. Transportation Research Board National Research Council *TCRP Report 2 Applicability of Low-Floor Light Rail Vehicles in North America*, 1995

30. Coifman, B. *IVHS protection at light rail grade crossings*, Proceedings of the 1995 IEEE/ASME Joint Railroad Conference, 1995

31. Swanson, J. *Light Rail Systems Without Wires*, Proceedings of the 2003 IEEE/ASME Joint Rail Conference April 2003

32. Maunsell Australia Pty Ltd, *Perth Light Rail Study*, 0284/05, August 2007

Chapter 4 Overview of Rail Infrastructure

Track

Track is the system that provides a running surface for rail wheels, and supports the rail vehicle. Track is easily one of the most important engineering systems for a railway, and is a central part of the design of any new rail system. Track is mostly standard in its design and configuration from many different railways, although there are some different types used for light rail systems.

Most rail systems use a fairly standard track system, with the exception of trams, monorails, and some light rail. For trams the rails are often embedded into the road, so as to allow road vehicles to pass over the rails as well as trams. Rails for trams have a separate and quite different design to normal rail. The shape of the rail, as well as the system by which the rail is held in place, is quite different.

Rails are made of steel. Some smaller rail systems run on concrete viaducts, but the vast majority of rail systems use steel rails. Train wheels are also often made of steel, and the behaviour of this steel to steel physical interface is very important. Surprisingly, the steel wheels of the train can often slide over the steel top surface, and when this happens the top of the rail and the wheel can be badly damaged. Care must be taken in ensuring that the wheel never slides over the rail, but rolls instead, and this requirement is central to the design of any rail system. One way to avoid this problem is to use rubber tyred trains, and this is occasionally done, such as the Montreal metro, but so doing adds a lot of cost as rubber tyres need to be constantly replaced as they wear.

Much of the track around the world is ballasted, which means the sleepers and rails sit on ballast. Ballast is made up of crushed rock, and major railways use substantial quantities of it. Sleepers sit within the ballast, and the ballast holds them in place. The major alternative to ballasted track is slab track, where the sleepers and rail sit directly on concrete. The track structure for ballasted track is shown below.

Figure 4.1 Track System

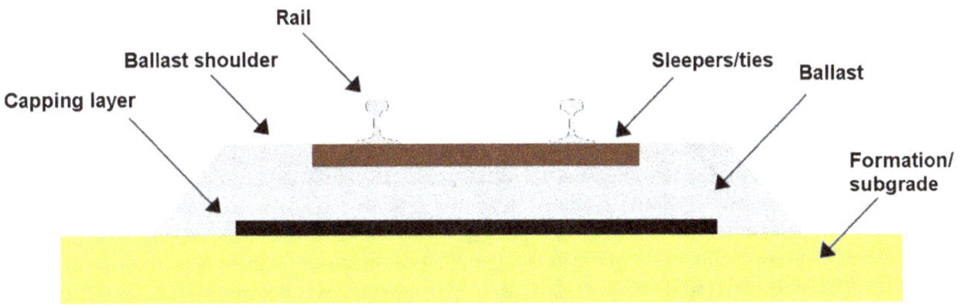

The function of each of the components of the track system is:
- The rail; supports the train, provides a running surface for the wheels of each train.
- Sleepers; which support the rails, hold the rails at a fixed distance from each other, and transfer the weight and load of the train into the ballast. Sleepers are often made of wood or concrete, although other materials such as steel or polymer are also used
- Ballast, which sits under the rails, and is made of hard crushed rock. Ballast distributes the load from trains, reducing wear, so that many trains can pass without causing serious damage to the track system. Ballast is a sacrificial item, which means it is designed to degrade over time. The degradation of ballast, and managing its replacement, is one of the key maintenance activities of any railway.
- The capping layer; which provides separation between the ballast and the subgrade. The capping layer maintains the separation between the ballast and the formation. The capping layer is sometimes replaced with geosynthetics, which is a type of textile matting, keeping the formation and ballast separate.
- Formation: which is usually the compacted ground underneath the track structure. The formation supports the track, and the condition of the formation is one of the key parameters for determining the maintenance of track.

Tracks are normally in pairs. Away from the track the ground normally has a fall to it, this is to allow for the water to run away from the track.

Figure 4.2 The Double Track System

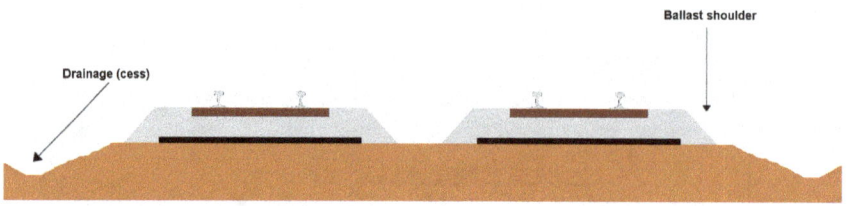

Drainage is very important for any track system. Drains need to be provided so that water can be removed when the track is rained on. Drainage, or the lack of it, can cause substantial problems in any rail system.

The rails are fastened to the sleepers with specially designed fasteners. The picture below shows the clips holding the rails to the sleepers.

Rail Track

If the reader looks carefully, notice that most of the rail is rusty, but on top of the rail there is part of it where train wheels sit when travelling over the rail. This patch of worn shiny rail is called the wear band, or the contact band, and it's important for a rail system to maintain this clear band of clean steel for signalling equipment to operate. The picture below shows it better.

Rail Fastenings

Rails are quite standard, and come in a number of sizes. Rail sizes are usually expressed in weight per unit of length, and in metric countries this is often 53 or 60 kgs per metre. Other sizes are also possible, with 40 and 50 also being common. In the large heavy haul freight networks in northern Australia, 74 kg/metre is now being used (as of 2012), which is a very large size and suitable for very heavily loaded trains with a high frequency. The imperial unit of measurement is pounds per yard, and 40 to 100 pounds per yard is common.

Increasing the size of the rail increases the size of train that can pass over the rails. For a light rail system, only a small rail is needed, and where small trains operate only small rails are needed. For larger trains, and especially freight lines, the rails need to be large to accommodate the higher weight.

Figure 4.3 The Rail Profile

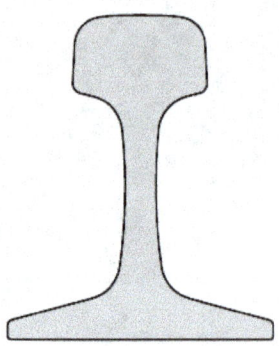

Above is a very standard profile for rails. The top is called the head of the rail. Different sizes of rail have slightly different shapes, but overall they mostly look similar to the rail shape above. Tram rails look significantly different, and monorails do not have rails, but just the one beam. The image below shows the profile of a tram rail, and it is designed to allow trains to run on it and allow road vehicles to drive over it as well.

Figure 4.4 Tram Rail Profile

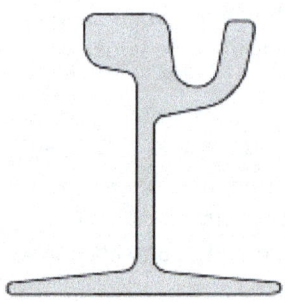

The ballast underneath the track plays an important role. The main purpose of ballast is to maintain and support the track, which is generally does well, but also to suppress vibration. Trains moving over tracks generate a lot of noise and vibration, and the ballast, surprisingly enough, suppresses this. Ballast is even used in tunnels, to suppress noise, again which is does quite well. It seems strange that ballast does this, but it does.

Ballast is made up of many small hard rocks. The amount of ballast placed under the track is not fixed, and more is usually better. Putting more ballast is expensive, as the stuff is unexpectedly expensive, and actually quite heavy. The best ballast if tough and rough, and locks together to form a tight bed for the sleepers and rails. Generally the harder the better, and quartz and granite are often considered the best materials, but many different types of rock are used. Railways often use materials that are found locally, to reduce costs and ensure the ballast does not need to be shipped very far.

Achieving the great noise reduction that ballast achieves is done through breaking down the ballast. Each time a train passes over the ballast, a small amount of it breaks into smaller pieces. Over a long period of time, such as decades, the ballast breaks down into such small pieces that most of it becomes powder. The powder intermixed with the rocky ballast is often described as fines. Once the ballast is full of fines it needs to be either cleaned, or entirely replaced, and both of these options are not cheap. Also, the track will be unable to hold track geometry, and this can be a real problem for high speed track where maintaining good track geometry is quite important.

So in summary ballast is a sacrificial item. This means that it is designed to be destroyed, which on most tracks it will be sooner or later. As ballast degrades, it gets smaller, and so the track starts to sink. Over a period of time the track can sink up to 200 mm, and if this occurs at a platform, train floors will be lower than the platform. For maintenance, railways often top up ballast as it degrades.

Ballast maintenance drives a very large part of the maintenance for a rail system. There is much to be said about what type of ballast to install, when to clean it, and when to replace it. These decisions are important for the maintenance of a rail system, and a good rail maintenance organisation will carefully consider how to make these decisions. For the purposes of rail transport planning, the choice of ballast, or even if it is to be used, can influence the way services are provided to customers. This very detailed and interesting topic is unfortunately a bit too long to be fully explained here; one of the many compromises needed to complete this book and not let it get too long. But to provide a very quick summary:
- Better quality ballast costs more, and degrades more slowly. Reducing the maintenance can sometimes mean spending more on the ballast when it is purchased
- Better quality ballast provides more track stability and the geometry degrades more slowly

- Providing more ballast when the track is installed, or deeper ballast, allows the load from trains to be spread more evenly and the ballast will degrade more slowly. An alternative is to use lighter trains, or a lower frequency of service
- The geometry requirements for high speed rail are very high, and so using ballast means that track geometry will need to be constantly checked

Below is a very simple illustration of how ballast degrades and its effect on track geometry. The diagram below looks at track side on, so we can see what happens when ballast degrades.

Figure 4.5 Track in Good Condition

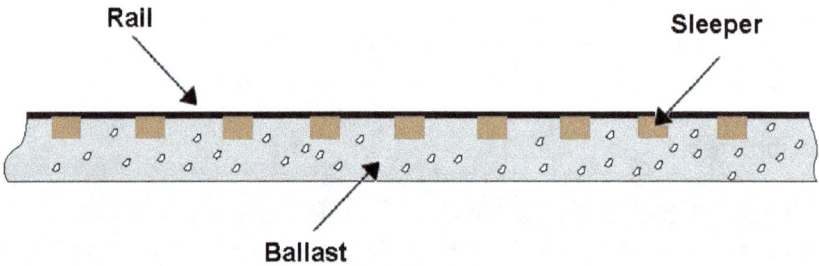

The track above is nice and flat and will provide a lovely smooth running surface for trains. Once the track has been used for a few years, and depending on a few things like the type of traffic, how much of it there is, and the amount of rainfall and the quality of the drainage, then the track will start to sink. When it sinks then it will start to look something like what is drawn below:

Figure 4.6 Degraded Track

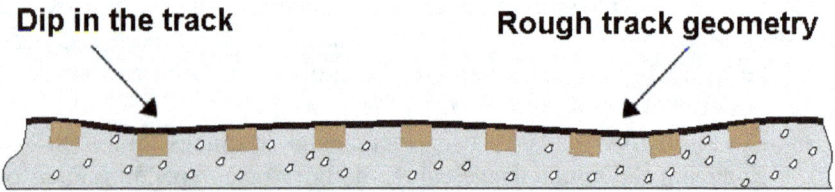

Again, the overall mechanics of track degradation have been heavily simplified here. There are a number of other track geometry parameters, and these also degrade, and need to be checked and measured by qualified maintenance personnel. Despite this, what is shown above is the most common cause of track geometry problems, and the one that usually determines much of the maintenance spending.

The degradation of ballast is a real problem for station design. It needs to be accounted for, and the track and rail position "moves around". This presents many problems, the most important of which, is that the platform gap needs to be increased in size. In some cases the platform gap is enormous, and this can be a real problem for people with disabilities.

The photo below is of tram tracks in Hong Kong that have been uncovered during maintenance work. Rarely is there any ballast for tram tracks, and as can be seen from the photo below the tracks are embedded into the road, and surrounded in bitumen. This type of systems does not allow the noise suppression that normally comes with using ballast, especially at joins, ie, where two rails are joined together.

Uncovered Tram Tracks in Hong Kong

So why is more slab track not used? Slab track, or putting the rails and sleepers onto concrete, seems to eliminate many of the problems associated with ballast. Ballast is expensive, and needs to be replaced after it has degraded. When it sinks it creates all sorts of track geometry problems, which can only be fixed with expensive track maintenance vehicles.

Slab track in Bangkok is shown below, on the Bangkok Skytrain. Note that on this track a third rail is also used, and it is located in between both running tracks.

Slab Track in Bangkok

Slab track is technically more complex to install. Problems with vibration usually mean that the concrete base can be damaged, and so vibration damping is needed. Whilst this function is normally provided by ballast, this is not possible with slab track, so some complicated vibration dampening scheme is needed. Different types of these have been designed and are in use, and quality control when they are installed is very important.

In some cases track may be designed for two gauges. Dual gauge track is sometimes needed in boundaries between areas with different gauges. Below is dual gauge track, this one is located in Brisbane, the inside rails are narrow gauge, and the outside are standard gauge. As Queensland uses narrow gauge, the inside rails are used more often than the outside ones.

Double Gauge Track

Signalling

The signalling system plays a critical role in any railway. Train movements are constrained by the signalling system. Trains are not like cars where they can travel along, and then stop when reaching an intersection. Almost all railways (excluding trams and light rail) operate on the principle that all rail tracks are divided up into sections, or blocks, and to enter each section trains need authorisation. For the most part trains are authorised to enter track sections using signals.

The signalling system is more than just signals, although this is the most obvious part of the signalling system. The purpose of the signalling system is to authorise the movement of trains, communicate this to drivers, and to keep trains separate so that one does not collide with another. The signalling system is composed of many different parts, including:
- Signals
- Track circuits and axle counters (train detection)
- Points installed over turnouts
- Signal boxes, and the control panel that display where trains are
- Interlockings

Signalling, like track design and the design of electrical power systems, is a huge area that has specialist people working in for decades, and there are courses and textbooks written on this asset system. Again, it is not possible here to provide anything but the simplest explanation of how this system operates.

Signals provide information to drivers of trains; the driver sees the signal, and then knows what to do. The driver has control over the motor of the train, and the brakes, and can instruct the motor to drive harder, or slower, or brake the train. He/she does this in response to what the signal displays. The driver almost always cannot determine the direction of the train, and so his control of the train is limited to setting the speed.

Some signalling systems do not have signals by the side of the track, but instead replicate signals in the driver's cabin. The driver can see the relevant indications on his control panel, and this is called "in-cab signalling". This style of signalling system is becoming more and more common, as it eliminates the need for lineside signalling, which is expensive to install and maintain. For the purposes of explaining how the signalling system works, it is helpful to examine how lineside signals work, as this can effectively explain how signals control the movement of trains.

The purpose of the signalling system is to prevent trains colliding with each other, as well as managing the passage of trains through the rail system. Trains stop by braking, and this means that the wheels use the rail to stop the train. As trains have steel wheels, and the rails are made of steel, then trains need to stop by braking through their wheels onto the rail. Steel normally slides quite well over steel, so trains need to stop slowly, and a typical trains moving at 70 kms/hr might need 500 metres to stop. Trains moving at higher speeds may need greater distances to stop, and the signalling system needs to inform the driver well ahead of time that there is a stop signal ahead, and then the train needs to be slowed so that it can stop.

Many rail systems require the signalling system to provide something called a "movement authority". This is the permission to move through a rail system, and to perform any movement. Many signalling systems grant movement authority for trains to move, often through the use of signals. More advanced signalling systems also use movement authorities.

Light rail and trams often use road signals for movement authorities. Trams may use traffic signals like road vehicles, although sometimes they have rail like signals that direct their movements. Signals on light rail and trams systems, where they exist, tend to be very simple. Light rail and trams also run on steel rails, and have steel wheels, so their ability to stop will be similar to that of any other rail vehicle. The steel on steel sliding problem, mentioned above, applies equally to trams and light rail vehicles but trams do not move very fast, and so can slow down in time to stop at red traffic lights. Modern light rail vehicles are equipped with magnets that latch onto the rail and provide additional deceleration. It's this new braking system that allows light rail vehicles to brake hard, and so use traffic lights as signals.

What colours are used on the signals, and how the lights are arranged, varies substantially from railway to railway, and from country to country. There is very little standardisation between countries, even within the same country. Even in Australia, which has only a rail system moderate in size, the style and structure of signals varies from railway to railway. This makes explaining signalling in a book of this type extremely difficult, as it's impossible to explain all the different scenarios, the US is different to French signalling, and so on. The method used here is to use NSW signalling, as the author is familiar with it, and it looks like traffic lights, so it's a bit easier to explain. Again, this situation is a difficult one, and there is no real best answer as to how to explain signalling systems in general.

The picture below is of a signal is the Sydney rail system. This one has two red lights illuminated, with a black background. This signal is described as a double light signal, as there are basically two signals, one of top of the other. The use of two heads for a signal allows the provision of additional information.

A Double Light Signal

The signalling system was designed to give drivers the warning time they need to stop the train, otherwise a collision could result. The most common way to do this is to put "signals" alongside the track to tell the driver what to do. As the driver drives his train he sees the signals, and based on what colours are displayed he knows what to do. It is the signalling system that determines the number of trains that can pass through a section per hour, and this is called the train frequency. The minimum time between trains is another important measure, and this is called the headway.

So who controls the signals? Signals can display many different meanings, and there needs to be some sort of decision making process to determine what is displayed. For road traffic lights many of these are controlled by computer, or sometimes by controllers at a control centre somewhere. Rail signals can be computer controlled, and many are, but many are also controlled by a person with a job description of "signaller", or in the USA and Canada a "dispatcher". The signaller sets the signals, and so controls the movements of trains. Signallers are physically located in signal boxes.

Signalling systems around the world can be divided into two broad categories; speed signalling, where the driver of the train is told the maximum permitted speed, and route signalling, where the driver is told the direction he will go, and not the actual speed. It might seem strange that the driver may not know where he is going, but in complex junction there might be many points lying in many different directions, and it may not be clear to him which track is the one that he will take. In a complex junction there may be ten or even more different possible directions, and the driver will need to know which one his train will take. Of course almost always the driver is not free to choose the path his train will take, but will need to follow the path chosen for him by the signaller.

Below are some lights and signals for the trams system in Hong Kong. At this turnout trams can go either to the left or the right, and the traffic light shows either a white line perpendicular up, or sloping to the left. This traffic light is operating as a route indicator. Trams can possible go two ways, to the left and right, to the tram stop ahead. The traffic light gives the tram permission to proceed, and in the middle of the picture is the route indicator, that displays how the points are set, so the tram driver knows where the tram will go. Route indicators such as the one below are more common in rail systems in commonwealth countries.

Hong Kong Route Indicator

There is absolutely no standard for signalling systems around the world. There are a very large number of different ways of constructing signalling systems, and signals can vary even within the same country. The enormous variety of different ways of building signalling systems makes it difficult in a book like this one to explain how this kind of system works, and it is necessary to find a common thread between the many different signalling systems. An attempt has been made below to do this, but the reader must remember that is impossible to explain anything more than the very basics of a signalling system.

What is described below is the British method of signalling. It is used in most of Australia, and places like Hong Kong and Singapore. It is obviously also used in the UK. The structure of the signalling is common to many countries, and has the basic rule of red/yellow/green, also used for traffic lights. This basic structure is also used in France and the US, but this is really the only commonality. For this reason these basic signals are described, and nothing more complex than this is explained.

The driver of a train needs to know the speed he should drive the train at. In speed signalling the driver is told the speed, but for route signalling a speed is not explicitly displayed. For route signalling the driver needs to have extensive route knowledge, and need to know the speed for different areas and different signal indications. This, for a large system, can be a lot of knowledge, and it may take years to train a driver to know all of the speeds in all of the different locations. Even in a route signalled railway (such as the rail system in Sydney) there is usually some information on speeds, and speed signs telling the driver his maximum speed are common. Information on speeds however is not complete, and for any speed other than a full proceed indication it may not be clear what speed the driver of a train should go, and experience will be his guide. To the casual reader this might seem pretty crazy, but in practice it is possible to successfully run a railway where the speeds in many situations are known only by experience.

The schematic below shows a very basic signal. The top part of the signal is called the signal head, and signals may have one or more of these. There are lights installed in the head of the signal, and there may be only one, or multiple of these. Remember that many railways do no structure their signal this way, but some do, and for the purposes of explaining how signalling works, this signal design is clear and easy to understand.

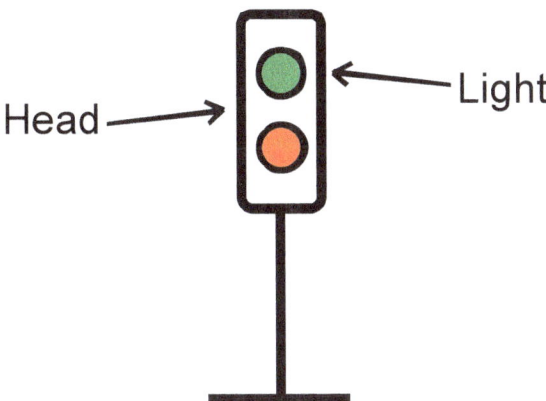

Notice that the green is on top, and the red is below the green. Whilst this is not always how signals are structured, this layout seems to be common. Normally only one signal light would be lit at any one time.

The "*aspect*" of a signal is its appearance, so if the green light is on we say that the signal is showing a green aspect. The "*indication*" of the signal is the meaning of the signal to the driver, and for a green aspect this will be a proceed indication.

So what do the colours mean? Well green means "Proceed", which is go at full line speed, at the place where the rail signal is located. The red means "Stop", which obviously means stop. These two colours are the minimum for any signal that can display different indications, but a signal can also be a single red light. Many more different meanings can be created, and some of these are discussed below.

Whilst in principle the signalling system is simple, in practice it is a bit more complicated than that. The interpretation of the signals can get quite complicated, especially in freight yards, and where there are many possible different routes. It can get even more complicated where there are level crossings and marshalling yards next to each other. A full discussion of what signals can display and what the meaning is far outside the scope of this book.

In practice the use of a two light signal has serious limitations, and so it is often not used, despite its simplicity. The table below shows a three light single headed signal, and the relevant indications. This type of signal is very common.

3 Aspect/Light Signals with Indications (Example)

Signal	Indication (meaning)
(green over yellow over red signal, green lit on top)	**Proceed**, travel at full line speed to at least until the next signal can be seen. This signal is called "**Clear**" in the US.
(signal with yellow lit in middle)	**Caution**, be prepared to stop at the signal in advance of this one. Drivers seeing this signal would reduce speed. This signal is called "**Approach**" in the US.
(signal with red lit on bottom)	**STOP**, do not drive any further than this signal. This signal is also called "Stop" in the US.

There are many other possible indications that can be created, such as for shunting moves, but these are not discussed any further.

The use of the three colours, red, green and yellow is very common. Where signals need to display additional information, then some more lights of the same colour may be added, or one of the lights may flash to provide a different indication. In the US there was a fourth colour, lunar white, which is a blueish white.

Where four indications are required to control the speed, then sometimes a fourth indication is used. In the US this signal is called "*Advance Approach*", and in Australia the name "*medium*" is commonly used. This indication is used to tell drivers that, 2 signals in front the current signal, that this signal is at stop.

A Fourth Indication	
Signal	**Indication (meaning)**
(flashing yellow signal)	Medium, driver should be aware that the second signal after this signal is at stop, and to be prepared to stop at that signal. Called "Advance Approach" in the US. To provide this indication, sometimes, the yellow light will flash, with no other lamp lit.

With speed signalling, the signalling system tells the driver the speeds, and for the US, the table below provides a rough guide as to what speeds are common. These names are

US Speed Signalling Speeds and Names	
Indication	**Speed (approx)**
Normal (full proceed)	Line speed (which depends on the

	location)
Limited	40 – 45 miles per hour (about 60 kms/hr)
Medium	30 miles per hour (about 45 kms/hr)
Low	15 miles per hour (about 20-25 kms/hr)
Restricted	15 miles per hour or less, and the driver should be prepared to stop quickly

The relationship between the signal indication and the most desirable speed the driver should drive at can be a bit complicated.

The signalling system includes more than just the signals that control the actions of train drivers. Another important component of the signalling system is the method of detecting the presence and location of trains, and this is commonly done with two pieces of engineering equipment; the track circuit and the axle counter. These items are able to sense when trains enter and exit fixed blocks of track, and provide this information back to the signalling system. The signalling system uses this information to make decisions about what signals should display, as well as provide this information to the signaller.

The heart of all signalling systems is the interlocking. An interlocking is the key device that prevents trains from running into another. In a junction, or a crossover, one trains passes in front of another, and it is possible for the two trains to collide. The interlocking checks that there are no trains in the way when a train is sent through a crossover or a junction. The interlocking takes information from the train detection system and makes some calculations, and then decides if trains can be allowed through junctions. Interlockings are very safety critical, and they must be designed with great care to ensure that there is no possibility that trains will collide with each other.

Signals are very important to calculating the capacity or headway of a rail system. This topic is extremely important for calculating how many people can be moved by a rail system.

Electrical (Traction systems)

Electrical power is often supplied to power them. Electricity is generated at a power station, or possibly locally and closer to the railway, and is then transmitted through transmission lines, to the railway. Once the power has reached the railway it is transformed down to the appropriate voltage, and then delivered to the trains.

Connecting an electricity network all this distance is expensive, and there needs to be a good reason to build the infrastructure that allows this to happen. Whilst it is true that the emissions from electrical power is mostly lower than from diesel locomotives, there are other reasons why electric power is preferred over diesel engines. These include:
- Electric trains are quieter than diesel trains
- Electric energy is much cheaper than diesel fuel
- Diesel engines produce a lot of smoke from combustion, and in tunnels the smoke is quite unpleasant for passengers
- Diesel engines require fuel, which in certain circumstances can ignite, and this is a fire risk which requires additional mitigations in tunnels
- And as mentioned previously, normally CO_2 emissions are higher from diesel fuel than from electrical energy supplied from a generator
- For high speed trains diesel trains are limited on the top speed to 250 kms/hr, which is too slow for many high speed rail services

Almost all rail services in major cities are electric, although there are some exceptions. Freight services are mostly diesel, although as with many things in rail, there are some more exceptions. In Australia the Mount Black railway line is entirely electrified, and very large amounts of coal are moved on that rail line, so it certainly is possible to electrify freight lines.

There are two main ways to supply power to a train, using overhead wiring, or a third rail. Overhead wiring is generally preferred, although it makes the rail line look messy. For overhead wiring the wires hang down from above the train, and then the train has a matching system that allows it to reach up and touch the wires. This part of the train is called the pantograph. As a general observation, overhead wiring is preferred as the live electrical wires are far above the track, so that track workers can walk along the track without the need to isolate power. Also trespassers are not in any danger when entering the rail corridor as the wires are too high.

The alternative to overhead wiring is a third rail system. Third rail systems are often used because they are cheap to install, and tunnels with third rail systems are smaller and so are cheaper. Many urban rail systems have third rails installed. One challenge with third rails is that anyone that touches them will be instantly killed, and they are at ground level and so easy to reach.

The schematic below shows how overhead wiring is often configured.

Figure 4.7 Overhead Wiring and Structure

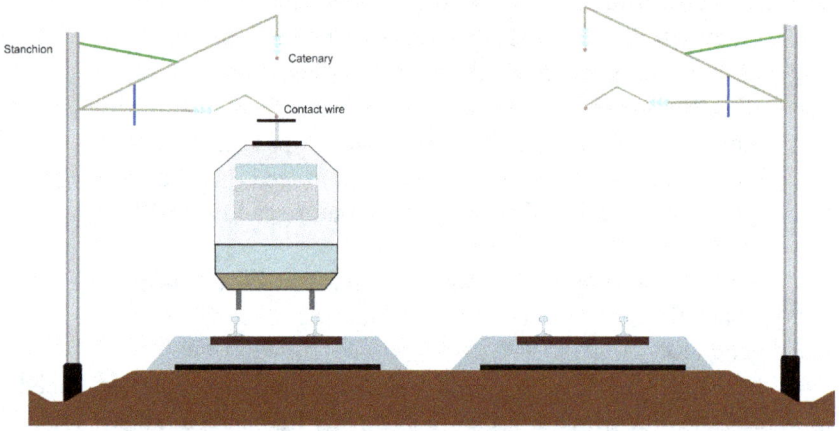

Overhead wiring needs to be supported and usually strong beams are concreted into the ground to hold the entire structure up. These beams in Australia are called stanchions, and are visually unappealing. Rail lines with no electric power are definitely visually more appealing than those with electric power. Recently there have been attempts to smarten up the appearance of rail lines with overhead wiring, with colours that are similar to the colours of the surroundings, with some success.

Overhead wiring structures come in many different shapes and sizes. The one below is for 25 kV, and is bolted onto a tunnel wall.

Registration and Contact Wire Support

Below is a pantograph that conducts electricity from the contact wire into the traction systems in the train. The top of the pantograph has a strip of carbon, and this wears as it rubs along the contact wire. The pantograph is pushed up hard against the contact wire with springs, and so if the contact wire is removed then the pantograph will spring up high into the air.

A Pantograph

Below is a substation in Perth for converting power. A substation is a truly ugly thing, but it is needed to convert and use the power successfully.

Substations also contain electrical power equipment, much of which is fatal to the touch. Preventing trespassers from coming into contact with any of the equipment in a substation is a key requirement.

A Substation

The photo below shows a number of third rails in and around a couple of crossovers. Trains need to maintain contact with the third rail, and if contact is lost then the train will come to a stop, not immediately, but relatively quickly. Notice how much cleaner and nicer the track looks, and the appearance of the tracks is really much better.

Ballasted Track in a Viaduct with Third Rails

Installing power onto railways comes with many problems. Electricity in a DC (Direct Current) system can leak away, and if the leak is large enough, passengers or the public can be injured or even killed. The leaking electricity can do damage through a chemical process called electrolysis, which can result in metals near to the track being reduced to a soup of unpleasant chemicals.

For AC powered systems, there are other different problems to a DC system. The power moving through the overhead can induce currents in nearby metal objects, which means that there is now electricity in something that should not have it. For example, pipes along a tunnel in a system with AC power can now have currents passing through them. Again, this problem needs to be managed, and specialist technical people are needed who understand the problem.

A problem often encountered in Australia is that providing power to rail lines requires high voltage power lines running from generators to the rail line. In Australia generators are often located in remote areas next to coal supplies, and transmission lines need to run through national parks. Providing maintenance to transmission lines is raises some issues, as trees may need to be cut down. This is especially difficult where the trees are protected or endangered. Running power lines through a national park is a real problem, as access roads will need to be cut, and no one wants to do that. Even for a very conscientious and diligent railway, managing transmission lines through environmentally sensitive areas is difficult and constant problems emerge.

Overall providing electrical power to trains can be quite technically complicated. Specialist technical people are needed, and their salaries are not low. From the perspective of rail system design, only when the case for electric power is clearly overwhelming should electric power be used. Electric power provides many benefits and is the correct solution in many cases.

Railways in the past often generated their own power, and owned power stations. In Sydney the railways owned White Bay power station, as well as the Ultimo Power Station, which was effectively the first power station in Sydney. Rail systems in Australia now rarely own any form of power generation, and this is not changing. There has been a trend in Australia in the past 10 years to move power generation back closer to cities, and this is sometimes referred to as distributed power. There is much to be said about the case for railways having some form of power generation, especially in countries where power is very expensive to purchase. The author is of the opinion that a railway possessing some form of power generation is not necessarily a bad thing.

Tunnels

Tunnels provide many benefits, the main one being the ability of a rail line to avoid obstructions and other immovable objects, and still provide a transport service. Tunnels require large amounts of specialised infrastructure, and so are costly to construct and maintain. No discussion of rail infrastructure would be complete without a discussion of tunnels.

Tunnelling is a challenging area of engineering. The soil conditions are important to the costs and challenges associated with tunnelling, and there is no real way to know what the soil conditions will be like without actually tunnelling. To get an appreciation of the ground conditions, a project may organise for test bores to be drilled to sample what the ground is like, and this will provide some information on what the ground conditions are like. Whilst test bores provide some information, the actual ground conditions won't be known until digging actually commences.

Tunnels, and the management of fire in a tunnel, will impact upon station design. A "standard" tunnel will have ventilation, although many do not. All the ventilation equipment will normally be located at a station. An underground station can have a large amount of equipment, located in several large rooms within the station, including ventilation. The need to ventilate a tunnel significantly adds to the cost of constructing an underground station.

The picture below shows a rail tunnel, with the photo taken from one end of an underground station. Rail tunnels are commonly black or very dark with not much lighting. In this case this tunnel is single bore, and the track is ballasted, rather that being slab track. Note that the lighting is very close to the floor of the tunnel, so that drivers won't experience flashing lights when passing them, something that in rare instances can cause epileptic seizures.

A Tunnel and Portal

Whilst underground stations are also strictly speaking tunnels, they are not referred to as such, and the tunnels connect two underground stations. The transition from station to tunnel is shown below, with the station being light coloured and well-lit, and the tunnel dark and black. The transition from station into a tunnel is called a portal.

Rail tunnels can be described in terms of the following:
- The length of the tunnel
- What type of traffic is permitted to move through the tunnel
- The diameter of the tunnel, or if not round, the cross-sectional area
- The type of ventilation

- If the tunnel is single bore or double bore, and the configuration.

So let's discuss each of these in turn.

The length of the tunnel is probably the most important parameter for any rail tunnel. Usually measured in metres, it is measured as a distance that a person following the rail track would walk, rather than a linear distance from one portal to another. A long tunnel would be over 1 km in length, although there are many tunnels over 10kms, these are a small percentage of the total number of tunnels worldwide. In the US tunnels less than 160 metres are not described as tunnels, and are not normally classified as tunnels (at least under NFPA 130).

Most rail tunnels have passenger traffic moving through them. The composition of the rail traffic is quite important for a rail tunnel, but a casual observer would probably not be able to tell from looking at the tunnel what type of traffic was using the tunnel. Putting either diesel freight or passenger trains through the tunnel may change the equipment installed into it, or maybe not. Most freight trains are diesel powered, and this fuel is carried on board the train, and fuel leaks and fires are possible. Diesel engines can also catch fire, and this is particularly the case with older or more poorly maintained locomotives. Diesel locomotives dramatically increase the risk in a tunnel, and typically are excluded from tunnels used by passenger trains.

The risk and challenge with rail tunnels is fires. As tunnels are confined spaces, any fires can quickly incapacitate any passengers in the train. The heat itself is not the danger, but the smoke produced from the fire. Small fires are often started through vandalism in trains, but large fires are rare. The hazard of a large fire has a very low probability of occurrence, but when they occur the number of deaths can be very large. Preventing fires, or providing some method of escape for a tunnel can greatly add to the cost of the construction of a rail.

The diameter of the tunnel is an important parameter. Most tunnels are roughly circular in shape, so it's possible to customary the cross-sectional area of the tunnel from the diameter, using the very simple formula $Area = \dfrac{\pi D^2}{4}$. A typical diameter for a rail tunnel is about 7 metres, and a typical cross-sectional area about 40 to 60 metres. Larger cross sectional areas make ventilation and management of the movement of air in the tunnel easier, and overall a larger tunnel is better than a smaller one. Trains need to push the air out of the way when moving through a tunnel, and where there is little room between the walls of the tunnel and the train then the power needed to move the train is significantly greater. Also very narrow tunnels will make the air hotter as trains pass through, and the heat can become very great.

The type of ventilation is also relevant, and there are a number of different types. Many tunnels have no ventilation at all, but for new tunnels ventilation is often installed. Ventilation is required based on the length of the tunnel, the frequency of traffic, and the cross-sectional area of the tunnel. Ventilation can be described as either transverse, or longitudinal. For transverse ventilation, air is pushed into the tunnel from the walls towards the middle of the tunnel, whereas longitudinal the air is pushed in from the end of the tunnel, from one end to another.

And the final part of describing a rail tunnel is its configuration, and it can be single or twin bore. The table below lists many of the different configurations possible for a rail tunnel.

Different Tunnel Configurations

Tunnel Type	Comment
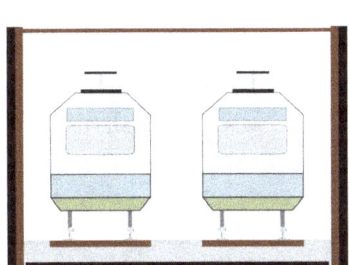	This is a single cut and cover tunnel. Cut and cover tunnels often have straight sides, unlike the curved sides of the other tunnels below. As cut and cover tunnels are often close to the surface, tunnels can be naturally ventilated.
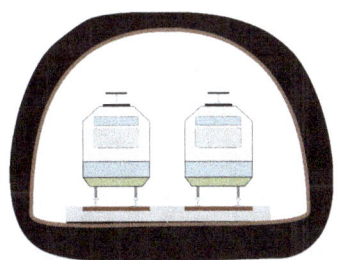	This is a tunnel with two tracks, in a single bore tunnel. There is no separate tunnel for escape or for service vehicles. The shape of the upper tunnel is often described as a horseshoe.

Different Tunnel Configurations

Tunnel Type	Comment
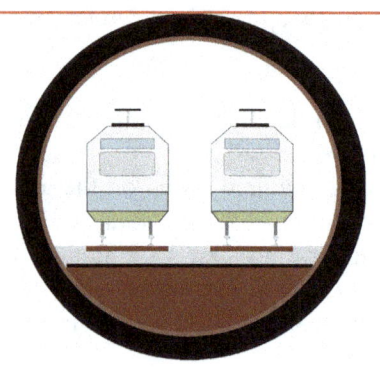	A tunnel with two tracks, with a circular tunnel. There is no separate escape nor service tunnel. This type of tunnel is common for deep tunnels..
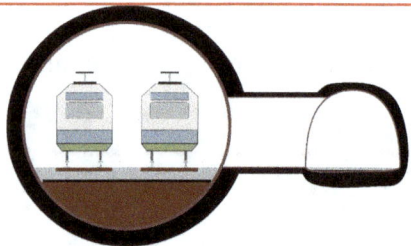	A circular rail tunnel with a supporting rail passage. This configuration is helpful if the need arises for an escape from the tunnel, and getting maintenance staff to equipment in the tunnel. The additional tunnel is expensive to construct.
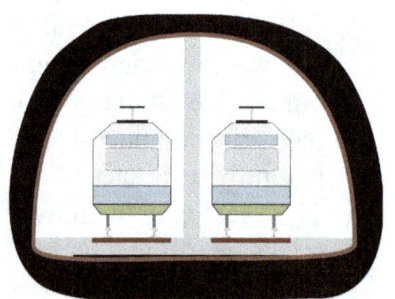	A horseshoe shaped tunnel, with a large concrete wall down the middle. The tunnel is split into two sections, which allows passengers to escape should the need arise down one of the two tunnels. This tunnel construction is commonly used in Hong Kong, and is relatively cheap.
	A double bore tunnel with cross-passages

Different Tunnel Configurations

Tunnel Type	Comment
	between each of the tunnels. This kind of configuration is common for long tunnels and those that carry freight.
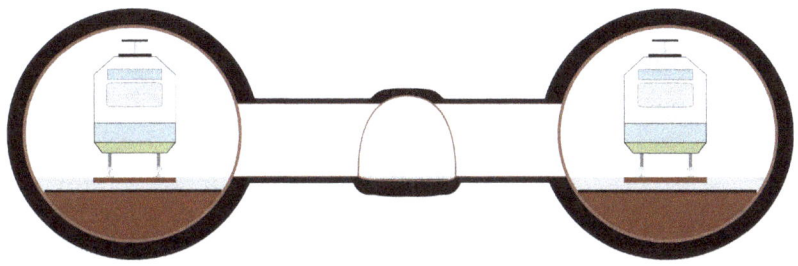	A double bore tunnel with a service tunnel in the middle, with cross passages. This is the configuration used on the Chunnel between England and France. This configuration is a very good one, and convenient for maintenance and escape from fires. Unfortunately it's really expensive.

Below is the layout of a twin bore tunnel in plan view. The key features are shown.

Figure 4.7 Rail Track through Tunnels

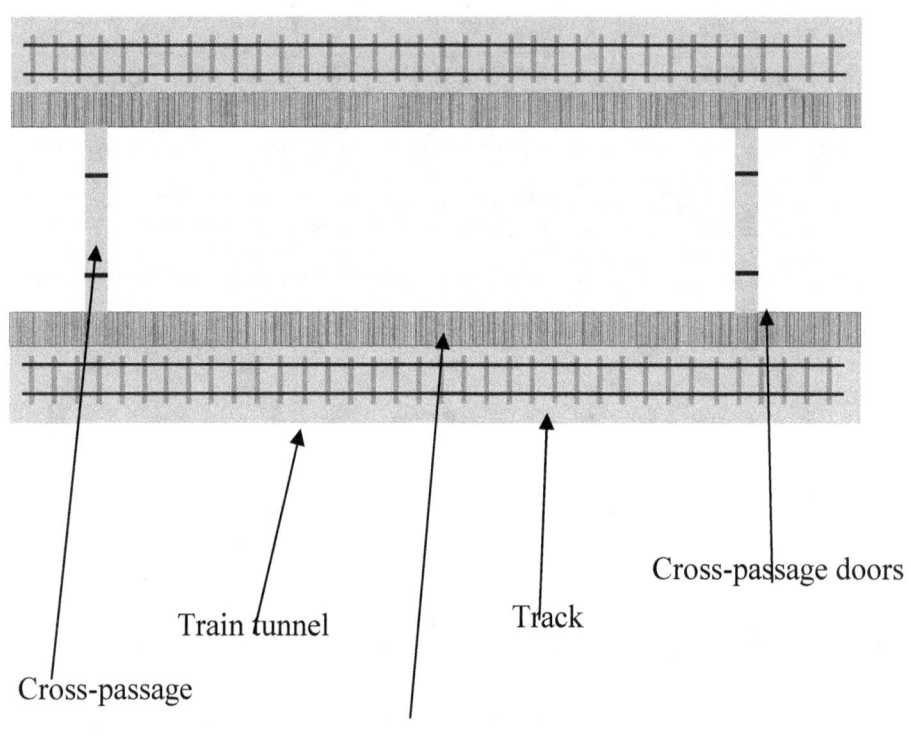

The main components of this tunnel system are:
1/ the tunnels
2/ the tracks
3/ the walkway next to the tracks
4/ the cross-passages
5/ the doors in the cross-passages.

We note that rail tunnels are with the two tracks side by side are normally built with side platforms, and those with twin tunnels are island platforms. Will this rule does not need to always be followed, it often is.

Bridges

Everyone knows what bridges are and what they do. Any large rail system will have dozens, if not hundreds of bridges. Bridges are used to get the rail system across natural obstacles such as rivers, roads, valleys, and other natural obstacles.

Bridges are an attractive asset for any rail system. They are usually low maintenance, and they rarely contain any moving parts. In some cases rail lines pass over draw or swing bridge, but generally this is uncommon. The Skelton viaduct in Yorkshire is one rare example of a rail system using a swing bridge, and the El Ferdan bridge in Egypt over the Nile is another.

Bridges need to be very strong, but constructed properly they are can last hundreds of years. The one below is over the Cooks River in Sydney.

A Rail Bridge

Bridges that move, such as swing bridges and drawbridges, have some safety issues. There have been a number of fatal accidents in the US on swing bridges. Bridges that need to be opened and closed can be a problem, and these are usually situated over bodies of water, and are installed to allow large boats to pass underneath them. Care needs to be taken that the train does not enter over the bridge when it is open, otherwise the train can plunge into the water, and that's not good.

One problem with rail bridges, especially where the railway passes over a highway, is that occasionally trucks with high loads will strike the bridge. When this happens care must be taken that the bridge has not been damaged, and sometimes it is damaged, and trains need to slowly pass over the bridge just in case it has suffered some damage. Raising rail bridges is an important part of investing into rail infrastructure, as the higher the bridge over the highway, the smaller the chance that there will be a collision. Where a truck does hit a bridge, it can make a terrible mess and the damage to the truck can be considerable.

A more complicated version of a bridge is a viaduct. A viaduct is a long section of bridges that are all connected together. Viaducts are often used over marshy or swampy terrain, or for high speed rail.

The Viaduct connecting Italy with Venice

The picture above is of the viaduct that connects Venice to mainland Italy. This viaduct is needed because the ocean separates the historical city from Italy, and so the viaduct is quite long.

Road and Pedestrian Level Crossings

Level crossings are places where road vehicles are able to cross rail tracks. The picture below shows a level crossing outside of Paris, and it has lights and bells installed. Level crossings are sometimes described as being an "at-grade" crossing.

A Level Crossing in Paris

Level crossings can have a boom or booms installed, which descends when a train is approaching the level crossing. The boom provides an additional visual aid to drivers that the road level crossing is alarming, and that a train is coming.

Level crossings are installed in huge numbers around the world. The majority of level crossings in Australia do not have any form of protection or warning system installed over them, and they are just a place where road vehicles can cross the track. Many level crossings only have lights and bells and no boom.

Level crossings can pose some serious risks to trains and users. Every year there are fatal accidents at level crossings, and people are killed. In almost all cases the driver of the road vehicle has crossed the level crossing without looking, and there has been a collision. There have also been accidents involving buses and can result in the deaths of dozens of people.

Level crossings are places of high risk for any rail system. The construction of bridges is a viable alternative, and bridges pose almost no safety risk to trains. The cost of bridges is not small, and replacing hundreds of level crossings with bridges is simply not possible for many railways operating on limited budgets.

Tram systems operate at road level, and so effectively the entire system is one giant level crossing. There are rarely fatal accidents involving trams, as the operational speed is rather low, and the drivers know to look out for cars. Low speed collisions between road vehicles and trams are however very common, and in one year there were over one thousand collisions such as this in Melbourne. Fatal accidents with trains seem to occur when the train is moving fairly fast, and the impact to the road vehicle has the energy to cause substantial mechanical damage.

Level crossings can be a part of the signalling system, because if the level crossing has bells and lights then the signalling system needs to tell the level crossing when to activate. A level crossing with no protection other than a sign has no connection to the signalling system. Complex level crossings can be expensive to maintain.

Papers have been written in the US where the benefits of installing lights, bells and booms has been analysed. The US has an extraordinary high number of deaths at level crossings, typically over 300 per year, a figure that would not be accepted in almost any other country in the world. The US government has had a long term plan to close, remove, or install lights and booms over as many level crossings as possible, and this program has been very successful in reducing the number of deaths per year. It is clear that booms work quite well in reducing the number of deaths at level crossings.

Another significant problem with level crossings is making sure that the lights and bells don't ring for too long. Car drivers quickly get bored waiting at level crossings, and they are tempted to drive around the boom after waiting even a short period of time like 1 or 2 minutes. Many of the accidents have occurred this way in the world over level crossings. In practice signalling systems have difficulties in allowing for the different speeds of trains, and so for a slow moving train the lights and bells may flash and ring for a time period much longer than a couple of minutes.

Sometimes there are pedestrian level crossings attached to road crossings. A pedestrian crossing is designed purely for passengers, and it operates in a very similar way to a road crossing. Pedestrian crossings are much smaller than road crossings, and have lights and booms. Pedestrian crossings in Australia at least are less common than road crossings.

There are also other types of rail crossings, but they are fairly unusual. There are sometimes crossings provided for animals, and in Sydney there is a horse crossing next to Rosehill Racecourse. Crossings for animals needs to be designed differently than for people, and more space needs to be provided, depending on the size of the animal. Given the rarity of level crossings designed for animals, they won't be discussed any further.

Control Systems

A control system for a railway is an engineering system that displays the position of trains and the status of signals. Control systems normally have a computer screen where trains and their position are displayed. Large rail systems have particularly large control system displays, and these can cover the wall of a large room.

Control systems display tracks as divided up into sections, and each section is displayed as either empty or occupied. Trains are often identified with some sort of alphanumeric code, such as 111A, which identified which run it is. Alternatively, the set number (ie the train identifier) can be displayed.

Control systems also allow the signaller to set trains to routes. This means that the signaller can set the direction of turnouts, and can direct the movement of trains. Remember that drivers mostly cannot set turnout directions themselves (although there are exceptions to this rule, once again), and this function is performed either by the signaller, or in modern times, a computer program.

Tram systems and light rail systems can also have control systems, but they operate differently, partly because of the simpler network design. There is often no track detection system for trams, or almost never, so trams need to be detected and found using a different system. GPS, or some system that effectively operates the same as GPS, can be used to locate where the trams are. On the control system the screen will show the location of the trams, but unlike a control system the trams can't be directed with points and track infrastructure to different routes. The control system for a tram system is much more passive.

A control system links in closely with the signalling system, but is not the same thing. The purpose of the signalling system is to prevent the collision of trains, and the purpose of control systems is to manage the movement of trains. If the control system is directed to allow two trains to collide with one another, then the signalling system will prevent it and send an alarm to the control system.

It is also common to refer to other systems that manage rail infrastructure as control systems. For example, a system that displays information on lifts and escalators may be called a control system. It is important to distinguish between the train control system, and a system that manages other rail infrastructure.

REFERENCES

1. Zhang, C. & Li, L. Zhang, D. & Zhang, S. *Types and Characteristics of Safety Accidents Induced by Metro Construction*, 2009 International Conference on Information Management, Innovation Management and Industrial Engineering, 209

2. Kimijima, N. et al *New Urban Transport for Middle East Monorail System for Dubai Palm Jumeirah Transit System*, Hitachi Review Vol 59, (2010), No 1

3. Murphy, E. *The Application of ERTMS/ETCS Systems*, IRSE Technical Convention Melbourne, Oct 2007

4. State of Florida Department of Transportation, *Central Florida Commuter Rail Transit Design Criteria*, October 2008

5. DB Netze *AG Network Statement 2014,* April 2013

6. Parsons Brinkerhoff *High Speed Rail*, Network, Issue No 73, Sept 2011, http://www.pbworld.com/news/publications.aspx

7. Lindahl, M. *Track geometry for high-speed railways*, Department of Vehicle Engineering Royal Institute of Technology, Stockholm 2001

8. Oura, Y. *Railway Electric Power Feeding Systems*, Japan Railway & Transport Review 16, June 1998

9. BSL Management Consultants *The Cost of Railway Infrastructure Status-Quo and Ways Ahead*, Presentation to the ProMain Council of Decision Makers, Brussels Nov 2001

10. Tateishi, Y. *Broadband Radio Transmissions in Railways*, JR EAST Technical Review-No 20

11. Zhang, W. et al *Pantograph and catenary system with double pantographs for high-speed trains at 350 km/hr or higher*, Journal of Modern Transportation, Volume 19, Number 1, March 2011

12. Eyre, P. *Signalling of the Southern Suburbs Railway*, IRSE Technical Convention – Perth, July 2007

13. Rail Industry Safety and Standards Board, *ROA Manual Section 01 Civil*

14. Kohel, J. *Optimised catenary maintenance measures on Austrian Federal Railways, Rail Engineering International Edition*, 2002 Number 1

15. Huth, P. *Overview of QR Signalling Principles*, IRSE Technical Meeting, Brisbane, July 2008

16. Kerr, D. Rail Signal Aspects and Indications, http://dougkerr.net/Pumpkin/articles/Rail_signal_aspects.pdf

17. Broderick, E. & Lemon, S. *Case Study: Application of CBTC on DLR*, IRSE Australasia Technical Meeting, March 2011

18. Thales *SelTrac CBTC Communications-Based Train Control for Urban Rail*, www.thalesgroup.com/security-services

19. Siemens Transportation Systems *GSM-R Terminals Flexible GSM-R Dispatcher Systems, Terminals and Cab Radio Solutions*, http://www.siemens.com.au/files/Mobility/RI/Documents/mob_gsm-r_terminals.pdf

20. Railway Gazette *Commissioning the world's heaviest automated metro*, Metro Report 2003

21. Thales *Netrac 6613 Aramis*, www.thalesgroup.com

22. Victorian Rail Industry Operators Group Standards Track Circuit Types Characteristics and Applications, Nov 2009

http://ptv.vic.gov.au/assets/PTV/PTV%20docs/VRIOGS/VRIOGS-012.7.4-RevA.pdf

23. Davey, E. *Rail Traffic Management Systems, IET Railway Signalling and Control Systems Course*, May 2012

24. Ancarani, G. et al *Mobile radio for Railway Networks in Europe*, June 1999

25. Hillenbrand, W. *GSM-R The Railways Integrated Mobile Communications System*, Dec 1999, http://www.tsd.org/

26. Mok, S. & Savage, I. *Why Has Safety Improved at Rail-Highway Grade Crossings?*, Risk Analysis, Vol 25, No 4, 2005

27. Klinger, R. *Radio Coverage for Road and Rail Tunnels in Tunnels in the Frequency Range 75 to 1000 MHz*, Vehicular Technology Conference, 1991.

28. Ahren, T. & Parida, A. *Overall railway infrastructure effectiveness (ORIE)*, Journal of Quality in Maintenance Engineering Vol 15 No 1 2009, pp 17 – 30

Chapter 5 Rail System Drawing and Configuration

The creation of any new rail line or extension would not be complete without drawing it. The visual interpretation of rail systems is a very powerful way of showing how a rail system is structured. Often the creation of a rail system starts with lines on a map. This book contains a number of different ways of rail systems.

Rail systems comprise of trains moving along tracks to get from one place to another. Trains are limited to operating on tracks, and trains cannot change direction without some tracks in that direction. There are different configuration of tracks that allow trains to swap from one track to another, or turn around. In almost all railways trains, when reaching the end of the line, need to be returned back in the direction from which they came. In this chapter are ways of describing rail lines, and how they are drawn.

Many different styles exist for drawing rail systems. The level of detail can vary considerably, and maps for passengers tend to be very simple, and maps for rail operators far more complex. In some countries rail maps are more complex that the very simple lines on a map, for example, rail system may be drawn to scale, or even with some geographical features added. In some cases rail maps provided to the public may be geographically correct, rather than a simplistic representation of the rail system. Some examples are provided below of the more common methods of drawing rail systems, but the reader should bear in mind that there are many different ways, and for brevity, only the more important ones are shown here. Perhaps the most common, and the most simple, are the maps where rail lines are drawn as straight lines, with different colours for the different lines. Many examples of this style of rail map are shown below.

For rail network designers, rail maps need to be much more complicated. The basic ideas behind constructing a more complex rail map are also elucidated below, and so it may become clear as to how to construct these. Many different types of maps are useful for the purposes of rail transport planning, and the map used will depend on the situation. There is no right and wrong way, just methods with different attributes.

Passenger Orientated Rail Drawings

Passenger orientated rail network maps tend to be very simple, and show basic information related to train operations and stopping patterns. Features such as interchanges, and where trains stop, are emphasised, and more infrastructure related information such as points and turnout locations are not mentioned or shown. Rail lines made available to the public are almost often in this format, and the look and feel is quite standard between different railways. Below is an example of a rail system drawing, that does not represent any particular place, which is passenger orientated.

Figure 5.1 A Simple Rail System

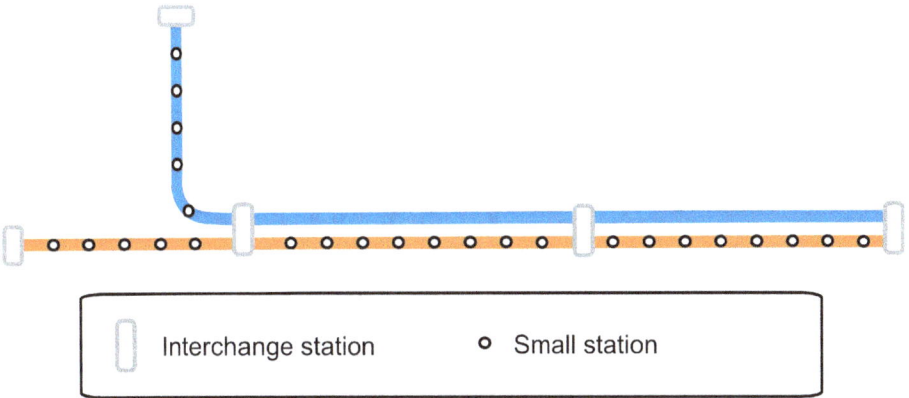

In this simple rail system, the blue and orange lines are drawn as separate lines, and there are many stations on the orange line where there is no corresponding dot on the blue line. This means that trains only stop when on the orange line, and not on the blue line. Trains on the blue line should travel faster than those on the orange, as the orange line trains are all stopping trains. Trains on both the blue and orange lines can interchange at the larger rectangular stations, of which there are only three.

A common misconception is that on a passenger rail map that lines drawn as different colours represent different tracks or different infrastructure. To the lay person this can be very confusing. Consider the rail system map below:

Figure 5.2 A Three Line Rail System

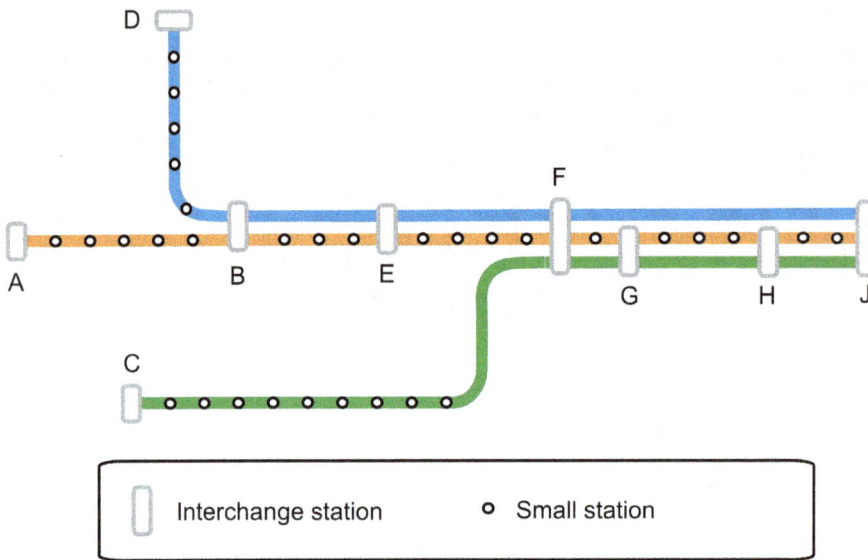

This kind of network design is quite common, although of course it is not the same as any other rail system in the world at the present time. Notice that there are 3 rail lines, and the blue line has only a small number of stops between stations B and J. The green line has additional stops at G and H, where passengers can interchange between the orange and green lines.

This rail system map is very useful for passengers, as it clearly shows which trains stop at which stations. For example, a blue line train will stop at E & F, but no stations in between. Any passenger travelling between D & J will know where they can and cannot alight from the train.

The drawing suggests that there are at least 6 tracks between F & J, and 4 between B & F. In practice there is no reason to have this number, and a very likely scenario in the above would be to have 4 tracks between F & J, and perhaps 4 between E & F, and only two tracks between B & E. Is is also not clear how many tracks there are between B & D, there may be 1, or 2, or less likely some other number.

If we take our example a little further, and say there are only 4 tracks between F & J, then most likely local trains will operate on two tracks, and the blue and green lines on the other two. Trains for the blue line will be

Rail System Drawing and Configuration Page 100

able to stop at stations G & H, but won't because they are timetabled not to stop.

An interesting question arises as to when a rail line is actually a separate rail line, and not just a branch, loop, link, or rail spur. In the 3 line system drawn above the blue line is drawn separately, as the stopping pattern is quite different from the orange line. Consider the rail line below:

Figure 5.3 One Rail Line with a Branch

Interchange/large station   o   Small station

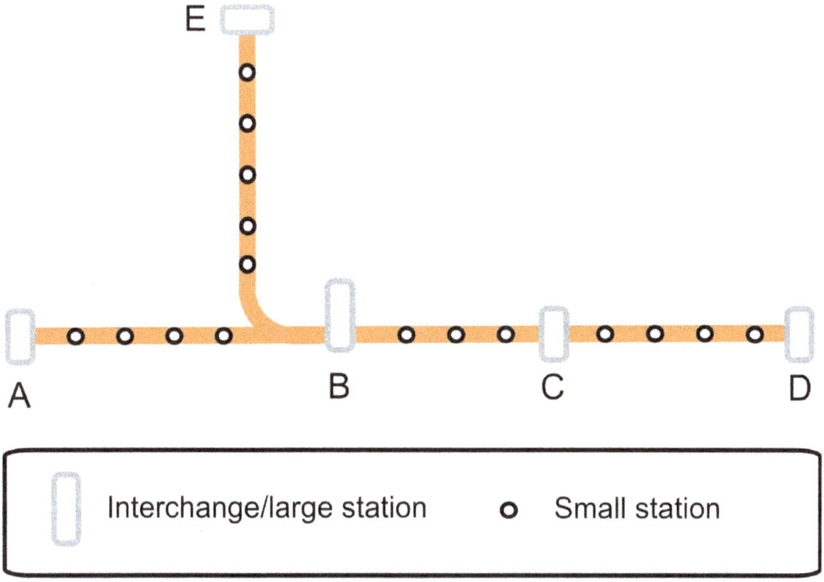

The drawing above shows a single rail line, with a branch or bifurcation. We would expect from a drawing of this type that trains do move from station D, to station E, and many stops in between. At station B passengers would need to alight if they wanted a train travelling along the other branch from the one the destination that the train they are travelling on would have.

The rail system below shows a shuttle service. A shuttle is a service that is separated from the rest of the rail system, that moves from one large station to another, typically over relatively short distances. The blue line below is a shuttle, and trains moving along B to E will not move through to any other station. This type of rail design is common. Typically both lines will be the same type of rail system, ie, both metros, or both commuter trains.

Figure 5.4 A Rail Line with a Shuttle

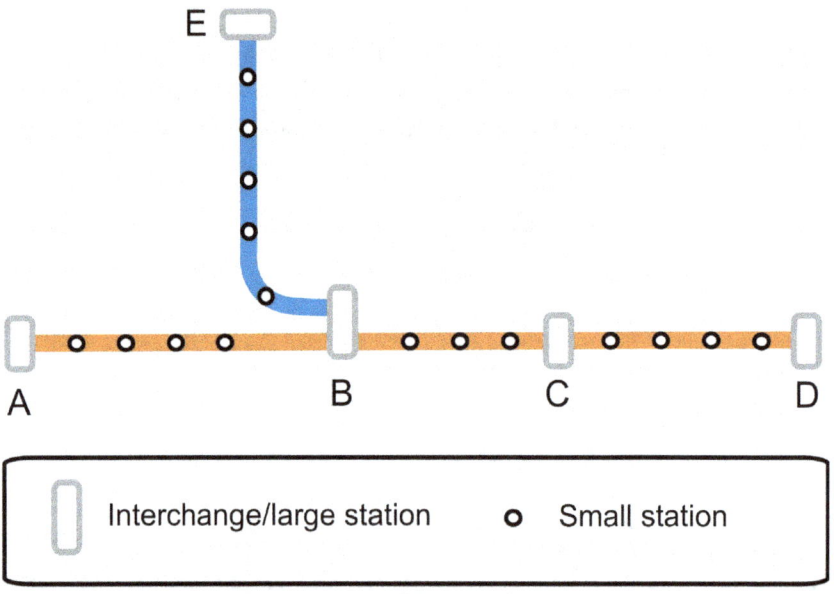

Below is another way of drawing a rail system that is sometimes used. The rail system below is made up of only 1 line, but it is drawn as 2. The top line is an express service, and the bottom an all stops.

Figure 5.5 One Rail Line with Two Stopping Patterns

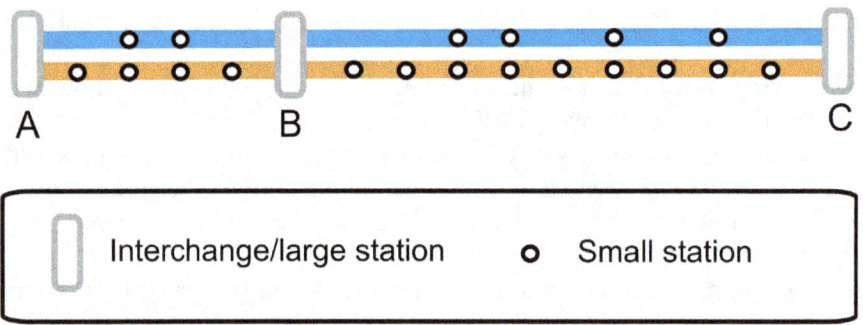

The way this system is drawn it may appear that there are three interchange stations, A, B and C, and many intermediate stations in between. This is not the case, A,B & C are larger stations, and passengers can interchange with any station where there is a dot on both the blue and orange lines.

Rail System Drawing and Configuration Page 102

In many cases there are other rail systems in and around the rail system being drawn. This is particularly common in Japan. The rail system in bright colours is the one being displayed, and the darker rail line with thinner lines is the one operated as a different rail mode, or by another company. The other rail system needs to be included to allow passengers to see the interchanges, but not much detail is required. This arrangement is shown below.

Figure 5.6 Two Rail Modes

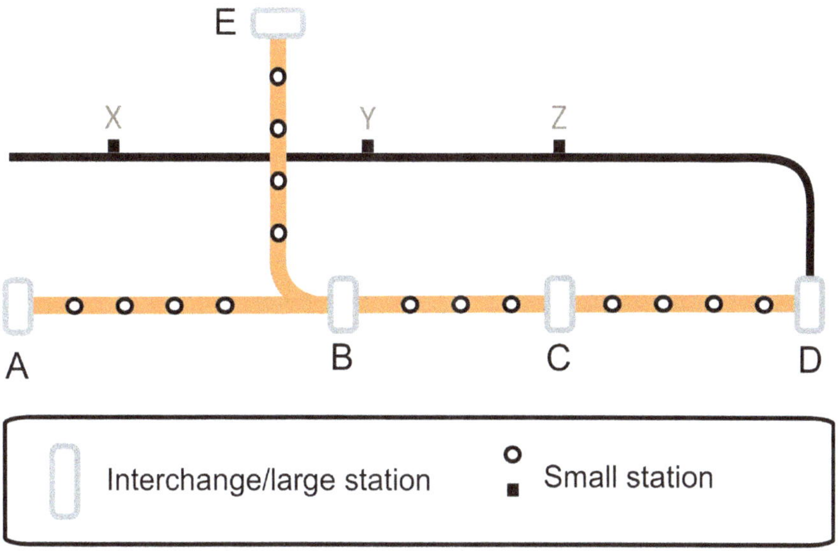

Whilst the drawings above are useful for the public, and demonstrate effectively where stations are and the services to them, this type of system drawing does not include much other useful information. Some of the pieces of information that are missing include:
- Stabling
- Turnbacks so trains can be terminated and sent back in the reverse direction
- Passing loops
- Any idea as to the number of tracks
- The number of platforms at stations
- Crossovers

For a train operator the above information, whilst not useless, is not on it's own enough to fully understand the rail system and how it operates.

Geographically Correct Maps

A geographically correct map of a rail system shows the location of stations and rail lines in comparison to an underlying map. Rail lines are drawn physically where they are, and not in the idealised way that passenger rail maps are normally drawn in. This type of map can be very helpful, but is less commonly used than the idealised maps above.

Geographically correct maps show the terrain and main features of an area, and the rail system within it. For example, lakes, rivers, and oceans are shown, and urban areas can be shown. For maps of entire countries, the main features that are show would normally be the boundaries of the country.

Passengers often find geographically correct maps difficult to read. For most passenger systems they are a little unsuited, but can work well where the rail system is relatively simple. One of the problems with a geographically correct map is that the spacing between stations in a real rail system often varies greatly, and this can make the maps a little confusing.

Figure 5.7 Geographically Correct Map of the Rail System in Newcastle NSW in Australia

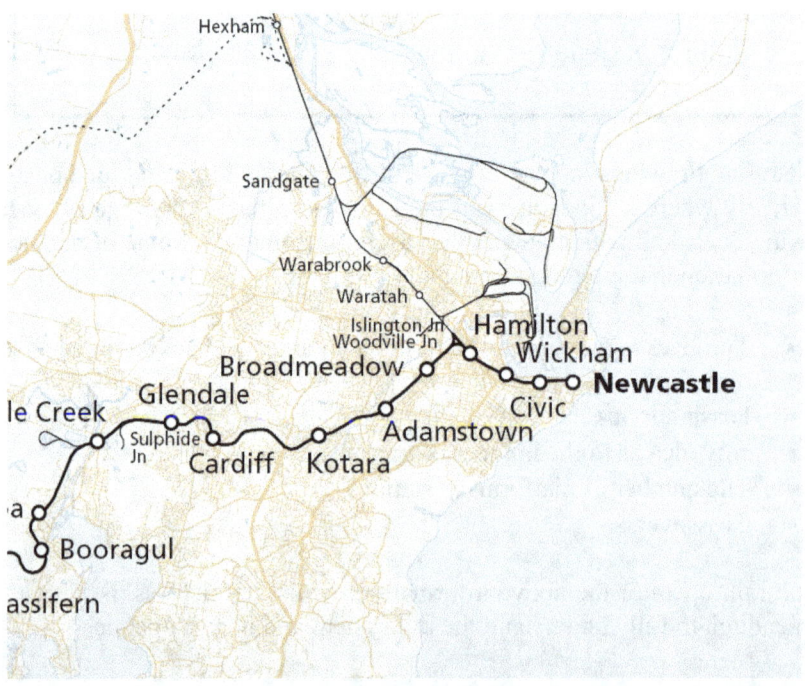

The map above also shows freight lines and the coal loader. Parts of this rail line have now closed. Bodies of water are clearly visible.

Detailed Drawing of Rail Systems

For much rail network design, detailed rail maps are essential. There are many different styles of drawing rail systems, and the one presented below is something of a compromise. Detailed design drawings of rail lines are very complex, and include all the different engineering items that are normally found in a rail system. Design drawings of rail systems are very difficult to read, and not included in this book because they are too complex for most rail transport planners to use.

The drawing method below does not include signals. As almost all signalling schemes are very complex, the signals themselves have a lot of detail and information that sometimes can make the drawing a little difficult to read.

The level of detail show below is useful to show places where trains can be stabled, and can be turned back. Many of the common features of a rail system are shown. The running direction of the rail system is also shown. Stations and platforms are also shown.

So here are the basic elements of a rail system.

Basic Rail System Elements

────────	A rail track, with two rails, and sleepers in between. Only one train can move along this track at any one time.
←────────	Possible direction of travel of a train
▭ (orange block)	A station
(turnout diagram)	A turnout, where the track splits, and the train can take one of two paths
←────→	One track, where trains can move in either direction. This is called bi-directional track.
────→ ←────	Double track, with trains moving in one direction on both tracks. This configuration is very standard, and could be described as the "normal" arrangement.
	This is an island

Basic Rail System Elements

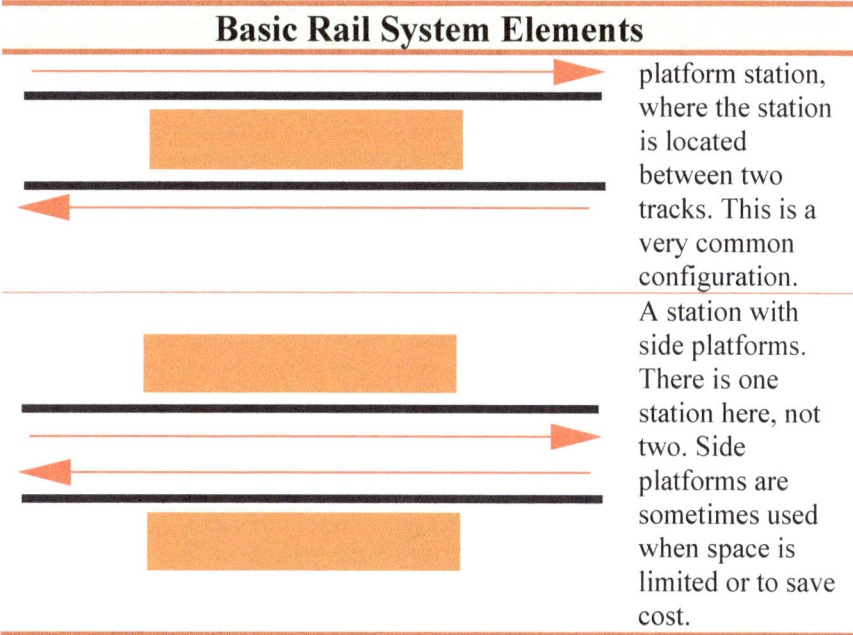

	platform station, where the station is located between two tracks. This is a very common configuration.
	A station with side platforms. There is one station here, not two. Side platforms are sometimes used when space is limited or to save cost.

More complex arrangements can be built out of these basic elements. The table below shows how configurations can be built up into more complex structures.

More Complex Rail Layouts – Crossing movements

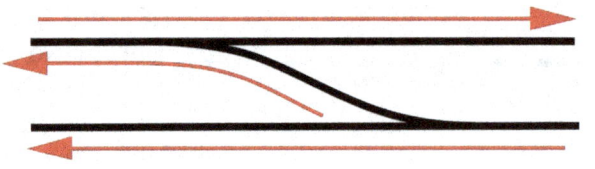

A crossover. Notice that part of the crossover is bi-directional, but most is not.

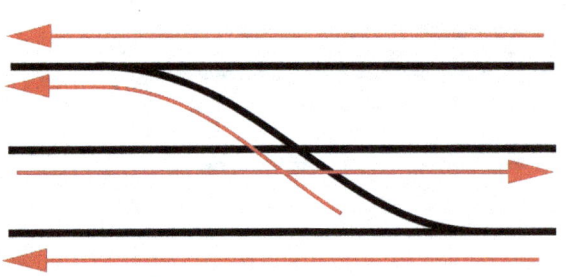

A diamond crossover. Trains crossing over would need to wait until the any trains in the middle had passed before crossing over.

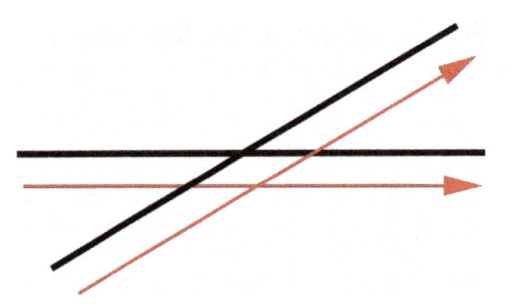

A diamond crossing, or just simply a crossing. Trains cannot change direction here, but do pass over one track to continue on their journey.

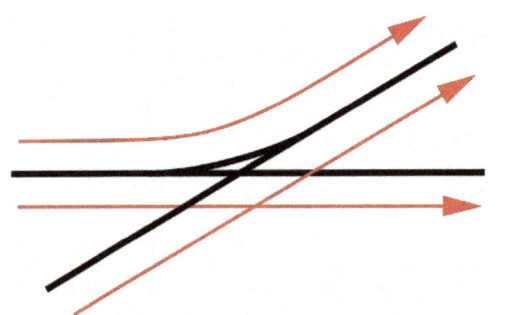

This unusual structure is called a single slip. Note that trains arriving from one direction can move in two directions, whereas arriving from another direction can only move in one direction.

More Complex Rail Layouts – Crossing movements

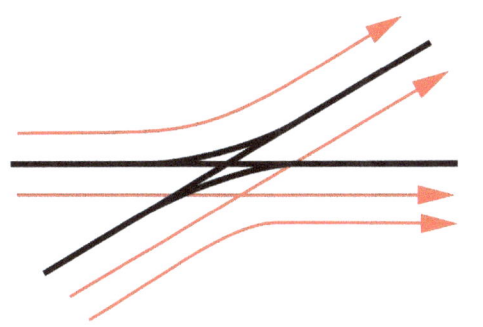

This is a double slip. The addition of this infrastructure adds a lot of flexibility to a rail system.

From an infrastructure perspective, the addition of turnouts (especially in large numbers) can create a lot of additional work and expense, and additional turnouts should only be added when really needed.

Drawing Junctions and other more complex structures

The elements show above can be combined together to create more complex ones. Common examples are shown below.

A junction is a place where rail tracks either split or merge together. Below 4 tracks on the left become two tracks on the right.

Figure 5.8 A Large Junction

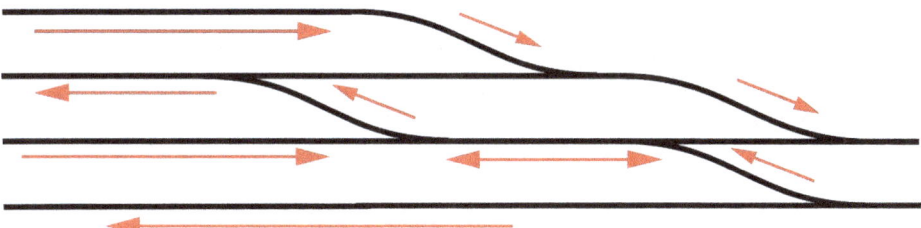

This junction is composed of 6 turnouts, of which 4 are in crossovers. Junctions can be far more complicated than the one above, and some junctions can be truly enormous.

A junction is a place where many of the above configurations have been installed, leading to quite a complex layout. Whilst the junction drawn above is quite simple, junctions get very complicated very quickly.

Crossing Loops

A crossing loop is provided for trains to pass one another, especially where there is only one track, but are sometimes used for more tracks. Crossing loops are also provided where fast moving trains need to pass slow moving ones.

The layout below best describes a crossing loop. A single track approaches the platform from either direction, and trains moving from left to right go to platform 1, and from right to left to platform 2. Thus trains are able to pass one another on the same track despite going in different directions.

Figure 5.9 Crossing Loop

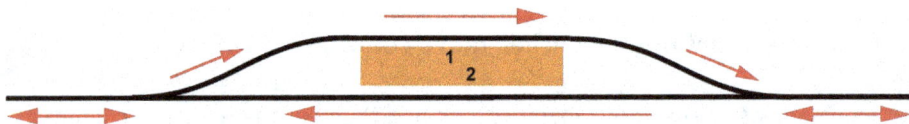

Crossing loops can be an effective way to allow trains to pass one another. Crossing loops are very common in regional and commuter networks, and also in freight networks.

Refuges

Refuges are a place where trains can be stored for hours or even days. They are almost always a loop, and do not have a platform. Refuges can be quite small.

Figure 5.10 Refuges

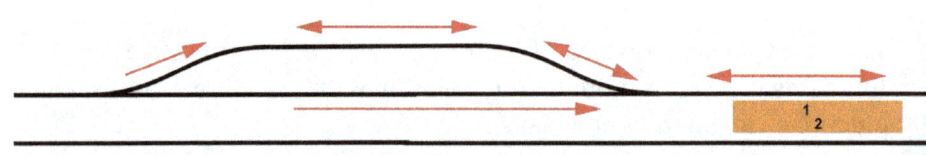

Refuges can be quite useful, and it is often necessary to store trains that are not in revenue service, and where no stabling is nearby. The two tracks are the ones that pass past the station. The refuge is not used for main line traffic, and the maximum permitted speed will be very low. The number of trains stored in a refuge will be small, typically only one or two.

Sidings

Sidings are used to store trains. Unlike refuges, sidings typically do not rejoin the main line. Sidings can be expanded to become very large, but the layout drawn below is not particularly large.

Figure 7.11 A Siding

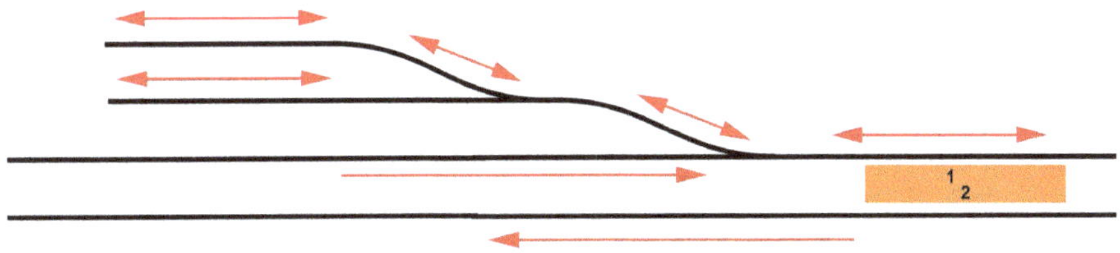

The bottom two tracks, the ones that pass the platforms, are mainline tracks. The top two are sidings. Sidings are a very important part of any rail network, and even a small network will need lots of sidings.

Termini

A terminus is where a rail line ends, and the passenger train will not continue in revenue service. A terminus may or may not have stabling, and where this is stabling then the terminus can be very complicated. Often however no stabling is provided, or very little, and the terminus is quite a simple design. Some standard designs are provided below, and there is no question some are better than others.

The termini presented here all allow trains to continue on. Most termini in a rail system will not allow trains to do this, and they must stop their journey and go back in the opposite direction. The termini presented here are common in large commuter networks, where trains frequently terminate, and express trains then pass continuing on. There can be several such termini in on one line, where trains with different stopping patterns

Goods Roads

A goods road is a track that passes round the station and other facilities, without providing for passengers to alight and board. Goods roads are provided to allow freight trains to continue their journey without disrupting passenger services. The layout below includes a centre terminating road. The goods line is drawn in green, and freight trains do not stop at the station, hence there is no platform number.

Figure 5.12 A Goods Road

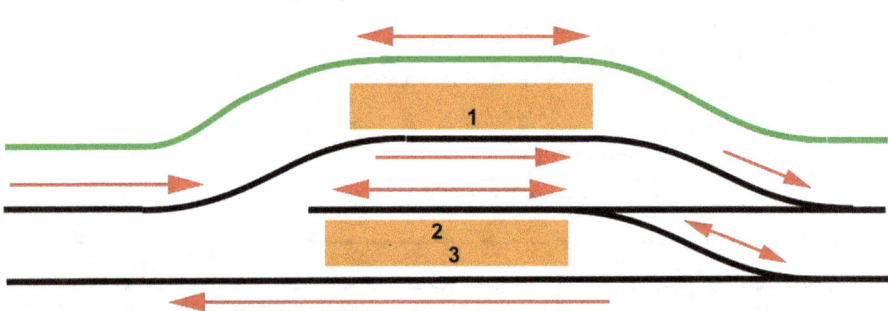

Goods roads are common in freight, regional and commuter networks, and unheard of in almost any other system. Some light rail systems, especially those constructed adjacent to a freight line, can also have goods roads around stations.

Perway Sidings

A perway siding is a place where track vehicles and other maintenance vehicles can be placed onto the track. Perway stands for permanent way, and the permanent way is the track and related components, such as rails, sleepers, and ballast. The maintenance of the permanent way requires large track machines, and there are different many of these. Sometimes, and this is especially true in large networks, it is better if track machines are put onto a truck, and craned into position. Once installed onto track, perway vehicles can then perform the maintenance that is required. Perway sidings are almost always unwired, so there is no overhead wiring, as machines vehicles are diesel powered, and cranes cannot be used where there is overhead wiring.

Figure 5.13 Perway Siding

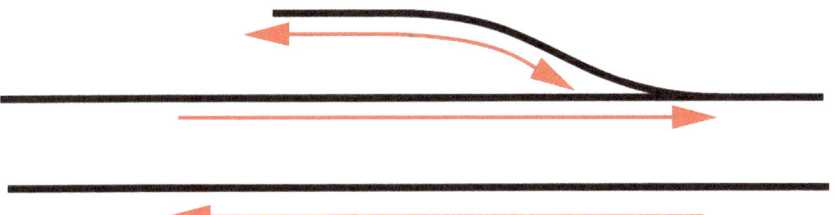

Junction for Four Tracks Becoming Two

Two track, normally with one track for each direction, can split and go in two different directions. The diagram below shows this with trains moving from right to left and there are two different ways trains can go. This type of junction is extremely common in most rail systems.

Figure 5.14 Two Track Junction

For four tracks it is important in many cases to allow trains to move between the two tracks that permit train movements in the same direction. Diamond crossovers allow this, and are shown in the diagram below. A diamond crossover is similar to a normal crossover, but crosses a track moving in the opposite direction to get to the other track. In the layout below there are 4 diamond crossovers.

Figure 5.15 Diamond Crossovers

As mentioned above, a double slip allows trains to move in 4 different directions through a single turnout. Below are two double slips. Double slips have fallen out of favour due to their complexity and maintenance challenges, and often are points of high use, so wear is high. Double slips allow substantial flexibility in the different directions trains can move.

Figure 5.16 Double Slips

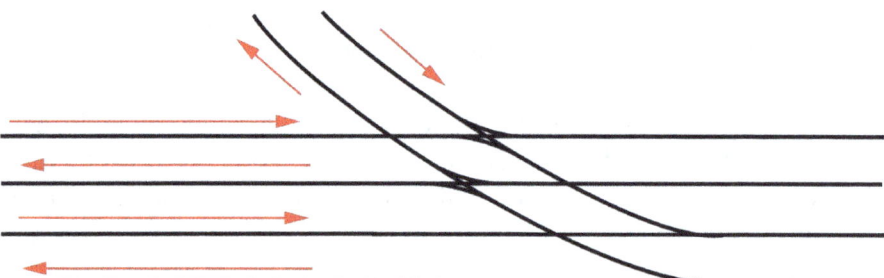

A triangle is a place where trains can move from one line to another. It is a meeting point of at least two rail lines, and sometimes three depending on the way lines are defined. Less obviously, triangles allow trains to be turned around, and face the opposite direction. The land in the middle of a triangle is entirely enclosed by rail lines, and can be used for any purpose a rail system might wish to use it for.

Figure 5.17 Triangles

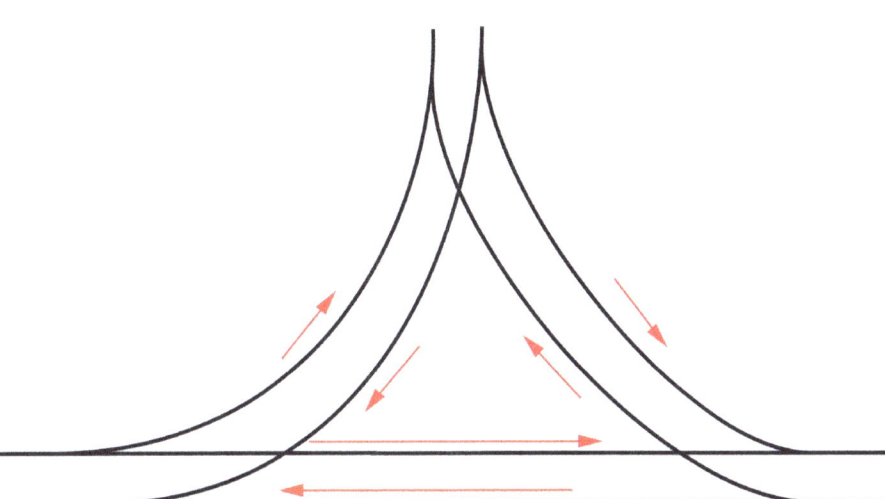

A loop is not a common feature in rail systems, but is used in some commuter rail systems in Australia, and also in Hong Kong in the tram network. A loop is very useful in allowing a train to change direction without stopping. Trains simply drive normally, and then are facing the opposite direction. Loops are difficult to deploy, but can be very effective in reducing turnaround times by removing a terminus.

Figure 5.18 Loops

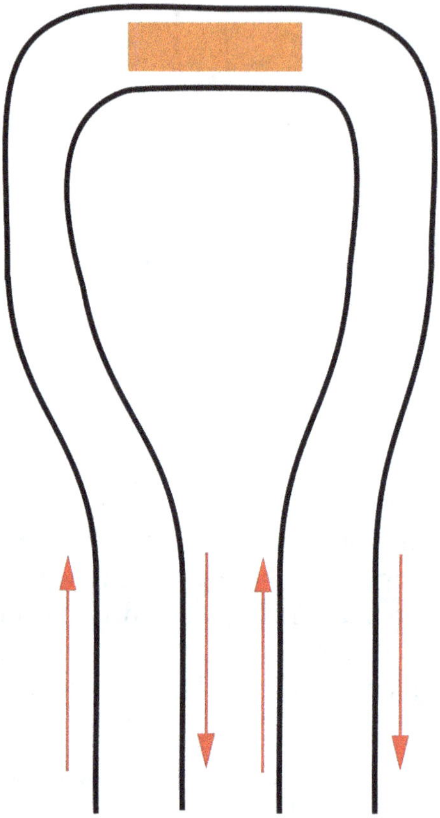

Drawing a new rail system

With all the different elements shown above, a complete rail line can now be drawn. An simple example is shown below.

As part of any new project or creating a new rail line, the new system would need to be drawn. To complete a drawing of the network, a number of key questions will need to be asked, and answers must be provided. For example:
- Where will trains be stabled?
- Where can trains be terminated from, and sent back?
- How many sidings are needed, the higher the frequency of trains, the more stabling, and hence sidings, that will be needed
- How is freight going to be managed, if at all?

Rail System Drawing and Configuration Page 116

So below is an example of what a rail line might look like.

Figure 5.19 An Example Rail Line

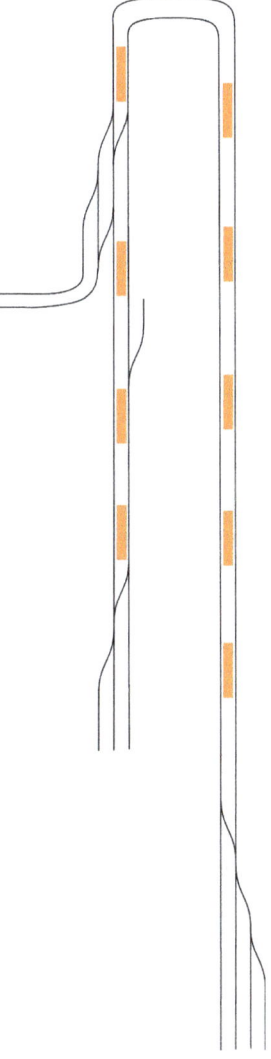

Chapter 6 Stations

Stations are what passengers see when entering and leaving a rail system. They are an important place for passengers, and play a large role in the perceived success or failure of a rail system. Stations also have a large amount of infrastructure, and the trend with modern stations is to provide more in terms of facilities to passengers in stations. Tickets are sold, and passengers provided with information on train running in a station.

The construction of stations are a large part of the cost of constructing a new rail line. This is especially so for underground stations, which need expensive ventilation systems to provide air to passengers, as well as providing an exit clear of smoke in the event of a fire emergency. Stations can, depending on the type of rail system, have a large number of facilities provided to customers, and the large number of these can make construction of the station rather expensive.

Some of the customer facilities that can be provided on a station include:
- Toilets
- Covered waiting areas
- Air-conditioning
- Vending machines and food stalls
- Information of all sorts, including tourist information
- Television screens showing news and other information
- First aid
- Internet kiosks
- Wifi
- Free water
- Mobile phone reception
- Prayer rooms
- Breast feeding rooms
- Lockers
- Services with baggage (such as long term storage)
- Sale of rail related souvenirs
- Shops selling all sorts of products
- Banking facilities
- Library facilities for long journeys

In any one station it is unlikely that all of these facilities would be installed at the same location.

Styles and Configurations of Stations

Stations come in a large array of different configurations, and can be described in terms of a number of simple parameters, which are commonly understood throughout the rail industry. Some of these are:

- Platform length. Typically platforms are raised and higher than both the ground and the track running alongside it, and the length of the platform is the linear measure from one end of the platform to another. Not all platforms are the same length as the trains that stop there.
- Height of the platform. This measurement is taken from the top of the running surface of the rail to the place where passengers stand to board a train.
- Number of platforms. Each platform normally has a separate track alongside it, although in some cases a very long platform may be classified as two separate platforms.
- Number of passengers through the station each day. This is counted through the ticketing system, and the number of barrier/gate entries and exits is counted per day.
- The role the station plays in the operation of the network. Stations may be very large and play an important role in the network or small and trains may stop there only rarely. Some stations are used only for special events. Alternatively, a station can be a terminus, where services terminate and do not continue, or am interchangestation, where passengers can alight from one service on one rail line, and then board a service on another line.
- If the station is underground, at the same grade as the ground, or elevated. These differences are important for the design and use of the station.

Some stations may have disused platforms, and these are not normally counted as part of the total number of platforms. Old stations may have a substantial number of these, and the numbering or identification of platforms may reflect this. At Rockdale station in Sydney platform numbering runs from 2 to 5, as platform 1 is no longer used, and the numbers have not changed since that platform was built over 50 years ago.

The station below is typical of stations in remote areas, and there is only one track at this platform. Trains moving in both directions stop at the same platform. There is no track on the other side. Also note that the station has no roofing, although there is a small area provided, a bit like a shed, where passengers can stand to get out of the rain. Stations of this kind are rarely manned with staff, as there is no booking office for staff to sell tickets at, or store cleaning implements, or any of the other accessories of an office.

A Simple Regional Station

This station has only one track, which has some advantages and disadvantages. A carpark on the side of the station without a track may be accessed without crossing any tracks, which for disabled passengers is a real benefit. Alternatively, the number of trains that can pass through this station will be limited to a small number per hour, as trains moving in both directions will need to pass over the same track. Another configuration possible with thinly used stations is that there is a loop around the station, allowing trains top stop at both platforms to pass one another.

We can see the facilities provided on this station, which is in outer Sydney. There is no booking office, so no staff will ordinarily be present to help passengers and sell tickets. Seating and lighting is provided, as well as a covered waiting area. The covered area will provide some protection from rain, but given its small size will provide shelter for only maybe 20 passengers, and no more. There are no vending machines, nor any screens providing information on when the next train is due. There are no barriers to restrict entry to the station, and passengers can move around freely. The reader may notice a small yellow box under the orange sign attached to the waiting area, which is a help point for any passengers who feel their safety is threatened. There are no lifts or escalators of any kind.

Whilst this particular station is in a remote area of Sydney, this configuration of station is very common in Australia. There are hundreds of this type of basic yet functional station across the country, and these exist in all states of Australia. They are cheap to construct, and maintain, and perform an important function whilst being relatively immune to damage from vandalism and weather. Some may feel that this type of station is somehow inadequate, but it is an efficient design that performs its function well.

The picture below is of a regional station outside of Paris. We may observe that this station has a clock, covered waiting areas, and is very long indeed. The platform height is also quite low, consistent with the platform heights across Europe and France especially. On the right hand side is a booking office, where tickets are sold, station staff work, and there is an air-conditioned office. Notice that the station has roofing over part of its length. Also notice that the two platforms are on the side of the track, and this configuration is called a side platform station. There is no obvious numbering on the station. Given that there is a waiting area and booking office on one side of the station, and not the other, this station is likely to be a commuter station, which passengers waiting to go to the city centre on one side, and using the other platform to only alight when returning from the nearby city (in this case Paris). This configuration is very common.

A Regional Station in Paris, Side Platforms

The station below is in urban Sydney, and is an island platform station. For this type of station the platforms are in the centre of the tracks, and trains move around the platforms. Passengers wait in the middle of the platform, and can wait in the same place for trains in either direction. Notice on this station there is a vending machine for Coke Cola drinks next to the wall of the old building in the middle of the platform. Express services bypass this station, and local all stopping services, which are slower, stop here with a low frequency.

A Suburban Station in Sydney, Island Platform

Island platforms are often considered superior to side platform stations. This is because:
- Rail staff can be placed in the middle of the island platform, to provide customer information, assistance, and sell tickets
- Toilets, if provided, need only to be located in the middle of the island platform
- In underground systems, island platforms are generally bigger, so there is more room for passengers to wait. For above ground stations with side platforms can be any size based on the nearby available land
- It's obvious where passengers should wait, but with side platforms passengers need to make a decision.

There are also some disadvantages to island platforms, and some of these are:

- Island platforms are typically larger, and this can particularly be a problem with elevated railways where space is quite limited
- Island platforms require tracks to move in a curve around the station. Notice in the pictures above that the tracks for the side platforms are very straight, whereas one of the tracks for the island platform needs to curve around the platform. If there are high speed trains not stopping at the station this could be a real problem.
- Side platforms can be convenient for passengers with disabilities, as they can enter one platform directly from the carpark. This can be very handy as there is no need to use a lift, assuming that the platform is on the side for trains going in the desired direction
- Island platforms are more expensive than smaller side platforms, especially in underground stations

Another type of station is one where passengers need to request the train to stop, to either board or alight. For heavy rail these stations are relatively uncommon, but for light rail are extremely common. For tram systems this is normal, and the waiting passenger would signal the driver to stop, usually with a movement of a hand. In the US this kind of station is called a halt. There are also a small number of stations like this in Sydney.

Stations for tram systems tend to be very simple, likewise for classical "light rail" systems. Tram stations are mostly called stops, and are more like bus stops than stations. Many of the stops are so small that that are almost invisible, and are can only be detected by a small street sign indicating that trams stop there. In some cases passengers may even need to board and alight from the side of the road to the waiting tram.

The photo below is a tram stop in Zurich. It is very basic, and there is an oval building alongside the tram tracks, which has a small number of shops in it. Note that the tram stop is just a flat space with no cover, no obvious lighting, and very little by way of facilities. This is common for tram stops, even in very busy cities.

A Tram Stop in Zurich

The photo below is a light rail station in Hong Kong. Light rail vehicles use this station to move passengers from the main metro line to apartment buildings in outer Hong Kong. From this photo we note that the platforms are quite high from the passenger walking surface to the top of the rail. Older light rail systems had this design, but this is now uncommon. Also note that the entire station is covered, but very poorly lit, and the platforms are very short. The photo was taken when standing on the tracks, something that is allowed with light rail and trams, but not with heavy rail. This station is a blend of a heavy rail station and a tram stop.

A Light Rail Station

In some cases the length of the platform may be shorter than trains which use the platform. Whilst this situation may seem a little silly, in some railways it is common, and passengers can only disembark from parts of the train there is a matching platform next to the door. Where there is no platform next to the train, people wanting to disembark may decide to leap from the train onto the ground below.

Regional trains can be very long because passengers need to sit down, making the passenger density in the train rather low. In some cases platforms where the train stops are not long enough, so doors will face nothing but grass or open space. Furthermore the drop down from the train door may be quite large, and so any passengers that attempt to alight down to the ground are risking injury. In rare cases most of the train may have no matching platform, and disembarkation may be impossible from several carriages of the train.

For obvious reasons it is far better if all platforms are as long as the train itself. In a metro or any other system that operates in an urban environment, this will generally be the case. In some rail systems that operate to remote places, where the number of passengers per day can be counted in the dozens, building a full station may not be appropriate. Alternatively, and this sometimes happens where the station is located next to a river or other body of water, it may not be possible to build a station to the length needed as space is severely constrained, and so a compromise is made. In many cases the local residents may be prepared to accept a reduced length platform as long as there is some sort of rail service.

For any railway that creates this situation there are a number of factors that need to be considered:
- Where passengers jump from the train and are injured, how will medical assistance be provided?
- Can the doors on the train be closed if there is no matching platform? This will require specialised controls to open and close specific doors
- What happens where a passenger does not know that their carriage does not have a matching platform, and cannot alight, and so are overcarried to the next station. Will a taxi be provided? Overnight accommodation? What happens if children are overcarried, is the railway going to allow them to find their own way home if they are overcarried at night?
- Which doors on the train are to be opened? Will it be the front doors or the back ones? Someone in the middle perhaps?
- How can passengers be informed that trains cannot provide exit to certain stations? Perhaps posters on station walls, or announcements to passengers.

Overall if at all possible stations should be constructed to at least the same length as the longest train, but in a small number of cases it may not be appropriate to do this.

Straight and Curved Platforms

Many station platforms in large metro systems are straight, and when trains arrive they will sit in a straight line from one end of the train to another. Many platforms are curved, and not straight, and this is common in large commuter rail systems. In Australia many stations are curved, some dramatically so, as building straight stations was not considered to be important until relatively recently.

A curved platform is shown below. This station is in Hong Kong, and has side platforms. Notice that the platform on the left is concave, and on the other side of the two rail tracks, convex.

A Curved Platform in Hong Kong

The problem with curved platforms is demonstrated in the diagram below. Train carriages are built straight in all cases, and can only bend or articulate where there is a coupling between carriages. Light rail vehicles can be articulated, which means that there can be a number of joins, which allows the vehicle to appear to be curved, but in reality is made up of many short straight sections. Commuter and regional trains especially can have very long carriages, 26 to 30 metres in length is common, and passenger doors will often be located at each end of the carriage. Placing a straight object alongside a curved one will mean that in some places the carriage will be close to the platform edge, and in others far away. In extreme cases the door/carriage floor may be over 30 cm away from the platform, and with such a large gap passengers can fall into it. This may cause injuries, or even death.

The diagram below shows the problem. The centre of the carriage is close to the platform edge, and any doors located there will not have a large gap. Doors close to the end of the carriage, and they are commonly located there on double decker carriages (bi-level), will be further away from the platform.

Figure 6.1 Platform Gaps

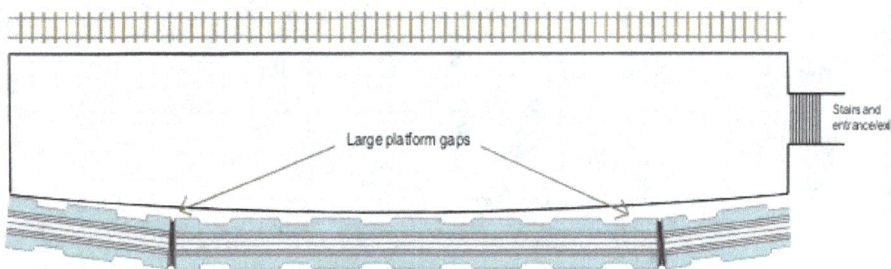

This situation is considered extremely undesirable. Passenger with disabilities, for example those with vision impairment, will struggle to contend with such a large gap, and may fall through. Passengers with wheel chairs will need some sort of mechanical assistance to cover such a large gap, and will not be able to cross this without help. Where gaps of this size exist, stations will need to be manned, and staff provided to allow wheel chair passengers to board the train. Typically a ramp is provided to wheelchair passengers to allow them to cross this gap.

Consider that where this assistance is not provided, and many regional and commuter trains are not staffed throughout the entire day, then wheelchair passengers may not be able to board a train at all. Alternatively, wheelchair passengers may not be able to alight, and may be overcarried to the next station that is staffed or where the platform and the floor of the train are close enough that the passenger can alight without assistance.

Also consider that mothers with prams may also struggle to get onto and off trains. There are a large number of different passengers who are disadvantaged by this station design.

Having said all this, there are some situations where a curved platform is unavoidable. Metro stations and stations will high volumes of passengers should always be designed so that they are straight, and this is a common requirement in the standards for passenger design. However, some very small stations may only have a very small number of passengers, and it may be acceptable for a rail line and corresponding platform to be curved. Consider that there may be laws and regulations that prohibit this in many countries, as this station cannot be used by those with disabilities, even when the number of passengers using the station is very small. This is the case in Australia, and in all future construction all platforms are straight.

Note that curved platforms can be both convex and concave. In the diagram above the platform shown is concave, and this is more common, as island platforms often contain a station building or other facilities in the middle, making the centre of the station wider than the ends. Concave platforms are much more common than convex, as many island platforms have two concave platforms.

So the reader has seen the need to have straight platforms, and the benefits this brings. Building rail lines with straight platforms raises many challenges also, and these include:
- Straight stations are a lot easier to achieve geometrically with side platforms rather than island platforms. Side platforms are not as suited for large passenger flows as island platforms.
- Island platforms, combined with straight platforms, will mean that the rail tunnels leading into a station may need to be twin bore, rather than single bore. A single bore tunnel may be impossible as it would be too large, so two tunnels are needed rather than one. This substantially adds to the construction cost
- Curves along any rail system with straight platforms will need to be sharper, as no curves are permitted along platforms, and curves in most rail systems are very common. In some cases the curves may need to be so sharp that maximum speeds need to be reduced, and so average travel speeds are reduced.
- In severe cases, especially where rail lines are following some geographical feature such as a river or a harbour, it may be impossible to construct entire stations, as the geometry does not permit the construction of a station without curves.

Straight platforms can be difficult to implement, and can present major design challenges. Clever design, and well thought out transport plans, can go a long way to manage this problem.

Terminal Stations

Large terminal stations are places where regional, high speed and commuter trains converge and sit to allow passengers to change from one train to another. This type of central city station is quite common, and in the US and Canada these stations are often called "Union" station. There are union stations in Chicago, Los Angeles, Toronto, and Montreal, and many others.

The most famous terminal station in the world is Grand Central Station in New York. In large cities there might be many terminal stations, for example, in Paris there are six. In all Australian cities there is only one in each city.

Below is an example of a small terminal station. This one is in Perth. Services leave here for some regional destinations, and almost all commuter trains pass through this station. The high ceiling provides a feeling of space. Notice the platforms are numbered, and there are text passenger information displays for each platform. As is common with terminal station, trains are waiting for their scheduled departure times at the station.

Perth Main Station

Terminal stations often have flashy designs to make them look more impressive. Open areas to give a feeling of space and to make the station look sexy and more cool. Large open areas are common in large stations, although there is no real reason why all stations should not be designed in this way.

Interchange Stations

Interchange stations are places where multiple rail lines are connected through the rail station, and passengers must alight to get to other rail lines. Passengers are able to move from one line to another and board another

train. Whilst many interchanges are designed well, many are not, problems with transport interchanges can be significant.
The ideal construction of interchange stations should allow passengers to easily and quickly move from one rail line to another. Ideally, interchange stations should have platforms close together, so that the interchange time is small. Good station design will allow passengers to interchange without going to far, and in Hong Kong it is possible to interchange between rail lines by moving from one side of an island platform to another. This is done by designing stations so that trains arrive on two sides of a platform moving in the same direction.

Some of the more common problems with interchange stations are:
- Two or more rail lines are far apart, and their interchange stations are far apart, and passengers need to walk large distance to get from one to another
- Poor signage means that it is not clear what direction to go to get to the other rail line
- Numerous flights of stair connect different rail lines together, which is a challenge for many passengers to negotiate
- Interchange stations that on maps appear close together but in reality are far apart
- Problems with ticketing, where tickets may not work from one line to another, or passengers need to go out of the paid area to reach the other rail line and do not realise they need to do so
- Some interchange stations are extremely large, and can be difficult to get around due to their size (such as Shinjuku station in Tokyo)
- Walkways between rail lines are little more than construction sites, with poor footing, broken surfaces, barriers around construction work, and poor signage.
- In some cases there may be multiple stations to interchange with, and signage needs to identify which is the correct one for passengers to walk to, and to get to their final destination.

The photo below shows a moving walk. A moving walk is similar to an escalator, but along flat ground. Moving walks do not have stairs, and are there to assist passengers in getting quickly from one place to another. Moving walks are common in airports, and also in large interchange stations. There are a number of large moving walks installed in stations in Hong Kong at interchange stations. The moving walk shown below is located at the Domestic Airport station in Sydney, where it is used to connect the two terminals together though the underground station.

A Moving Walk

Components of a Station

Platform screen doors have become increasing common around the world. They are suited in metro stations or at stations where there is significant crowding. To work properly the doors on the station need to line up with the doors on the train, and this is usually only possible with ATO (automatic train operation), where a computer drives the train. A human driver will rarely be accurate enough to allow a rail system to use platform screen doors.

Overall platform screen doors seem to be becoming more common, especially in Asia. Below is a picture of some platform screen doors in Singapore, and as with just about everything in Singapore, it's very clean and shiny. The platform screen doors below are full height, and completely the station from the tunnel in which the train moves.

Platform Screen Doors

Platform screen doors have a number of benefits, including:
- It is very difficult for people to commit suicide at stations with platform screen doors
- No one will be pushed under a train from overcrowding with platform screen doors
- The air-conditioning load for the station will be lower, as the air from the station will not mix with outside air
- The station looks better, as passengers cannot see the dirty tracks and tunnel, but instead see the clean shiny platform screen doors.

No discussion of any asset in a rail system would be complete without mentioning the disadvantages:
- They are expensive
- They can fail, and this can delay trains
- Their use is limited to trains that are at least partially computer controlled, as drivers cannot stop their trains with the accuracy needed to position the train next to the platform doors.

The lines painted on the floor to direct passengers. These are common in major metro lines where the number of passengers is very large. Passengers alighting move through the middle of the doors, and on the outsides wait for passengers to alight before boarding the train.

The doors above are full height doors, but it is not necessary to do that. Below is a picture of some platform edge barriers in Tokyo, which provides many of the benefits of full length doors. In terms of passenger flow and safety the half height doors work quite well, but do not assist with air conditioning. Also note the advertising screens on the walls across from the platform.

Platform Edge Barriers

Concourses are the area above or near a station where many of the entrances and exists are connected. Passengers move throughout a station from the concourse, and it is often above the station. The photo below is of a metro station in Hong Kong. Long concourses like this are common in underground metro stations, where the station has the additional purpose of allowing people to move around the city without catching a train. In the front of the picture are the barriers that provide entry into the station proper, and on the left is a walkway to the other end of the station. The concourse here is above the platforms where the metro stations stop, and as the metro trains are quite long, the concourse also is quite long. The area behind the barriers is sometimes referred to as the "paid area", where passengers need to buy a ticket to enter.

A Metro Station Concourse

Some of the stations in Hong Kong serve as major thoroughfares without the need for passengers to catch a train. Pedestrian interconnections through a railway station can be beneficial to the movement of people around the station. Stations may be connected through overpasses, and passengers can walk along these to get to the next station without riding a train. In some cases pedestrian overpasses or shopping centres can extend for several kilometres, connecting several stations together.

The picture below is of a station in Osaka where the platforms are on both sides of the train, and doors are opened simultaneously on both sides of the train. In practice passengers enter form one side and exit from the other. This type of station is sometimes called the Spanish solution, because it is commonly used in the Barcelona metro. Passengers get on through one side of the train, and alight from the other. This structure of station is able to move more people quickly.

Barcelona Style Platforms for a Terminus Station in Osaka

The station configuration above is sometimes used in terminus stations, and in stations with very high numbers of passengers. This configuration can be very effective in reducing dwell times.

Passenger information is a very important in a rail system. Information provided to passengers can be much more than when the next train arrives although this is also very important. The picture below shows a simple rail passenger information screen in a metro station in Paris. The information is very basic, but provides what passengers need.

Passenger Information Sign in Paris

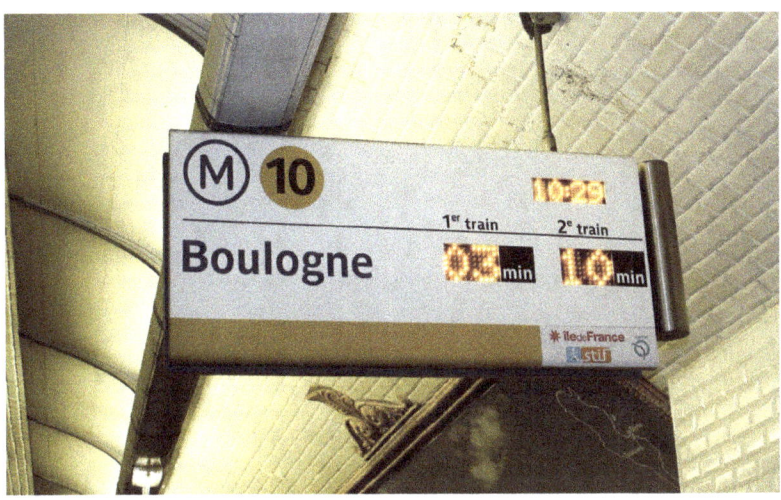

Information about the local area can also be provided to passengers. This includes exits, where important landmarks are located, and how to get there from where passengers are standing. This is called wayfinding.

Maps should be provided and easy to read. Network maps in particular should be freely installed in any station. Below in the two smaller photos are geographical maps provided in two different stations. The one on the left is of the metro network in Tokyo. The one on the right is the regional rail system of Taiwan.

Geographically Correct Maps in Stations

Tickets are sold on almost all rail systems, and provide a right to passengers to ride on the system. Paper tickets, previously very common, are a type of ticketing system called "proof of payment", where customers buy a ticket and use that ticket as proof of purchase. Tickets are almost always sold on stations.

Becoming more common are smart cards, where money is added to the card and then it is used to gain entry to the station. Smart cards obviate the need for large numbers of paper tickets, and more commonly money is added to smart cards through credit cards and machines specifically provided to do this. Providing enough ticket machines is very important. Below are some ticket machines in Western Australia. On the right is an add value machine, which is used to add money on to their smart card. In the middle are the machines for selling old style paper tickets.

Ticketing Machines in Perth

Stations are places where large numbers of people move through each day. Advertising can be a very valuable source of revenue, and many railways take advantage of this and build different types of signage and information. Stations can be a very good place to locate advertising signage, and all sorts of different products can be promoted through signage. In Hong Kong signage is very common, and much of the flat space is devoted to signage.

Advertising is not limited to signage. This display is for digital cameras, in a display cabinet in Thailand. This one is at Chit Lom station in Bangkok, and seems to contain actual digital cameras. Promotions in stations for different products can take a variety of different forms.

The photo below is of a different type of passenger information. Very long trains, in particular regional and HSR trains, have numbered carriages and can be very long. Their length, and use of reserved seating on HSR trains, means that passengers need to know where their carriage is located. For HSR services where the dwell time is only a couple of minutes at any one station, passengers need to know where their carriage is located along the platform, and so these signs are provided along the platform to provide this information.

Stations Page 139

Passenger Carriage Information

Underground and elevated stations in major rail systems are almost always protected from the rain. There is complete coverage of the railway station, and heavy rain will not effect the movement of passengers and trains. In regional or commuter systems, almost all stations will be above ground, but not elevated, and be exposed to the elements. The station below is common in some rail systems and the covered area is very small. This station is in Perth in Australia, and like many stations in that city has almost no coverage of the platform.

An Uncovered Station

For small stations there is no real reason why the entire platform should be covered. During rainstorms passengers can wait under the small shelter

Stations

provided, and this will be adequate in most cases. For larger stations, lack of coverage can be a problem, as passengers will want to avoid getting wet, and will all wait under whatever cover is provided. Where the covered area is small, it will be come very crowded, and when boarding any trains there will be delays are the passengers will all crowd into one or two doors. This can create serious problems with dwell time, as passengers will attempt to board trains only through train doors next to covered areas.

Stations that are only partly covered will need less cleaning, as rainwater will wash away any dirt, especially where the station is designed with a slight slope on the platforms to allow rainwater to run away. Sunlight can sterilize the floor of any platform, in time, so this means that sanitising agents may not be needed to clean the platform. As a general rule, stations should only be covered if needed, and there is nothing wrong with leaving a station partly uncovered.

Access in and out of Stations

Trains are large, and in many cases there are two or more tracks making up any rail line. Passengers need to be able to get from outside the rail corridor to the desired platform to catch a train. They need to either go over the top of the rail corridor, or beneath it.

The raised section over a station is called the concourse. Concourses are quite common, and often stairs may lead to the concourse from both outside the station, and from platforms.

The design below is a common one, and the concourse is connected to both the platform and the outside of the station through a ramp, and not stairs. For a side platform, where there are no barriers, this solution is quite acceptable, and there are only two ramps at this station, one in view and the other to the left. The ramp allows passengers to get over the tracks entering the rail corridor. Also the ramp allows wheelchair passengers access across tracks.

A Station Ramp

Ramps are a cheap and practical solution to providing access to stations for those with disabilities. Ramps also are unlikely to fail, and require very little maintenance, unlike lifts and escalators.

There are national and international on ramp design. Normally ramps must be design to be below a certain grade, and a steep ramp will be difficult to those with disabilities to use. Also, long ramps need to have landings, which is a flat space where people with wheelchairs can rest during the ascent of a ramp.

An alternative to a pedestrian crossing over a station is for passengers to cross at the same grade as trains. The pedestrian crossing above is a common way to allow passengers to cross the rail tracks, but obviously there is a safety risk. The trend in modern railways is to avoid using this type of infrastructure, as there can be fatalities to the travelling public.

A Station Lift

Mobility aids are a very important topic with stations. Adding mechanical aids to a station will help disabled people use the station more effectively, but they can be very expensive to install. On the left is a lift which can move people from the concourse to the platform. This type of free standing structure is extremely expensive to install as there is no other structure upon which the liftwell can use for support, and so it needs to be a free standing structure.

Escalators are often also used to move people from and to the platform. Escalators are very popular because the speed up the departure of people from the platform once passengers have alighted. Escalators can be provided individually, in pairs, or in groups of three or more.

A Station Escalator

Light Rail Stations

One of the advantages of light rail and tram systems is that they can be designed with little separation between the rail system and road vehicles and often at the same grade. This reduces the cost of construction, and makes them very accessible to public transport users, as they are at street level and usually not buried deep underground. In many cases these systems have no separate right of way. Trams often operate down the middle of roads, and in many ways are treated the same as any other road vehicle.

As light rail and trams are located in and around roads, the question arises as to the placement of track and rail corridors in comparison to where roads are located. The right of way for rail may or may not be separate from road vehicles, and a large number of different configurations are possible, and some of these are shown below:

The figure below shows a rail corridor in the middle of a street, with road vehicles on either side. This is a common design for light rail stations, and the use of a separate right of way for rail track is a good idea. For this design passengers will need to cross the road on one side or the other of the station

Stations Page 144

to exit the corridor. Passengers will also need to cross the tracks to get to the other light rail station to go in the opposite direction to the one in which they came.

Figure 6.2 Light Rail Station in the Middle of the Street

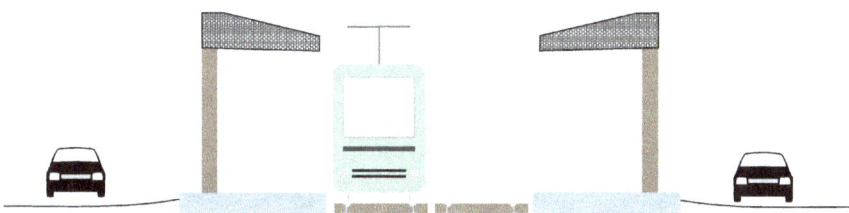

Below is another configuration for a light rail station, and the light rail station is on the left. The road is separate from the light rail station, although alongside one another. The light rail station is an island platform, so passengers will need to cross one track to get to the side of the road. This configuration is a very good one, as road and rail traffic is separated.

Figure 6.3 Light Rail Station on the Side of the Street

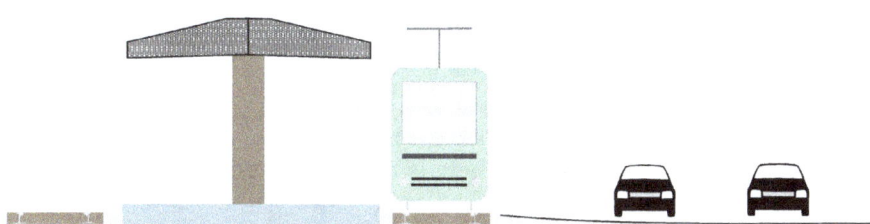

The light rail configuration below is extremely common in tram systems, but is also used in light rail systems as well. Road vehicles and rail share the same right of way, and mix freely. Whilst road vehicles can overtake trams, the converse is not true. This structure can work quite well, and is common in Melbourne with the large tram network there. One of the drawbacks with this structure is that passengers who wish to board and alight onto the tram must cross roads with fast moving vehicles on it, and the potential for an accident is quite significant. This configuration, whilst cheap and easy to implement, is not the safest, and is generally not recommended unless it cannot be avoided. There are however, many instances in a large tram network where there is no alternative, and this configuration is suitable.

Figure 6.4 Mixed Light Rail and Road Traffic with some Separation

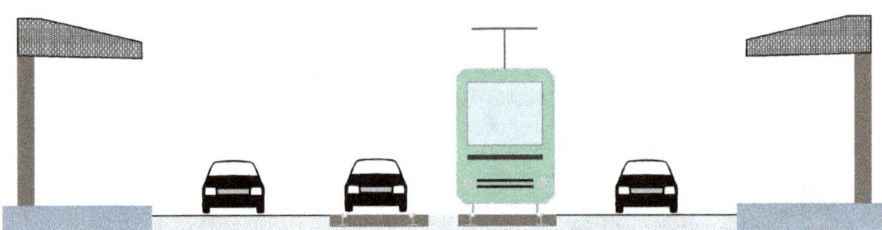

Also notice with the above configuration that road vehicles drive on the steel rails that support the light rail vehicle. Where the width of the road vehicle and rails are the same, it is possible for the road vehicle to slide along the rails, and not be able to stop when needed. This is particularly a problem in the wet, and accidents can be quite common.

The light rail configuration below is a poor one, but also somewhat common, especially in Melbourne. There is no separate right of way for rail traffic, and so road vehicles and trams/light rail share the same space. There is no way for road vehicles to pass the rail traffic, which is likely to be slow. As trams/light rail stop to allow passengers to board and alight, these vehicles will stop and wait at the tram stop. As the rail vehicle waits at the stop, road vehicles need to wait also. For a very busy street, passing through a congested shopping area, the travel speed of the tram/light rail vehicle may be very slow, to the point where there is no point in providing the service at all.

Figure 6.5 Mixed Light Rail and Road Traffic

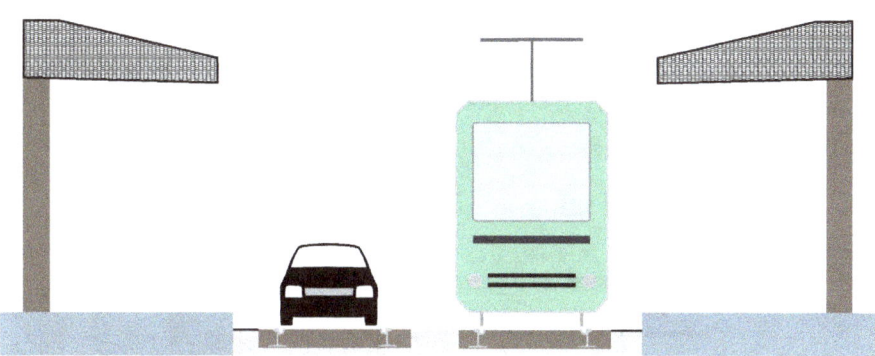

Tram systems were once very common in many parts of the world, especially Europe and North America. Almost all of them have been removed, and only a small number exist in their old form. One of the major contributing reasons for this was the use of the configuration above, which blocked road traffic and greatly contributed to congestion. The survival of the Melbourne tram network, now the world's largest, was because the configuration used above was rarely used, and so problems with congestion were avoided. The configuration above should only be used when absolutely necessary, and when there is no alternative.

Network Design around Stations

The design of the rail system in and around stations affects the way trains stop and arrive at those stations. Passenger trains typically terminate at stations, and not at other places in the network, as then passengers can be disembarked as far as possible into the train's movement to its final destination.

What is drawn below is a series of different configurations for stations that allows for a large degree of operational flexibility. The choice of what network design to choose depends on what is needed at that point in the network. Below are a series of different configurations that can be used.

What is presented below are a series of network configurations where trains can be terminated and sent back in the opposite direction. This can be achieved in a variety of different ways, and depending on the configuration determines the way trains are managed.

The layout below allows for trains to be terminated on the middle road between platforms 1 & 2. Trains making their way along the bottom track can terminate on platform 2, and then move to the terminal road. Once there then the train can move in the opposite direction, normally once the driver has moved from one end of the train to the other. The train can then make its way to platform 1, where it can board passengers and move off to the right of the page.

Figure 6.6 Terminal Road

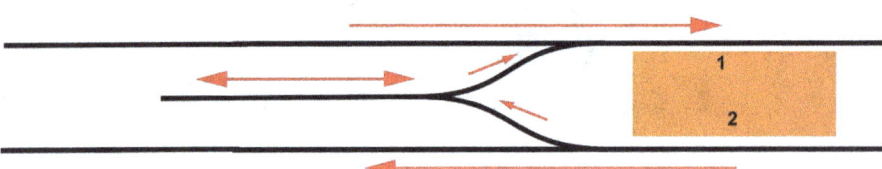

One of the advantages of the layout above is that trains can dwell in the terminating road waiting to be sent back. This feature can be very useful where there is a defect or failure in the train, and it needs to be moved out of the way from other trains.

In the layout below trains are terminated on platform 1. Trains can be terminated from either direction, but only onto platform 1. This will block trains moving from the left to the right, but trains can effectively change direction. This type of layout is inferior to a layout with 3 platforms, but is a common and effective way to get trains to be able to terminate.

Figure 6.7 Terminating in Both Directions

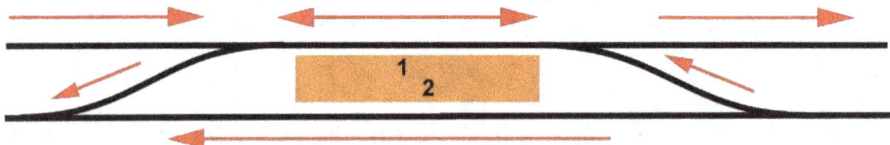

Notice that trains can also continue along from right to left, and stop at platform 1. Notice that it is not possible to terminate trains on platform 2.

In the layout below there are three platforms, and two tracks turns into three at the station. Trains can be terminated on platform 1, and sent back to the right of the page. Trans can also be terminated on platform 1 and sent back to the left. This layout is very versatile and can provide a lot of operational flexibility for an operating railway. This type of layout is also useful for storing a slow moving train, which can be stored on platform 1. Platforms 2 and 3 are still useful for trains moving in their normal direction.

Figure 6.8 Terminating on No 1 Platform

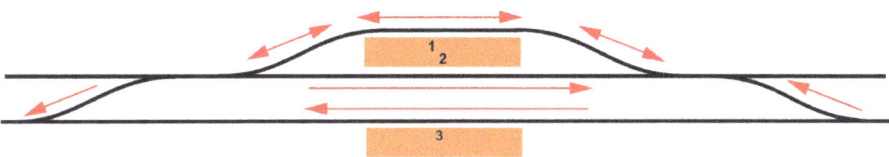

One problem with this layout is that it requires additional space. For an underground railway this additional space can cost money, and quite a lot at that.

The terminus below operates slightly differently than the one above. Notice that trains can terminate and stand on platform 2, and can wait there for a while whilst trains pass through platforms 1 and 3. The track next to platform 2 is sometimes known as a terminating road. This layout only allows trains to be terminated in one direction, from right to left. The advantage of this layout is there is no need for terminating trains to cross the path of any other trains, and so headway is not impacted.

Figure 6.9 Centre Terminating Road

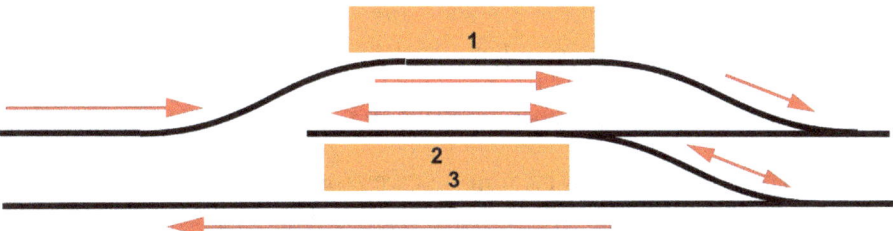

In the layout below trains terminate on platform 1. This layout is considered inferior to the other two above because trains need to cross in front of trains passing through platform 2 to get to platform 1. However, once there, trains can stand on this platform for some time until needed. Again, trains can only be terminated in one direction, from right to left, rather than from left to right.

Figure 6.10 Terminating Road away from Running Lines

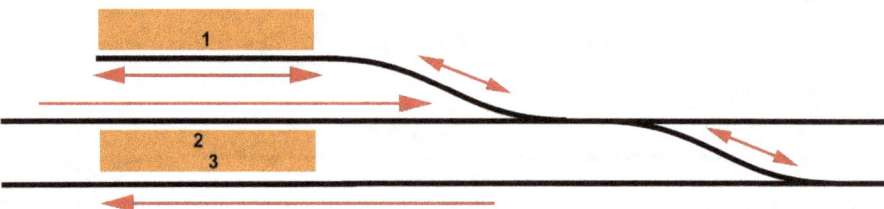

The layout below is a simple layout that minimises the use of space. Trains can be terminated on either platform, and then sent to the right. This structure of station is particularly useful for sending trains back to the right. One of the challenges of this layout is the use of a diamond crossover, which can require extra maintenance.

Figure 6.11 Terminating Station with a Diamond Crossover

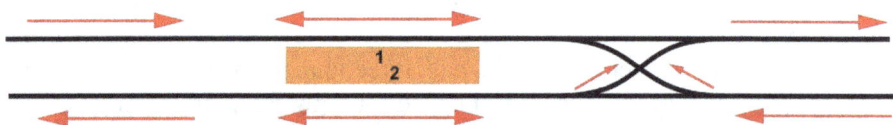

The station layout below is a little more complicated than the ones above. In this layout there are 3 platforms and this is used to manage trains which are either making their way to or coming from the right hand side. There is a two track junction on the right, and trains are being managed at the station. Junctions such as the one below are common in many different types of rail systems, and adding operational flexibility to move trains around.

The layout below allows trains to be put from branch line (the one going up to the top), onto any platform. Trains sitting on platform 2 can also proceed to either direction. Trains sitting on platform 1 can also move either to the left or the right.

Figure 6.12 3 Platform Station with Junction

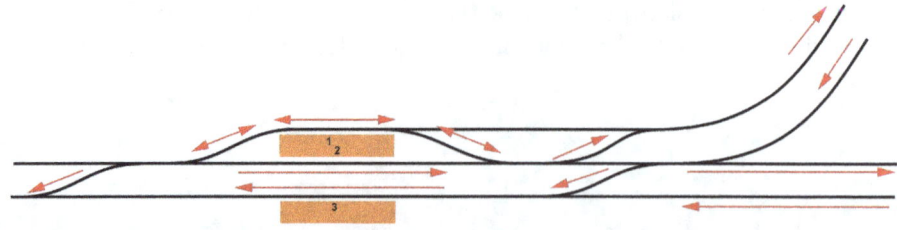

Stations Page 150

The layout below is for a terminus. A terminus is where a rail line ends and where many trains cease to be in revenue service. Terminus's are a very common feature of any rail system, and even metro systems have them. The layout below has 5 platforms, and is a common type of terminus.

Figure 6.13 Terminating Station

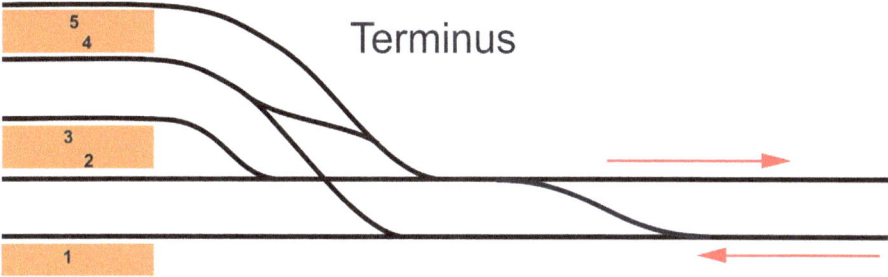

The layout below is a Spanish style terminus. This means that trains that terminate at the terminus can open their doors on either side, and typically passengers disembark on one side and then embark on the other. Spanish style stations are able to move large numbers of passengers quickly and efficiently.

Figure 6.14 Spanish Solution Style Terminus

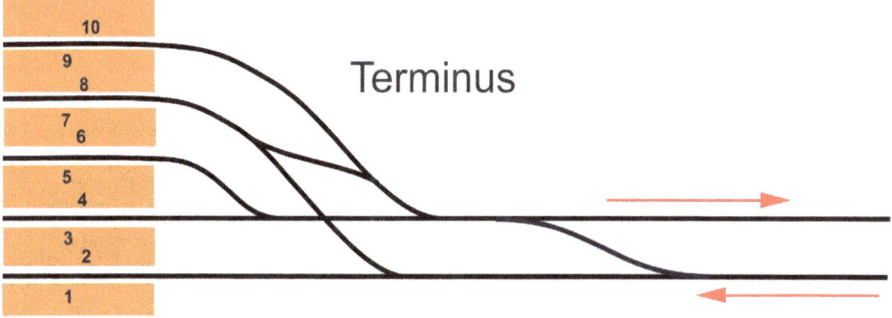

Chapter 7 Structure/Loading Gauge, Geometry, Heights and Grades

Track is at the centre of any rail system. Most of the infrastructure sits around the track, and the size and position of the track is important to how the infrastructure is laid out. Grades influence that infrastructure around the track, and stations for example are typically placed the grades are low.

Track and space around the track is very important for the choice of what rollingstock can use the track. Many different types of trains cannot accept large grades, and where the space around the track is small then the rollingstock will need to be small as well. In many ways, the track will affect many other rail systems, which is why it is so important. An understanding of the features and restrictions of the track is important in any rail network planning exercise.

Loading and structure gauge is a term that applies to the space through which a train moves. Structure gauge is the space that the infrastructure must stay out of for a train to make its way through a rail system. This includes platforms, where platform edges must not intrude into the structure gauge to the point where a train will strike the platform when entering a station. Platform strikes are uncommon, and when they occur can cause serious damage to a train. Usually the paint is stripped from the side of the train next to the platform.

Loading and Structure Gauge

Railways have specific terms for describing the space required for a train to pass through on a network. These terms are commonly used, and understood between countries. These terms are a rare example of some jargon that is used in Australia/UK and the US interchangeably. They are:
- Structure gauge
- Loading gauge
- Kinematic envelope

The structure gauge is a defined space around the track, into which no equipment or infrastructure is permitted. If any equipment strays into that space, then a train may strike it as is comes past. The structure gauge is the space allocated to trains to pass along the track and is larger than the train that passes through it, to allow for movement of the train and any possible slight deviations of the train from its design size. Trains are never as large as the structure gauge.

Structure gauge is what infrastructure maintainers use for maintaining clearances. They need clear cut guidance on what the structure gauge is, and any large railway and many smaller ones will have detailed standards on structure gauge and what sizes are required. It is not sufficient for an infrastructure maintainer to be told the loading gauge, as this is information is not useful and cannot be used for maintenance purposes.

The loading gauge is the area in which a train must fit in when stationary. Loading gauge is relevant to rollingstock and its design. It's important because the loading gauge determines which trains can be procured, what size they are, and hence their capacity. Loading gauges play an important role in determining the capacity of a system.

The kinematic envelope is the space through which a train might move, taking into account superelevation (cant), the suspension of the train, the end throw and centre throw. Calculating the kinematic envelope is a process called dynamic gauging. Calculating the kinematic envelope can be a paper exercise, and there are formulas that describe how to do this. The kinematic envelope increases where there are curves, as the curves result in the end of the train protruding away from the track.

Whilst changes to structure gauge are a common type of rail transport project, the cost can be high. Changes to structure gauge are very expensive, and can involve large scale changes to infrastructure. To complete a change from one structure gauge to a larger one, every point in a rail system or rail line at that structure gauge needs to be converted, it's not sufficient to convert some or even most of the track. There is no benefit for doing most of it, and so one problematic point in a rail system can stop the conversion to a larger structure gauge.

In many cases the maximum possible loading and structure and loading gauge is difficult to change. Train lines often pass next to structures and buildings that cannot be moved or demolished, and so it is not possible to change the width of the train, or the space through which the train passes. Some stations are heritage listed, and so major changes are not possible. In these cases rail operators need to manage their rollingstock as best they can, given the constraints on size. Problems with the maximum permitted size of trains can be very expensive to manage.

Loading gauges do not need to be square or rectangular. The diagram below shows a typical profile of a loading gauge. The shape down below is typical of what a loading gauge outline looks like. Whilst not always this shape, they often are, and so a train that is a perfect rectangle would not be permitted to operate on many rail networks if it were above a certain size.

Figure 7.1 Typical Loading Gauge

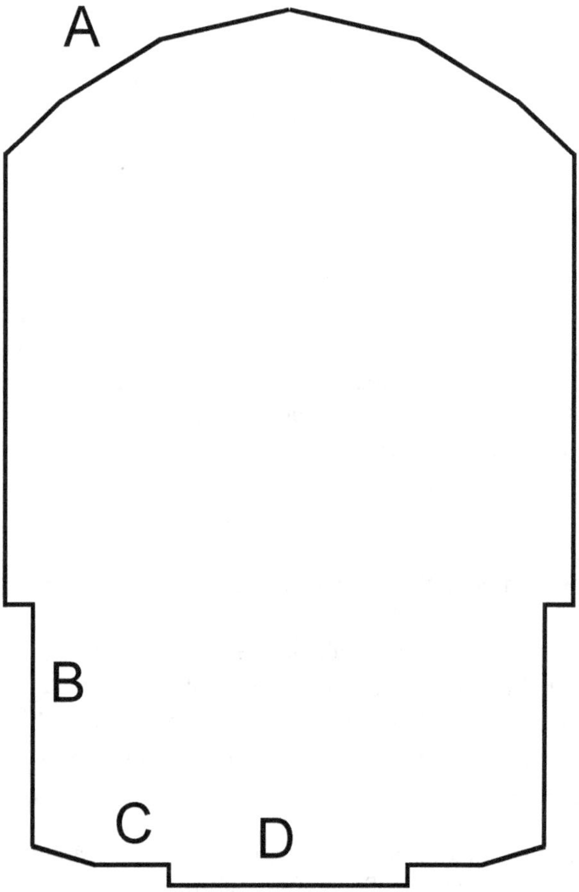

The letters in the diagram above refer to various parts of the outline. These are:

A/ This is the curved part of the roof of the train. Most passenger loading gauges are curved, and this allows the construction of arch shaped tunnels,

which are cheaper to construct than tunnels with rectangular ceilings in many cases.
B/ There are often cut-outs for platforms for passenger trains. There is always a risk that passengers will fall between the train and the platform, and it's best if this gap is kept as small as possible. One way of managing this is to have the train overhang the platform, so that the gap is minimised.
C/ For the bottom of the train the loading gauge is flat and even all the way across, and is higher is some parts compared to others. In the schematic above the corner is cut out (same as D). This is to allow the many different types of rail side devices to operate and exist. Also the ballast is sometimes too high, and so contact with the ballast is minimised by having the train higher than the track.
D/ This is the lowest part of the train, and where the train runs along the track.

The kinematic envelope should be within the structure gauge, even for curves. If the kinematic envelope extends to the structure gauge or beyond it, then trains may strike objects and structures next to the track (such as platforms). The kinematic envelope needs to fall within the structure gauge.

One way to determine the kinematic envelope is to run different trains along the track and see what happens. Whilst this is possible, it is far better to calculate the kinematic envelope, because if a train strikes an object it tends to make a bit of a mess, and the damage can be substantial. Also once a rail line is constructed it can be a bit difficult for the structure gauge to be changed, so any errors can have a very long term impact. So for most rail projects, the kinematic envelope will be calculated first before construction begins.

So of the things that need to be considered in the calculation of a kinematic envelope are:
- The superelevation of the track
- Track movement
- The suspension of the train
- Loads on the train, for example, fully loaded passenger trains compared to empty ones
- Rail wear
- Tilting functions of trains, including both passive and active tilt
- Curves in the track

Structure, loading gauge and the kinematic envelope are most relevant to a railway in tunnels, but are also important at stations and particularly at platforms. Tunnels have very limited space available, and increasing the size of the tunnel once constructed is a messy and expensive business. If a train can't fit into a tunnel, there is little a rail organisation can do to get it to fit in, other than making major engineering changes. Some things can be done, and trains with hard suspensions and very little movement in the springs that support the train can move through slightly smaller tunnels. Also, trains that move at lower speeds can also fit into smaller tunnels, as they bounce around less when moving at lower speeds. Where a railway needs to move a large train through a small structure gauge, this can sometimes be achieved with dramatically reducing the speeds of the train to a point where the railway is confident that the train will not strike any object.

If a train strikes an object (again, such as a platform) the result can be very bad indeed. Whilst a glancing blow may not be very serious, a full impact with a fixed object is really a train crash, and passengers can be killed. That's really bad, so railways will put a lot of effort into ensuring that trains cannot collide with anything fixed. One of the key responsibilities of maintenance staff is to ensure that a collision does not occur.

Vegetation often will grow into the space where the train runs. Trees often line rail corridors, and as trees grow they can come into contact with passing trains. This can be very common in some networks, and it's common in Australia. It's mostly harmless for trains to brush alongside trees, and most tree branches are quite soft. Trees can present problems to the overhead wiring system, or reduce the visibility of signals so that drivers cannot see them. In these situations trees can be a problem, or when they fall over in a big storm this can also block running lines.

In some cases trees may be planted on stations. The branches of trees may grow to the point where they intrude into the structure gauge, and even strike a train. Trees on stations, where they are healthy and continue to grow, will need to be routinely pruned to keep them outside of the structure gauge

It has become common to calculate the movement of trains, and the swept volume resulting from this, with software, and some packages have been written which work quite well. The software can visually display and calculate the movement of trains through tunnels, and so any problem areas that need to be addressed are identified. Whilst a hand calculation is possible, this method is increasingly rarely used. The calculation of the structure and loading gauges and a key part of the planning process, but given the technical detail necessary, and the cost, and the level of detail needed to carry out the analysis, this would typically be done very late in the process (but definitely before construction).

Loading gauges, as mentioned above, often have complicated shapes. To simplify things, they are often described in terms of height and width.

Figure 7.2 Simplified Description of Train Size

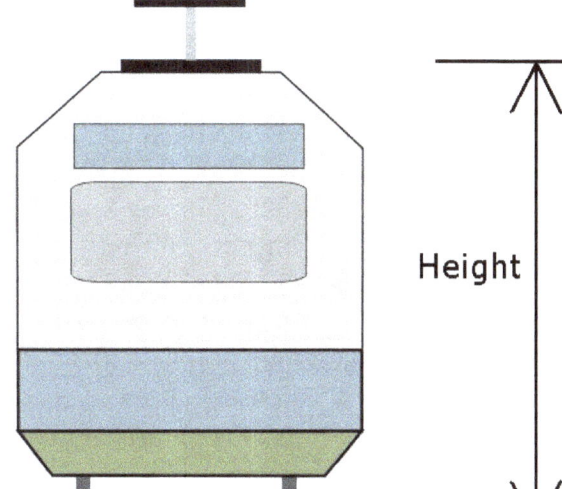

The pantograph above the train is not normally included in the loading gauge. In practice the pantograph is spring loaded so it can move up and down, and can usually be pushed down almost flat with the top of the train. Where the pantograph sits there is usually a hole/recess so that it can be strapped down, i.e. when transporting the train by sea. The space in which the pantograph is sits into is called the pantograph well.

Below are some common loading gauges. It is only a small selection of the large number of loading gauges currently in use. Worldwide there would be hundreds of different loading gauges.

Table of Loading Gauges

Country	Name	Width	Height
UK	W6	2820 (9 feet 4 inches)	3965 (13 feet)
	W7	2778 (9 feet 1 inch)	3966 (13 feet)
	W9	2996 (9 feet 10 inches)	3967 (13 feet)
	C1	2744 (9 feet)	3772 (12 feet 4.5 inches)
(high speed)	UK1	2720 (8 feet 11 inches)	3965 (13 feet)
US, Canada, Mexico	AAR plate B	3250 (10 feet 8 inches)	4620 (15 feet 2 inches)
	AAR plate C	3251 (10 feet 8 inches)	4720 (15 feet 6 inches)
	AAR plate E	3252 (10 feet 8 inches)	4800 (15 feet 9 inches)
	AAR plate F	3253 (10 feet 8 inches)	5180 (17 feet)
European Union	UIC-A	3150 (10 feet 4 inches)	4320 (14 feet 2 inches)
	UIC-B	3151 (10 feet 4 inches)	4321 (14 feet 2 inches)
	UIC-C	3152 (10 feet 4 inches)	4650 (15 feet 3 inches)
Germany	G1	3153 (10 feet 4 inches)	4280 (14 feet 0.5 inches)
	G2	3154 (10 feet 4 inches)	4650 (15 feet 3 inches)
Spain/Portugal	Iberian gauge	3300 (10 feet 10 inches)	4300 (14 feet 1 inch)

Superelevation (Cant)

Superelevation is the difference in level between the two rails. It is common for the two rails to be at different heights, and it is a very useful thing to do in many different situations. The height different between the two rails is show below.

Figure 6.3 Simplified Description of Train Size

Superelevation is also called cant. Superelevation is installed in track to allow trains to be able to move through curves faster, and so reduce travel times. It is a cheap and effective way of improving the efficiency of track.

Platform Heights

Rail lines typically have stations with the same platform height. It is possible for one rail network to have varying platform heights, with one line having a different height than another. For anew rail line being constructed, the designers of the rail line have a choice as to the platform height, although this decision is often an obvious one, or a very discrete one. There are advantages and disadvantages for setting the platform height either high or low.

Standardising platform heights in a rail network greatly aids efficiency and reduces cost. This is the ideal, and new modern networks are constructed such that all the platforms are the same height. However, in many older rail systems, there is more than one platform height, and potentially there could be several different standard heights.

Platforms are may not be at the same height as the train floor. It is preferable for modern train systems to have the platform as close as possible to the floor of the train, and at the same height, but this often does not happen. The photo below shows the regional tilt train in Taiwan, and note that the floor of the train is higher than the platform, and there is a step between the train and the platform.

Taiwanese Train with Door Flaps

Platform heights installed in rail systems have been decreasing over time. This is especially true for trams and light rail, where platform heights are dropping significantly. Trams often run at street level, and stepping into a high floor tram can be quite daunting, especially for people with disabilities. It's best for disabled people getting into trams to have the floor as low as possible. It is seen as desirable to reduce the height of platforms as much as possible, and rollingstock manufacturers are often keen to announce any reductions in floor heights of their products.

The step fills the space between the train and the platform. The step is often slightly higher than the platform, so that if the platform is curved or too close to the train then the step won't hit the platform.

It is engineering challenging to make the floor of the tram very low. Ultra-low floor trams have had some significant engineering problems, with cracks developing in the body of the trams, which were quite serious and needed substantial repairs. The lower floor puts higher forces on the body of the tram, and these stresses can cause higher maintenance costs and maintenance problems.

Ultra-low floor trams, notwithstanding their engineering problems provide a better service to customers. The step up into the tram is a small one, often only 180mm, which is low. This is enough for people to comfortably enter the tram from road level, and so this technology is still being developed (and perfected).

Low floor trams are higher than ultra-floor trams, and are about 300-350mm from the ground or platform, or about 1 foot in the English imperial system of measurement. Most people can negotiate this kind of step up from the road.

Higher speed trains will generally require higher platforms, at least as high as 550mm. The higher platform allows for structural changes in the rollingstock that make it stronger, and allow for higher speeds. Trams and light rail vehicles with ultra-low floors are limited in speed to about 100 kms/hr, or perhaps even lower.

There are many different platform heights in use around the world today. The variety is enormous, although attempts are being made to standardise to specific heights. It seems that 550mm is the minimum height for larger commuter trains, although 760 mm platforms are also used. In Australia and Hong Kong platform heights of 1100mm are used, which is high enough that if passengers fall off the platform onto the tracks then they will injured from the fall.

Where the platform is a different height to the floor of the train, the preference is to make the floor of the train higher. Passengers will step up into the train, and not down. It is considered by some that it's dangerous for passengers to step down into a train, and so this configuration is avoided if at all possible.

Rarely rollingstock is designed that can accommodate different platform heights. This can be achieved through steps that can vary in height to allow for the different platform heights. Rollingstock with this feature can be very expensive.

European Union decision 2002/735/EC specifies that high speed trains should be designed to a platform height of 550mm or 760mm. However, for trains that operate in the UK 915mm was specified, and for the Netherlands

840mm was specified. Even within a standard designed to force uniformity between member states, there is significant differences in the platform heights.

In designing a new rail line or more stations, and where platform height are different throughout a network and there is a need to extend the system, system designers face a number of choices:
1/ modify the existing platforms to a standard height
2/ have two different sets of platform heights, and different rollingstock that is designed for each
3/ continue with different platform heights, and order specialised rollingstock that can accommodate different platform heights.
4/ Design very long platforms that have two different heights, and so able to accept different trains with different floor heights

It's always best to have one standard height throughout a rail system, but there are many examples where this was not possible.

Grades

Grades and their presence in a rail system impacts on many things. Rollingstock needs to have larger motors to climb the grade, or more locomotives. Also maintenance on the rail infrastructure increases for grades. Where the grades are especially large specialised trains are needed to negotiate the grades.

Grades should not be installed at stations where possible. In some cases it may be necessary to install a grade at a station, but this is very undesirable, and should only be done where absolutely necessary.

Grades are calculated as below:

Figure 6.4 Grades

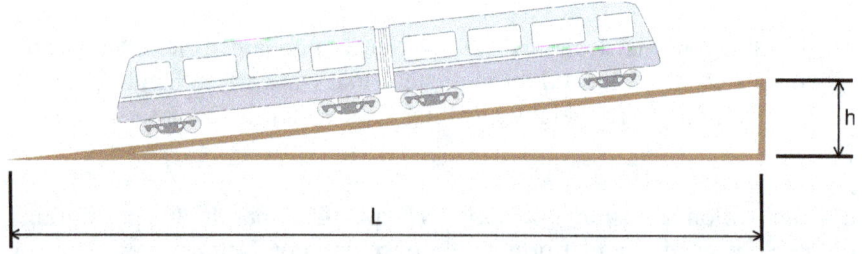

Grades, or sometimes called slopes, can be expressed as percentages, based on this simple formula:

$$Grade = \frac{height}{length} \times 100\%$$

In Australia and the UK grades can be expressed as 1 in X, where X can be found from the formula below:

$$\frac{1}{X} = \frac{height}{length}$$

Which can be re-arranged to give:

$$X = \frac{length}{height}$$

Another way of expressing grades is using this symbol (‰). This symbol is similar to a percentage, but actually means the parts out of 1000. So a 1% grade would be expressed as 10‰. This symbol is common in continental Europe, for the maximum possible grades that a particular type of train can climb. On Wikipedia the symbol is referred to a "*per mille*", which is Latin for per one thousand.

So, the conversion tables for the grades are:

	Grades and Conversions		
%	UK/Australia	Degrees	‰
1	1 in 100	0.57°	10
2	1 in 50	1.15°	20
3	1 in 33	1.72°	30
4	1 in 25	2.29°	40
5	1 in 20	2.86°	50
6	1 in 16.6	3.43°	60
7	1 in 14.3	4.00°	70
8	1 in 12.5	4.57°	80
9	1 in 11.1	5.14°	90

Grades and Conversions

%	UK/Australia	Degrees	‰
10	1 in 10	5.71°	100
11	1 in 9.1	6.28°	110
12	1 in 8.3	6.84°	120
13	1 in 7.7	7.41°	130

Most rollingstock is quite limited in the grade that it can climb. Common limits for the grades that rollingstock can climb are listed below, with some comments:

Maximum Acceptable Grades

Rollingstock type	Max grade	Comments
Trams	6% or 10% with specially designed rollingstock	Some trams are specially designed to climb high grades
Light rail	6% or 10% with specially designed rollingstock	As more vehicles are combined into a consist, the total possible grade may be reduced
Commuter rail	3%	These trains are not designed to climb high grades
Regional rail	3%	
Freight	1.5%	Typically higher grades make the freight service uneconomical, as more locomotives are needed
High speed rail	1.5%	Higher grades tend to have a large speed penalty
Monorails	6%	Able to climb fairly steep grades
Metros	3%	Steel on steel metros
Metros (rubber tyred)	12%	Very large grades can be accepted

A typical limit for a grade at a station is 1 in 100. Whilst larger grades can be accepted, it is generally preferable to limit grades at stations as much as possible.

Grades are very important for any rail network design. They place powerful restrictions on the nature of the network designed. A system with low grades has a much better efficiency than one with high grades. The reduction of any grades is one of the key measures in improving the efficiency of any rail system.

In many cases the designer of a rail system may have no choice but to install high grades. Where this occurs, the type of rolligstock may need to be modified to accept the higher grades, and the power system design to allow for the higher grades. Where the grades are very high a specialised solution may be needed to allow the system to be built.

Grades are an often forgotten feature of rail network design. Low grades allow the choice of more efficient rollingstock, and fewer motor cars (power rollingstock carriages) are needed. Maintenance costs are also lower, as grades in track cause high forces and this means more maintenance.

Freight is particularly impacted by high grades. Where grades are high then energy consumption is higher, which reduces the economic efficiency of a freight movement.

REFERENCES

1. European Commission, *Tracks for Tilting Trains*, Fast and Comfortable Trains (D8), July 2005

2. Mancini, G. et al *New developments with the Italian solution for tilting trains: optimisation of tilting system on new generation of Pendolino trains*, www.uic.org/cdrom/2008/11_wcrr2008/pdf/R.2.4.3.5.pdf

3. Alessandro, E. New Developments for Tilting Trains, November 2001

4. Government of South Australia, Department of Planning Transport and Infrastructure, *PTSOM Code of Practice Volume 2, Track Geometry CP-TS-956*

5. Mochizuki, A. *JRTR Speed-up Story 2 Part 2: Speeding-up Conventional Lines and Shinkansen*, Japan Railway and Transport Review No 58 Oct 2011

6. Lindahl, M. *Track Geometry for high-speed railways*, Department of Vehicle Engineering Royal Institute of Technology, Stockholm 2001

7. Persson, R. *Tilting Trains Technology, benefits and motion sickness*, Thesis submitted to Royal Institute of Technology Stockholm, 2008

8. Forstberg, J. et al *Influence of different conditions for tilt compensation on symptoms of motion sickness in tilting trains*, Brain Research Bulletin, Vol 47, No 5, pp 525 – 535, 1998

Chapter 8 Approaches to Network Design

Introduction

The design of any network needs to allow trains to efficiently move around the network. A poorly designed network can have a powerful effect on the speed, cost and utility of the network, and the rail system will be dramatically underutilised. One of the key objectives of any rail transport design is to provide the right level of services to the right places, and one of the best ways of achieving this is through good network design.

Network design for transport networks has traditionally been somewhat mathematical. One branch of applied mathematics is Operations Research, which is concerned with applied mathematics and solving complex industrial mathematical problems. Network design for transport is often discussed in papers on Operations Research, and as a consequence this topic can be very complicated and mathematical. This is not how this topic will be discussed in this chapter, and complex mathematics will be avoided.

For any major transport plan, a network design will be needed. Whilst individual projects may not change the network design, large strategic plans will need to make some decisions on the size and scale of the network, and where locations are connected together. Tough decisions are needed, and this area is not an easy one. How should these decisions be made? What is the best approach? The approach taken in this chapter is to outline many different possible network designs, and discuss their strengths and weaknesses, and hopefully this will provide some guidance.

For any large city or country, the number of different network designs can be extremely large. There may be hundreds of different potentially feasible designs, and the large number can be very challenging to manage. Rail lines can be drawn on maps in a huge number of different ways, and filtering out all of the different options can in many cases be a near impossible task. This chapter provides examples of different network designs, and the more designs that are generated as part of the design process of a rail system, potentially the best one will be better.

Any possible network design will be limited by some practical constraints. In theory, almost any rail network design is possible, and these different designs are only limited by imagination. In practice things are not so easy, and constraints are placed on possible network designs. A constraint is a limitation placed on the network design, which must be followed. Typically rail systems are not built under oceans, but may cross between islands, for example. Some of these constraints are obvious, others less so. For example, it would be very unusual for a rail system to have a station in a cemetery, or in a garbage dump, or have entrances inside churches or temples.

For rail systems the available land, topography and ground conditions can also play a very large role in deciding where to build a new rail line. In many cases the choices are quite limited, mostly because land has been reserved in only one place and that's what needs to be used, or because land is difficult to acquire, or there is some public policy reason as to why land cannot be acquired. The availability of land is a powerful constraint, and where land is available is often where a rail line is built, even if the location of the available land is not in an ideal place.

Other constraints include the ground conditions, especially for tunnelling. Building tunnels through sand, next to seas or other bodies of water is normally a very bad idea, as the water will seep through the sand and into the rail tunnel. There are many other problems, such as large hills, immovable obstructions, heritage buildings or national monuments and other problems that will cause the rail line to have only a small number of options on where it can be placed.

Similarly with any rail tunnelling project, there are often underground obstructions that can become obstacles to any underground railway. Large buildings can have very deep car parks that can be so low that a railway line becomes too deep and cannot go under them. In many countries there are archaeological sites that can be powerful barriers to any underground excavation. Also other rail and road tunnels can be in the way of any new rail project. These limitations can be so powerful that there may be almost no design choices left for any network design.

Rail transport often involves the movement of passengers in and around large cities, or from one large city to another. Within large cities, major centres within the city may need to be connected, and this can largely drive the creation of any new rail system. Rail network design is often best optimised by connecting these centres together, and this removes many of the potential different options for network design. Major transport hubs, especially where there are large bus stations, should be connected, and so the challenge often becomes how to connect them.

Avoiding Mistakes with Network Design

Rail network design is a large area with many different possible solutions for any one planning problem. This makes the construction of general rules for network design difficult, and this entire book is about assisting with those choices. Notwithstanding the complexity of the planning problem, there are some specific problems that clearly should be avoided, and they are listed below. It is by no means an exhaustive list, and some of the key things to avoid with network design are:

- Building a rail system with lots of curves so that average speeds are low
- Building a rail system where many pieces or rail lines are unconnected to one another
- Building a rail system that misses major population centres (excluding freight systems)
- Building a rail system that is difficult to access, or located in places that take a long time to reach, such as deep in the bottom of a valley
- Connecting cities to one another that do not need to be connected, or where cities closer together should be connected first
- Building a rail line where it does not reach the centre of a city, or a place that clearly needs to be connected, such as a major regional centre
- Building an intercity rail line that does not connect to the transport network in one or both cities at either end of the line
- Placing two stations next to each other, where interchanges should be possible, but with a major obstacle in the way, so that passengers moving from one station need to make a time consuming or difficult journey
- Building a passenger rail line to pick up people in areas with low populations
- Constructing stations deep underground so that they are difficult to access
- Designing rail systems that are very wasteful of energy

Most of the list above represent major blunders, but almost all of them exist in one form or another in operational railways around the world. In some situations they may represent an acceptable solution to some localised difficult problem, but overall these situations should be avoided where possible.

So, taking the opposite of the rules above, we can identify some of the principles for good rail network design to be:
- Rail lines should be as straight as possible
- Station selection needs to be made carefully to keep the average speed high
- Lots of grades should be avoided in any rail system, especially high grades in only one position
- Underground stations should not be too deep
- Major areas of population and major commercial centres should be connected
- Good interconnections with other transport modes, and other forms of rail transportation, are very important
- Average speeds are always important
- Power and energy consumption is important and should be minimised

The ideal for any rail system is to build a cheap to maintain system that has high passenger volumes. In many cases there is a tradeoff between speed and connecting to major centres, and the more places that are connected the lower the average speed.

Whilst most of this chapter is directed towards passenger traffic, the ideas are the same for freight. Freight rail traffic is also time and cost sensitive, and where possible rail lines should be as straight and flat as possible.

There is a standard layout and structure for rail systems in large cities. This structure seems to be relatively consistent from country to country, and so can provide a useful template for the design of any new rail system.

A Standard Rail System for Large Cities

In large cities the configuration below is a common one. This schematic represents the "normal" situation for any large city, where most the different rail systems are represented. The city below is not based on any one city, although there are many cities with this structure, but is an idealisation of what would be considered "normal" for a theoretical city. A good example of a city with this design is Toronto in Canada.

Figure 8.1 A Standard Urban Rail System

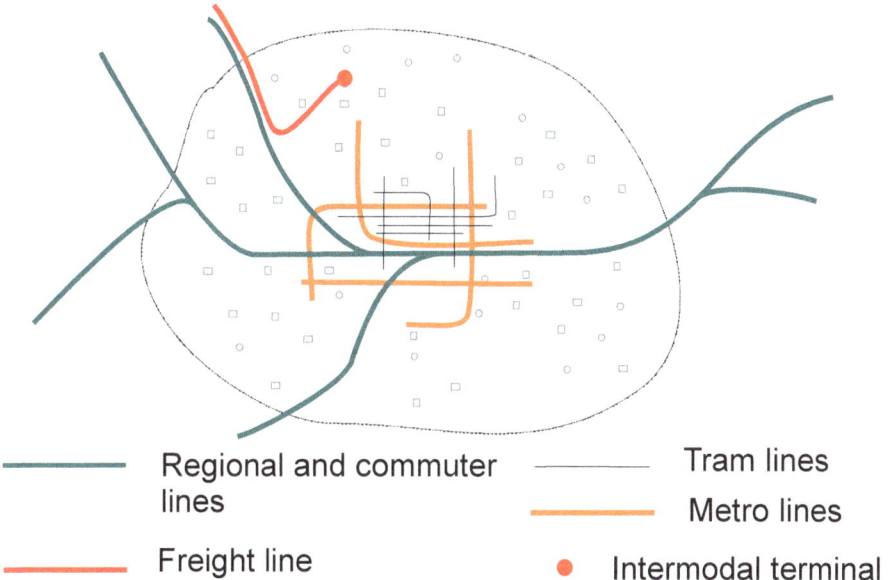

So what we see here is:
- The tram system, or possibly a light rail system, in the centre of the city, serving high value locations but at a low speed
- The metro system, which covers the centre of the city, but also the fringes of what is sometimes called the "inner city", which is suburbs located close to the centre of the city
- The regional or commuter system, which goes outside the boundary of the city. High speed rail systems may also share tracks with regional and intercity trains
- A freight line in the suburbs, which brings intermodal freight from other cities and countries into the city. The intermodal terminal is normally located in an industrial area, away from the city centre, where land is cheaper and where it won't detract from the appearance of the city.

More rarely, there are also some other rail lines present in a large city, such as a monorail, or a tourist railway. Also not shown is an automated railway connecting different terminals in an airport to one another. Some or all of the elements of the above city can be missing, but the larger the city, the more likely it is that all these elements will be there. The most common rail system to be missing is the tram/light rail system, which can only be installed if there is room or the will for it to be installed.

Larger cities tend to more closely follow the rail system structure above, although very large cities such as Tokyo can be quite different (and there's only a couple of them really). For smaller cities, such as with populations under 3 million, and especially under 2 million, many other choices are possible, and some of the rail systems in a big city can be combined together. Some of the possibilities are:

- The metro and the light rail system are combined together, forming an intermediate capacity metro, such as Porto in Portugal or in Vancouver
- There is no light rail system, and the metro is much smaller to accommodate the smaller population, such as Helsinki
- There is no or very little light rail or metro system, and the regional railway operates as the main rail system, such as Sydney
- The metro system replaces any commuter or intercity system, and is the main system, such as Singapore (excluding some very small lines, such as the rail line from Woodlands to Malaysia)
- More unusually, most of the rail system is replaced with a more uncommon rail system, such as a monorail, such as Chongqing in China

The choice as to the best system will depend on the local factors, the structure and size of the city, and the culture and vibe of the city.

The above network configuration can be used as plan for future rail construction. The above configuration has been proven to work well in many different cities and environments time and time again.

Some Examples of Network Design – Single Lines

The analysis of network design here is split into two main categories; single lines on their own, and a rail system with multiple lines. A rail system that has multiple lines can often be examined through dividing up the system into single line sections, and then characterising them as below.

To simplify things, the examples below are constructed in terms of cities or towns, and a rail connection linking them. The city at each end of the rail line could also represent a major centre within a large city. Conceptually this is the same as another city or town.

The two cities below have been connected using a rail line that is relatively direct with a minimum of curves. The rail lines get into the centre of both cities, and the line connecting them is reasonable straight.

Figure 8.2 A "Good" Intercity Connection

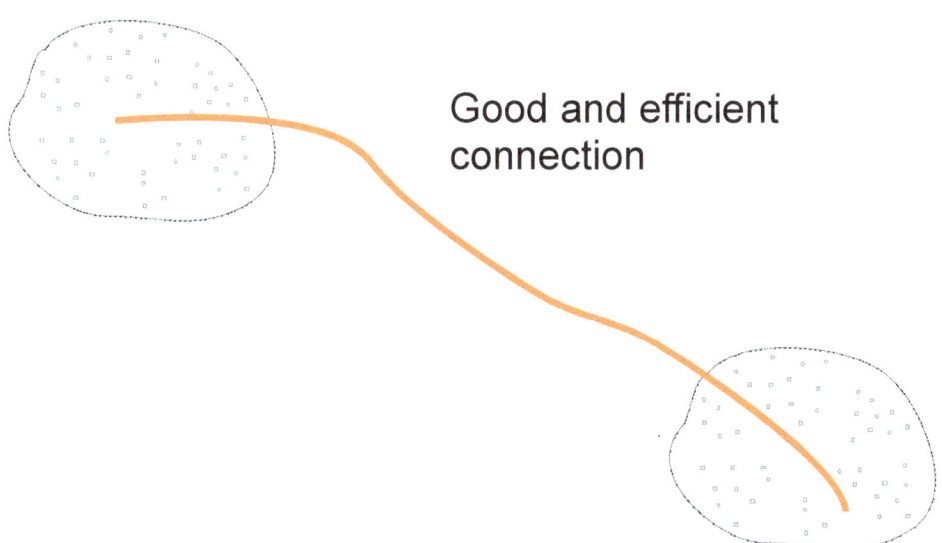

This is in contrast to the line below, which is a very poor design. The main problem with the connection below is the length of the rail line, it is long and has many curves, which will mean that trains have a longer distance to travel, and travel more slowly as curves require lower speeds to negotiate.

Figure 8.3 A Poor Intercity Connection

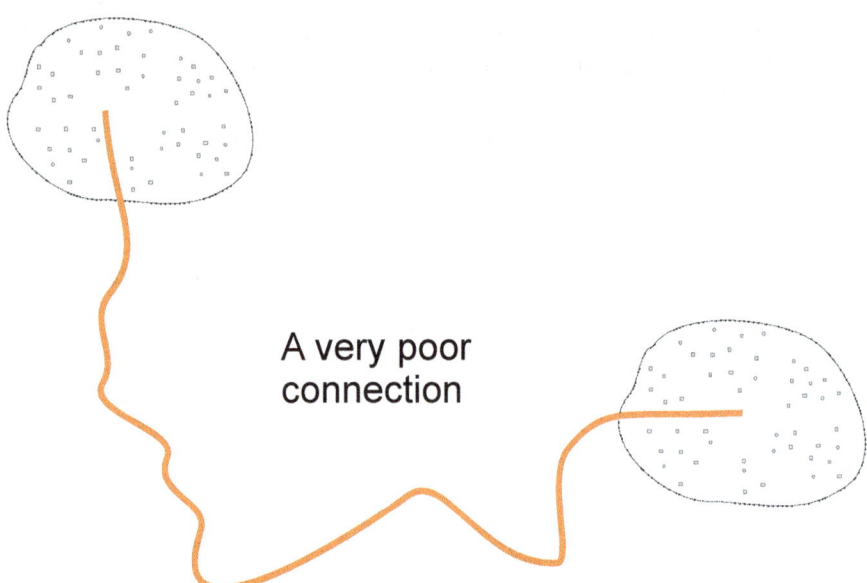

Remember that intercity traffic, and most rail travel, is very sensitive to the travel time, and a slow travel time will normally dramatically impact upon passenger numbers. A rail line like the one above is unlikely to be of much value, and may be cheaper to construct, but will be used by only a small number of people.

This problem also seems to be particularly acute with freight networks, which rarely seem to follow straight lines or the most direct path between where they start their journey or their final destination. Freight traffic is also very sensitive to grades, which means that a more direct route between two places is often impossible as the grades as too steep.

There are other network design problems that are also serious. Consider the network design below where there are three cities, and a need to connect the smallest of the cities to one of the other two. The smaller city will most likely have strong links and numbers of passenger movements to City B, as it is so close. City A has been connected to city C, and this may be because city C is slightly larger than city B.

Figure 8.4 Network Design with Multiple Cities

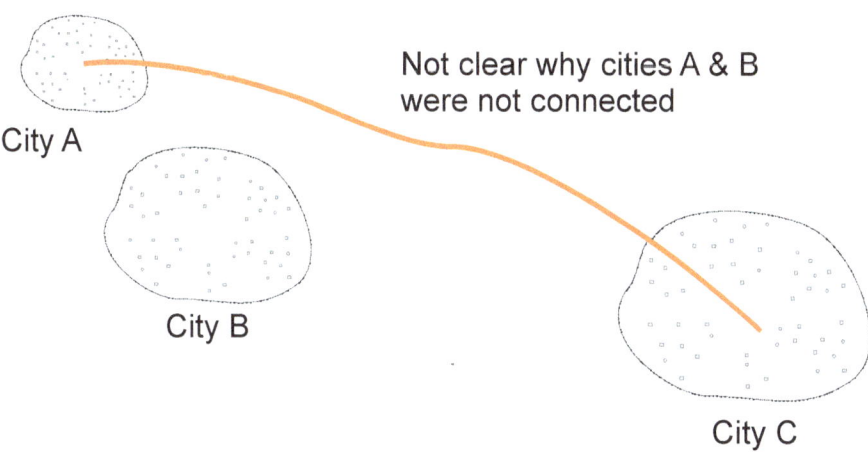

This type of rail transport connection creates many problems, other than the obvious one where the two closely located cities are not connected. It also encourages people to travel from A to C, when B is much closer. This may increase the number of long distance trips, which will sometimes be replaced with car journeys, which may cause road traffic to be higher than it needs to be. A much better network design is shown below, and of course A & B have been connected, so that this journey is now available.

Figure 8.5 Network Design with Multiple Cities

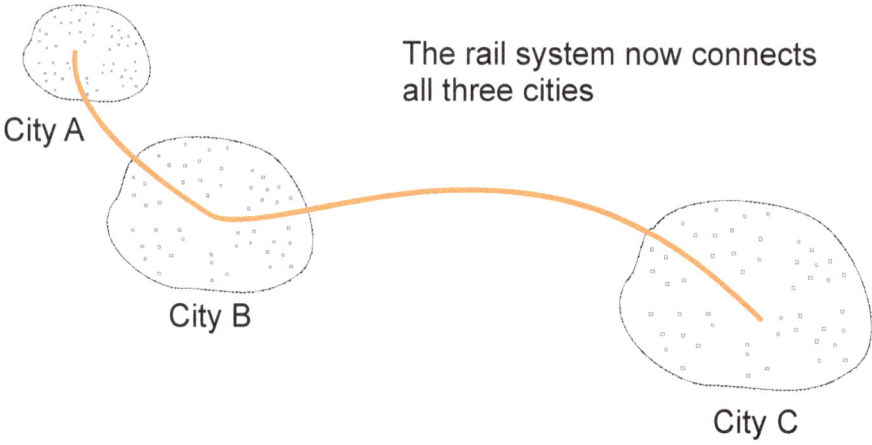

This design is far superior, and connects all the cities in a logical order. This network design will increase the number of passengers travelling between B

& C, and so services will be more frequent between A & C (or probably will be, if services are not terminated at B).

Another mistake that is sometimes made is to have trains enter into a city, and then reverse out again having made a stop in the city or town. Below is the normal structure of a rail line passing through a town, and it enters from one side and then leaves from the other. Presumably there are other towns on both the entrance and exit side of the rail line leading into the city.

Figure 8.6 Network Passes through the City

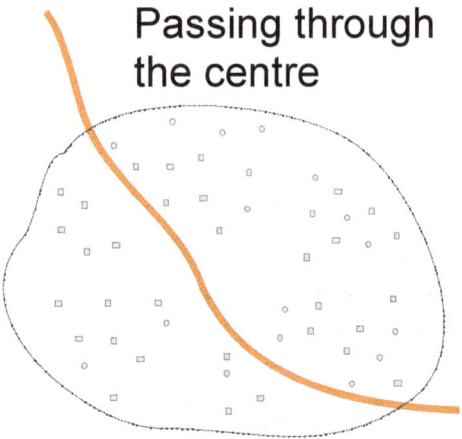

Below is another possibility, one that is not a good idea, but is done occasionally where there is no other choice. The rail line enters the city, and then the rail line terminates in the centre of the city. In the schematic below it is possible for a train to travel from city A to C through B, and to get out of city B a train would need to follow the same route that it used to get in. The train is essentially backtracking over the path it has taken to get into the city.

Figure 8.7 Trains Reverse out of City B

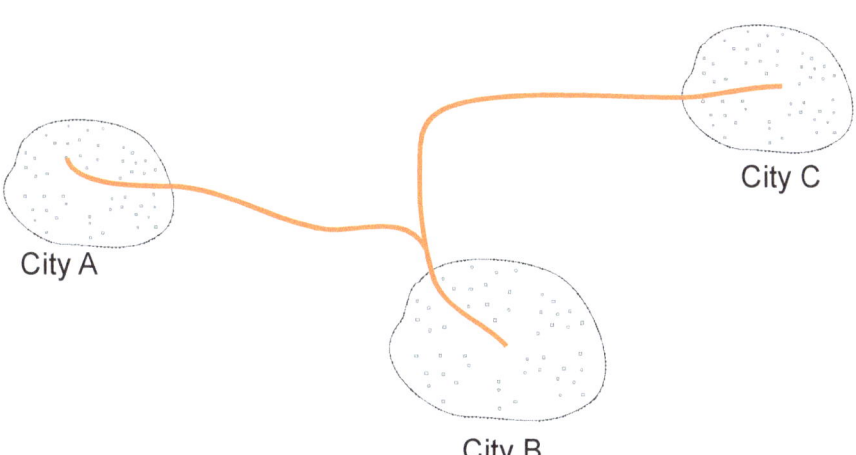

When the train arrives into city B the driver would need to change ends, and trains will leave the city in the reverse direction to the one it entered. Passengers will need to turn around, or flip seats around to face another direction (or sit facing backwards). Where the seats in the train are facing both forwards and reverse then maybe nothing is needed to be done.

The rail line from Venice to Rome has this structure when entering and leaving Florence. This rail structure, despite being sometimes unavoidable, is messy and inefficient, and should be not be utilised where at all possible.

Terminating trains early

Trains do not need to travel the entire length of all rail lines. A terminus or turnback can be installed at almost any station, and this can allow trains to be used more efficiently.

The schematic below shows a common scenario and potentially how trains can be managed. The main line runs from station A to station D, and the branch runs from B to E. A common rule is that trains can be terminated at any large station, but in metros and monorails systems trains normally only terminate at the major stations at the end of the rail line.

Figure 8.8 A Branch Line

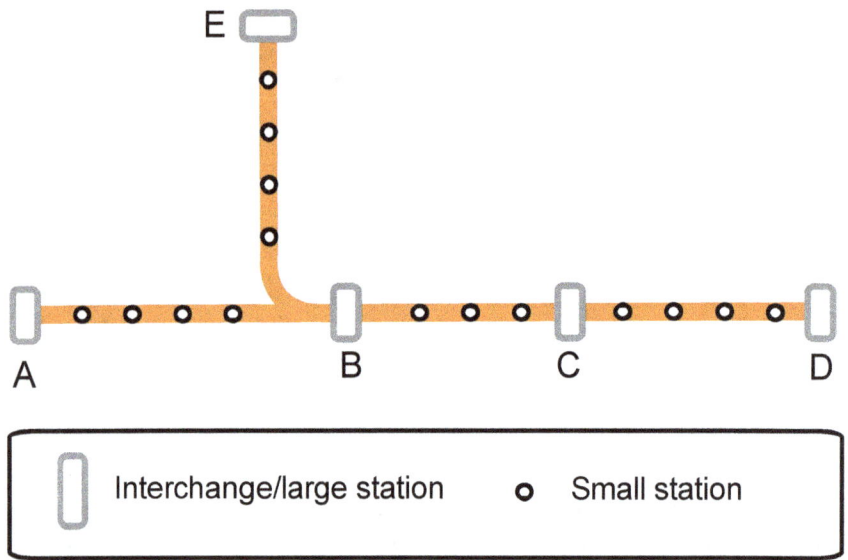

Trains can operate from A to D, but the number of passengers between A and B may be very low. If this is the case then trains may be terminated at station B, and sent back towards C and D. It is possible to terminate half or even most of the trains at station B, rather than send trains onwards. The branch line between stations B and E can also operate as a shuttle. Trains can be terminated at station B and then sent only along the branch line. The creation of shuttle lines has been discussed below.

Terminus's can be installed with significant cost, and can be expensive to maintain. A terminus can provide significant operational flexibility, and can be used to effectively manage a network. The main benefit of a terminus, such as in the schematic above, is to minimise the amount of rollingstock needed to provide a rail service along the line above. Rollingstock is expensive, and managing it efficiently can significantly reduce the cost of operating the network. Often if trains are terminated early, then the number of trains sets needed to provide a service drops.

A rail terminus or turnback should normally be provided at a large station. Whilst in theory it is possible to install a turnback at a small station, so doing means that trains are travelling to this station almost empty, as the train will terminate there and few passengers will use the station. The optimum solution is to install turnbacks at the largest stations, and when trains are being turned around, passengers can join the train.

Loops

A loop is sometimes put at the end of a rail line, so that trains can turn around without stopping. They are common on tram systems, and also for freight lines, especially ones that move bulk materials. They are less common on passenger lines, such as a commuter rail system or a metro, but are sometimes installed. Sydney has a loop in the centre of the city, which is heavily used by many train services each day.

The loop below is on the tram system in Hong Kong, and this one is located at Shau Kei Wan. Tram and light rail systems often have loops, and the benefits of installing a loop are quite significant. Whilst it is a little difficult to see on the photo below, the yellow tram has doors on the side facing the photographer, and the black tram does not. It is possible for trams and light rail vehicles to have a driver's cabin at only one end of the vehicle, and this can save space. Of course to achieve this there needs to be loops at each end of the tram or light rail system, so that the vehicle can turn around.

Tram Loop in Hong Kong

Loops have a number of benefits, and these include:

- Trains do not need to turn around, so the capacity of the rail line can be higher
- There is no need for a driver to change ends, which on many trains takes 5 – 10 minutes, and this time can be used for driving the train
- There is no need to divide or amalgamate trains, as the train does not break its journey

Of course it should be noted that for trams and light rail a loop can be quite small, maybe only 20 to 30 metres across. For metros and commuter rail, or any heavy rail really, a loop will need to be a number of kilometres across, so it will be very large, and quite expensive to build.

Freight systems seem to make the most use of loops. Loops for bulk materials are extremely common in Australia, and almost all collieries and loading ports are structured as a loop. A loop allows the freight train to slowly move around and either load or unload its cargo, and once complete the freight train makes its way back to its departure point to pick up some more material. It is expensive for freight trains to be shunted and trains marshalled and built up, so it needs to be avoided whenever possible. Freight loops are often operated in tandem with unit trains.

Loops seem to be less common for intermodal traffic, and this seems to be related to the land available to move containers. Intermodal terminals are often severely constrained for space, unlike coal ports in Australia which are built away from towns and have plenty of room. Intermodal terminals at ports are often located next to the port where containers are loaded and unloaded, and these are usually terribly cramped. A loop requires quite a lot of space, and most of the intermodal ports in Australia just don't have the space for a loop. The same can be said for intermodal terminals located away from port in cities, again, there is rarely room in an industrial suburb for a freight loop, and a siding is much more common.

The disadvantages of a loop are the cost, and the additional space required to install one. The land is often not available, and unless the rail line is being constructed away from residential areas, the land is very difficult to find.

Multiple Branch Lines

Rail lines can be split to cover more area than a single line. Radial designed systems often contain a large number of splits, and they can perform a very useful function. However, it is possible for a rail line to bifurcate too often,

Approaches to Network Design Page 180

and the rail network below is a rail designer's nightmare. There are far too many splits on the right hand side of the network below.

Figure 8.9 Multiple Splits

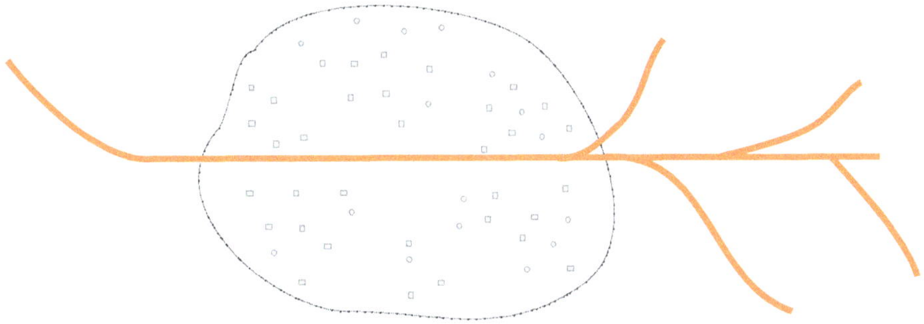

In this situation there would be many problems, but clearly the main problem would be that rail services from the right had side would not be able to get into the middle of the city, because too many lines feed into the centre. The left hand side of the network would be extremely congested, and there would be a very high number of services, regardless of whether these services were needed or not.

When confronted with this kind of rail nightmare, an operational railway has a small number of choices, and these include:
- Close one or more of the lines
- Convert one or more of the shorter lines to shuttles, so that services on this line don't operate all the way into the city centre
- Add additional tracks to the left hand side of the rail network so that there is somewhere for all these services to go
- Build another line into the centre of the city, and put some of the rail lines on the right hand side into this new line

For an operational rail network to balance this passenger loads on rail services in this network would be difficult or maybe even impossible. Another potential problem is of course that the rail line on the left hand side of the network does connect to any destination of any consequence, and so it is highly unlikely that all the services feeding into this line would be needed.

The schematic below shows what the rail system looks like when it has been repaired. The different colours represent different lines, and note that there are now two lines, whereas before there was only one. Also note that network has been extended on the left hand side, and now there are two termini for trains to terminate at and to be turned around. There is also a shuttle, in brown, on the bottom right hand side. This network design is a vast improvement to the one shown above.

Figure 8.10 The rail line re-balanced

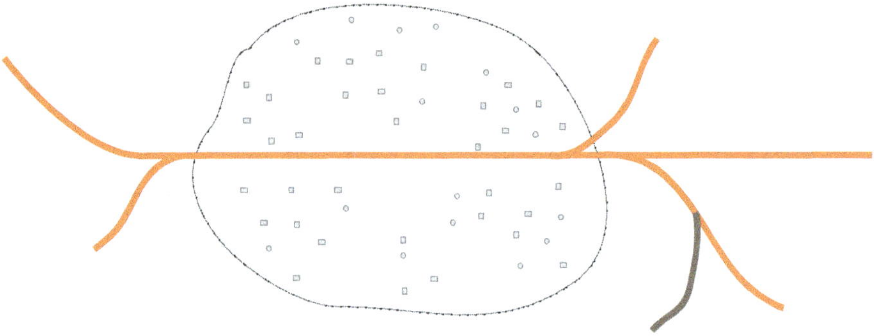

Rail Lines Passing Through the Centre of Cities

Rail lines often move passengers from suburbs into the centre of cities. This very common movement pattern occurs because city centres (CBDs) are congested, and parking, if it is available, is very expensive. This frequently means that in some cities the only rail lines that exist are ones directed at moving people from the suburbs into the city.

A pendulum line is one that passes through a large important destination, and then out again. Often considered to be the hallmark of high quality network design, a pendulum line can bring passengers into a city centre, and then take people out again. Pendulum lines are so described as trains move in and out of the city like a pendulum.

The scenario below shows how to get a pendulum wrong, and in this case the rail line doubles back on itself. The problem with this design is that passengers will alight from the train at the city centre, because then the train returns close to the direction it came from. Passengers will avoid this rail line because it will be quicker to travel from one arm of the rail line to another by another means, often private road vehicle. If the rail line continued through to the other side of the centre of the city, then passengers who needed this transport movement will remain on the train.

Figure 8.11 A poorly designed pendulum line

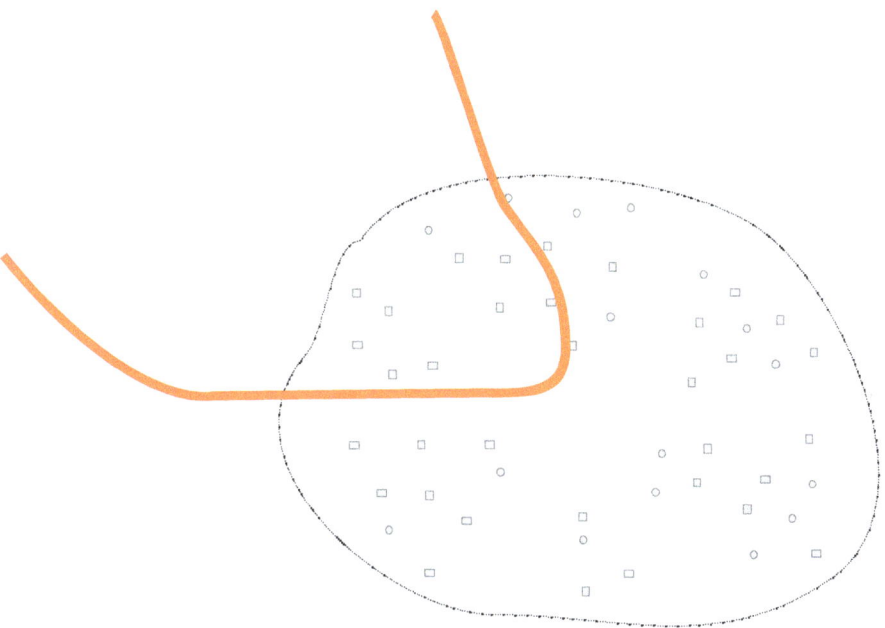

As always there are advantages and disadvantages for everything, including pendulum lines, and the advantages are:
- Trains passing through the city centre and pick up and drop off passengers at the same time
- Trains do not need to terminate, and change direction, so no time is lost at the terminus, which increases the efficiency of train use
- Passengers that wish to travel from one side of the city to the other can do so without interchanging

So it would seem that a pendulum line is a really good idea and should be the standard in rail transportation planning. However, in practise there are problems, and some of these are:
- In actuality it is almost impossible to balance the passenger load on one side of the city to the other, as there will almost always be more passengers travelling to stations on one side than another. This leads to some trains being overloaded on one side of the city, and relatively empty on the other which is undesirable
- There are often natural barriers preventing rail lines passing entirely from one side to another, such as river or a mountain

- Most passengers are probably travelling into the city centre, and would not be interested in continuing their journey into the suburbs to the other side of the city. As a rail path it may not needed
- In order to get the rail line through the city centre, the rail line needs to be positioned so that its path does not pass through some immovable object, and this location for the rail line is not ideal.
- Terminating trains in a city centre allows them to sit at the platform, and passengers can comfortably make their way to their seat without being rushed, and settle in for the trip home

So it really isn't clear if installing pendulum lines is a good decision of not, but some of the critical factors in making this decision are:

- Can a pendulum line even be built, is there a sensible place to put it?
- Will the number of passenger coming into the city be the same or similar on each side of the city?
- Which choice is cheaper; building the pendulum line or having two separate lines?

Some Examples of Network Design – Multiple Lines

Rail systems are often made up of multiple rail lines. A rail line is a part of a rail system in which trains traverse in one continuous trip from one end to the other. Rail lines are often separated from one another, but can also combine together and run alongside each other. Many network design decisions concern the design of multiple rail lines.

In the design of a passenger rail system, the system design is often described in terms of rail lines. Separate lines have services that are separate from one anther, and are timetabled independently. Multiple rail lines can share tracks with one another, and maybe some of the track will be separate. Alternatively they may be completely separate, and share nothing at all. This can be a little misleading. Perhaps the best way of considering a rail line is that services are separate from the rest of the network.

Things are simpler when designing a rail system with only one rail line. Where there are multiple rail lines, then the relationship between these lines needs to be decided. The relationship between the different rail lines can be very important for rail network design.

Junctions vs Interchanges

When rail lines pass over each other, there is a decision needed as to if the lines connect, or if there is no connection at all. Where rail lines converge, there is a junction that provides the ability for rail lines to merge together. Junctions are expensive to maintain, and create timetabling problems, and many rail systems installing junctions to connect two or more rail lines together.

This is an important decision, and in complex rail networks large number of rail lines might cross each other. Where rail lines are unconnected, but cross one another, they will be grade separated, so at different levels/heights. There is no real reason why rail lines should all be connected, and in the schematic below there is no connection other than the interchange for passengers. Trains themselves cannot move from one line to another. This network structure is commonly used for metros, and intermediate capacity metros.

Figure 8.12 Two rail lines, passenger interchange only

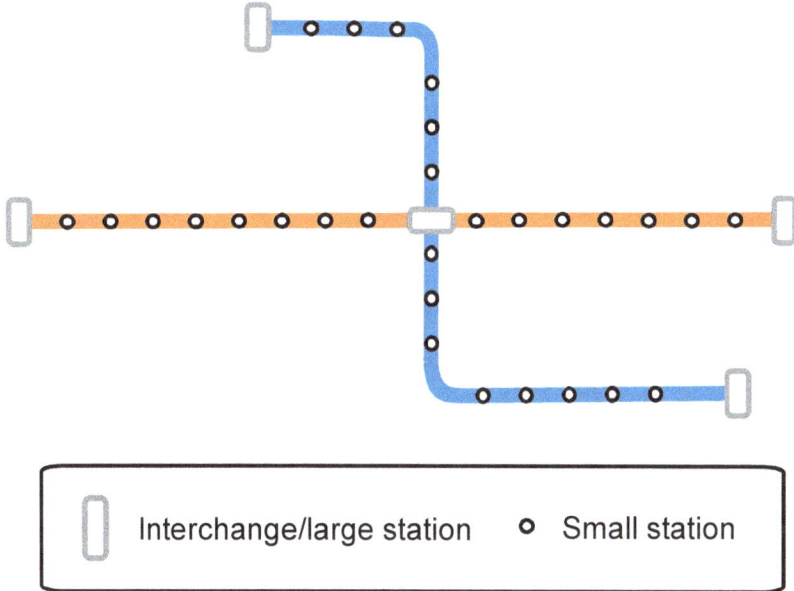

Alternatively, there are many systems where rail lines do connect, and it is possible for one rail line to connect to the other. The picture below shows how this works, and the green line is a path for trains to move from the blue line onto the orange, although it is not drawn this way. The green line is not an extra line, but rather a pathway that trains can take. Whilst it might seem that trains moving along the green line are separate from both the blue and orange lines, in practice there is probably no separation between the rail lines that are alongside each other.

Figure 8.13 Three rail lines, multiple paths possible

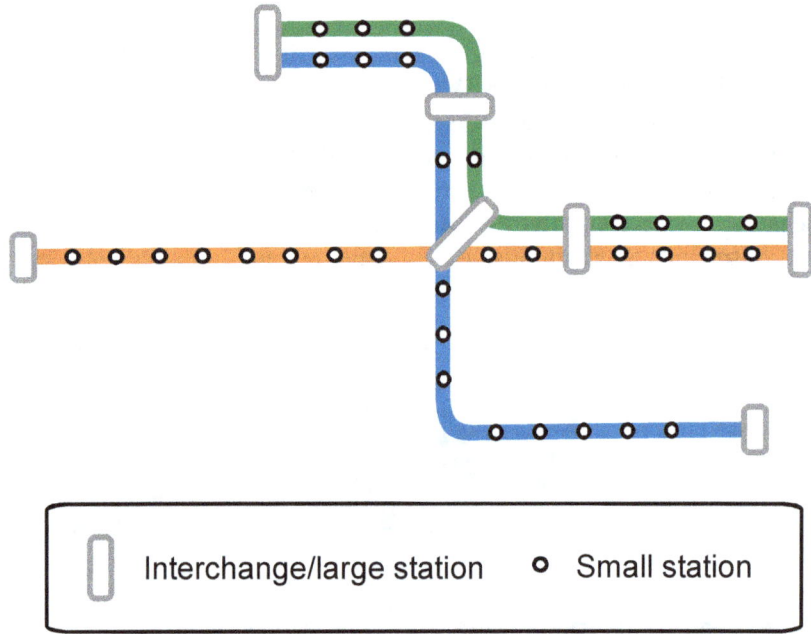

Where a railway can send trains to any direction, it is possible to tailor services to the needs of passengers. Multiple pathways are possible, and so in theory this must be better.

Of course there are also disadvantages, and these are:
- The rail network is more complex when providing this kind of connection, and the timetable will be more complicated and difficult to create, and for passengers to understand and use
- Incidents such as engineering failures will impact more of the network than where the network is separated
- Infrastructure is needed at the junctions to allow the different train movements
- Passenger information systems play more of a role, as passenger now have more options. This can be expensive in terms of maintenance and support

- Connections means turnouts, and this means a signal box somewhere with signallers managing the network. This is expensive
- The turnouts in the connections will need to have signallers managing them, and be thrown when trains need to go along a different path. This can increase the minimum headway.
- Trains when purchased will need to be able to be compatible with both rail lines, rather than just one. This can make rollingstock purchases more expensive.

Whilst one connection might seem fairly easy to manage, large numbers of connections in a complex network can make the system so complex that passengers have difficult knowing where to go. The number of possible combinations of routes will increase dramatically, and finding a pathway through is a little like navigating through a maze. The trend in Australia has been to attempt to minimise the number of different paths, as it confuses passengers.

Metros almost never have connections between lines, and this is one of the secrets to their overwhelming success. As connections are costly and messy to manage, passengers in most metro systems will interchange from one line to another. Even in a relatively short journey a passenger may interchange two or three times. No connections means that trains can operate more frequently, as trains do not need to wait for turnouts to move from one position to another.

Tram systems commonly have many connections, and a large tram network is full of them. Inter-connections between lines are very frequent in Melbourne, and the network map gets quite complicated with the number of different possible combinations. Connections (ie turnouts) are cheap in a tram system because the entire network is almost always at the same level, ie, one line normally does not pass over the top of another (of course there are exceptions).

Freight systems can also be quite complex, and full of interconnections between lines. Freight traffic can have a large variety of different destinations and departure points, and a large freight network will have an extremely large number of different possible paths for freight trains to use. In a combined passenger/freight system much of the complexity may be because of the freight system and it's need to send freight trains in many and varied directions. In some freight systems essentially everything is connected to everything. Where a passenger and freight line is mixed together, then the rail system can be extremely complex, and very difficult to manage. This challenging situation really needs its own chapter, and perhaps another book.

High speed rail lines do not normally cross each other, as they are so expensive to construct it is unlikely there would be 2 in the same place. Where there are 2, it is best for these rail lines to be grade separated, with a flyover to allow trains to pass over the other rail line without hindrance.

It is with regional and commuter trains that many of the decisions are needed with creating connections. Regional and commuter services may have many different paths and stopping patterns, and the number of different possible combinations can be very large. A decision should be made on an economic and public benefit basis on when to include a large junction, or not, but in practice these types of networks have large numbers of connections. This difficult area is not discussed any further in this book, but it is possible to analyse the cost of the junction and the number of passengers who get a benefit from the presence of the junction.

Shuttles

A shuttle is a train that moves back and forwards, captured within one part of the rail line. Shuttles terminate early, and often travel between only two stations. Shuttles require passengers to disembark at the connecting station, and then to transfer to the shuttle service. A shuttle service can be constructed on the branch line in the schematic above.

Shuttles usually only service a very small number of stations. Whilst 2 stations seems common, there is no reason why this number should be 2 and not 3 nor 4. Shuttles can connect lines that many people on the main rail line would not want to go down. Shuttles are a solution to the problem of how to balance the movement of trains down many separate lines.

Some examples of shuttles are:
- The Disney train in Hong Kong that connects the main metro line at Sunny Bay to the theme park
- The tourist shuttle from Beitou to Xin Beitou in Taipei, that connects the main metro line to the tourist area with the volcanic hot springs hotels
- The train in Sydney that connects Lidcombe station with Olympic Park, where the 2000 Summer Olympic games were held

- The Carlingford line is Sydney is operated as a shuttle, as the number of people wishing to catch the train from that line is very small

The network structure of a shuttle service is shown below. Trains start and finish on separated lines, and do not move along the entire length of the rail network, as shown below.

Figure 8.14 A shuttle and main line

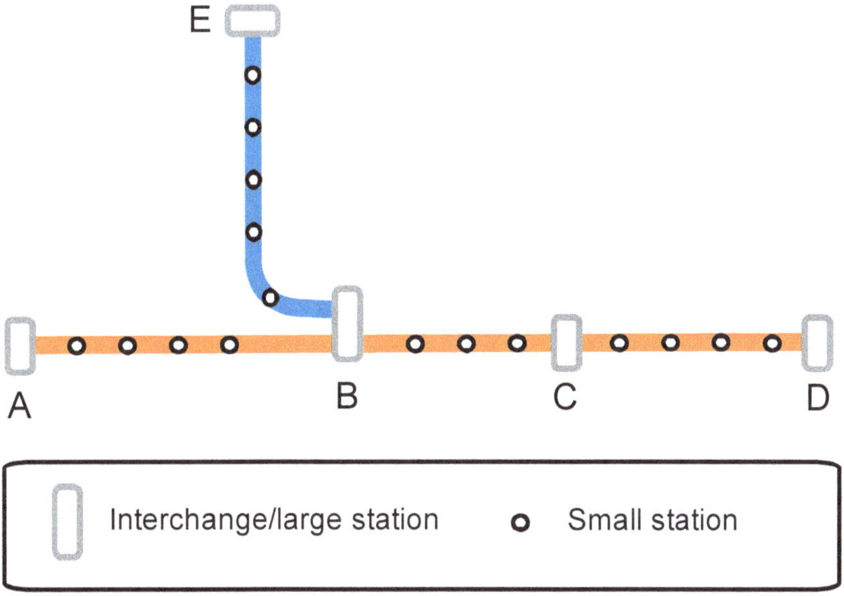

Shuttles are often unpopular with passengers, as they need to change trains and this can be time consuming. Passengers want to get settled on their train, read a book if they are sitting down, and then arrive at their destination. Interchanges, especially where they are poorly designed, which they often are, are extremely unpopular with passengers, and installing them will result in a far lower level of service. Shuttles also result in longer travel times, as the interchange time now is included in the total travel time.

In some cases shuttles are used because the other rail line is a different type to the main line, such as a monorail connecting with heavy rail system, or more commonly, a light rail system connecting with a heavy rail. In Taiwan very unusually a cable car system forms a shuttle service, because the steepness of the terrain, which is integrated into the transport system of the city of Taipei. It must be remembered that where a different type of rail system is used then a shuttle is almost always the result.

Shuttles are extremely popular with rail operators, as they divide the network up into sections and this makes the network far easier to manage. Problems with one line can be contained to one line, and the complexity of the network is far lower. Rail operators are often tempted to convert small lines into shuttles, but can be prevented from so doing by the government, passengers, the local community, and politicians (which is not necessarily a bad thing).

Some lines may operate as combined lines during part of the day, such as peak, and as shuttles during the rest of the day. Alternatively, on weekend the line may operate as a shuttle, and on a weekday as a combined line. Many variations are possible.

Perhaps the greatest importance of a shuttle is that it is often used when problems occur on a train system. Some rail systems are very prone to problems, and when these occur then trains can be formed into a shuttle service on either side of the problem.

When designing a rail system it is often tempting to create a shuttle. Where there are a small number of stations that need to be connected to the system, and there is limited capacity, then one solution is to use a shuttle. Overall it's best not to create shuttles, despite their cheapness and ease of construction, as they are generally not popular, but they can be a cost effective solution to a transport problem.

Two Rail Lines Sharing Stations

Rail lines can be combined together to provide a higher and more frequent level of services than with divided lines. The schematic below shows how rail lines might appear when not combined together.

Figure 8.15 Two rail lines running side by side

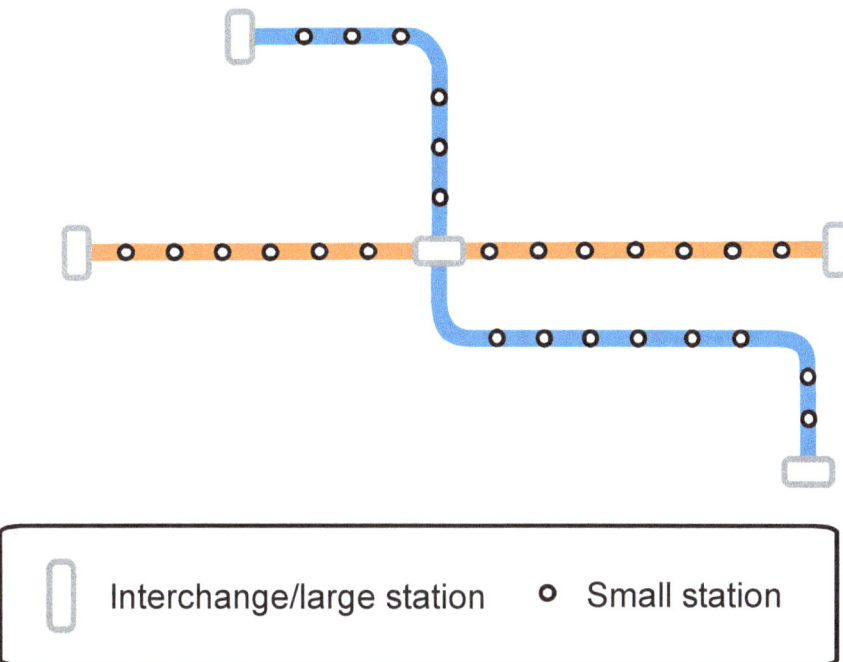

Note in the schematic above there is an interchange at one point, and the lines run parallel for a large part of their length. The alternative is shown below, and in this schematic the lines have been combined for their common length.

Approaches to Network Design Page 191

Figure 8.16 Shared Stations on Two Lines

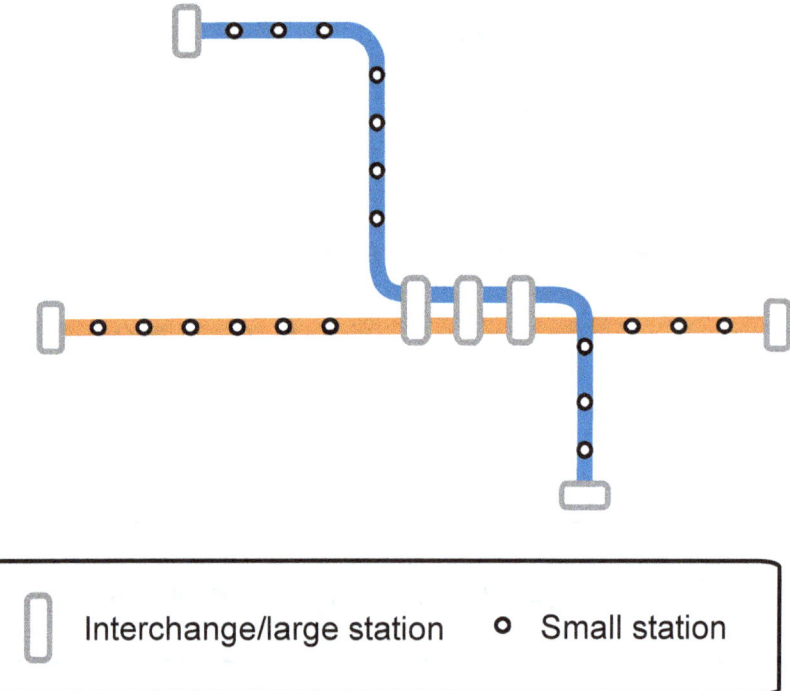

The network lines are drawn as being side by side, by in reality these lines often would be running over the same track. In Hong Kong there are rail lines that run along side each other and are entirely separate This type of decision, whether to combine lines together, is a common one, and there are, like all the different decision needed in this section, advantages and disadvantages. There are a number of papers written on the design of transport networks, with a very heavy focus on buses, and the combined structure is almost always seen as being superior, but this is not necessarily the case.

So some of the advantages for sharing stations between different lines are:
- The number of services will be higher over the combined section, providing passengers with a higher frequency of services
- The construction cost of a combined system is lower, as either the stations are shared, or the track is shared.
- For high value locations such as the centre of cities, having lines operate together is better as people want to go to specific locations that both lines connect to

However, there are some disadvantages, and these are:
- If lines A & B are very busy, then combining them together will result in a lower number of services compared to separate lines, where tracks are shared.
- The coverage of the city or area will be better if the lines are separated, as there are more stations
- If there is a disruption on one line, then this disruption will impact the other line, as there is a common section in the middle. Separated lines are more reliable in general

So overall the recommendation is that rail lines should be separated if the traffic warrants it, and this is common in very large cities. This is especially the case for metro systems, where rail lines should almost never be combined. In smaller cities, with a small amount of rail traffic, combining rail lines together can make very good sense, especially for rail commuter traffic, or regional trains, where the train frequency would be too low to otherwise provide a good quality service.

Grid Layouts vs a Radial Design

Grid networks are very common, especially for large cities with multiple metro lines. The basic idea is that the entire city, or the centre of the city, has a very good level of service and is covered with a grid of rail lines. This type of network is unsuited for freight networks, but can be ideal for large cities.

Figure 8.17 Rail Grid Design

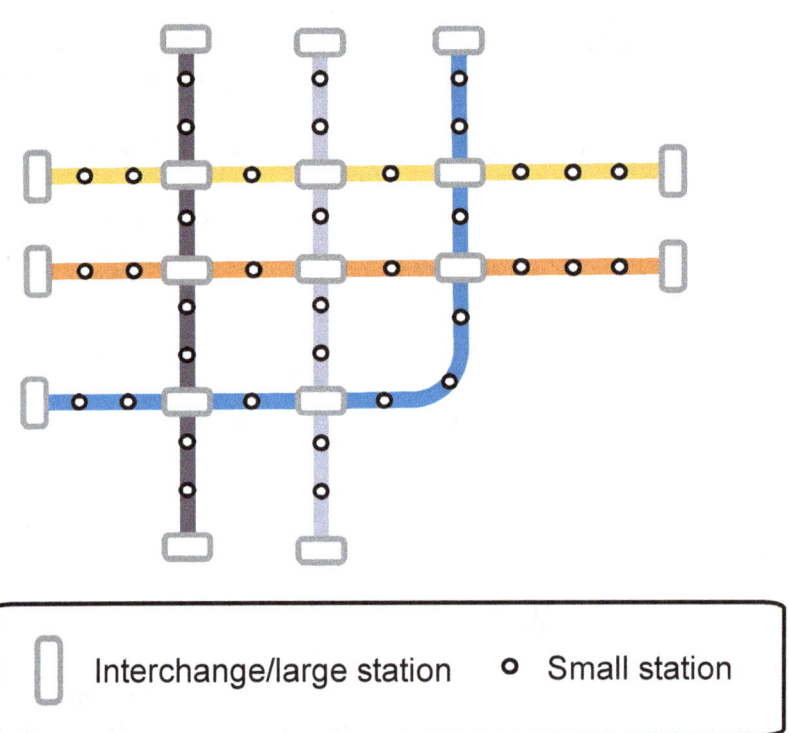

Grid networks almost always require passengers to interchange between lines, but of course there are exceptions. The author's experience of Tokyo was that the rail system was dominated by rail services moving as in a traditional grid, but a small number of services were moved from one line to another, such as the express train to Narita airport.

Grid designs have a large number of interchange stations. In the relatively simple design above passengers can interchange at no less than 8 stations. A grid design will often require numerous interchanges for passengers, even for short trips.

The alternative to a grid design is a radial design, where trains radiate out from a central point. Radial designs are common in commuter and regional networks, where rail services move from the centre of the city to the suburbs and outlying towns. A radial design is shown below.

Figure 8.18 A Radial System Design

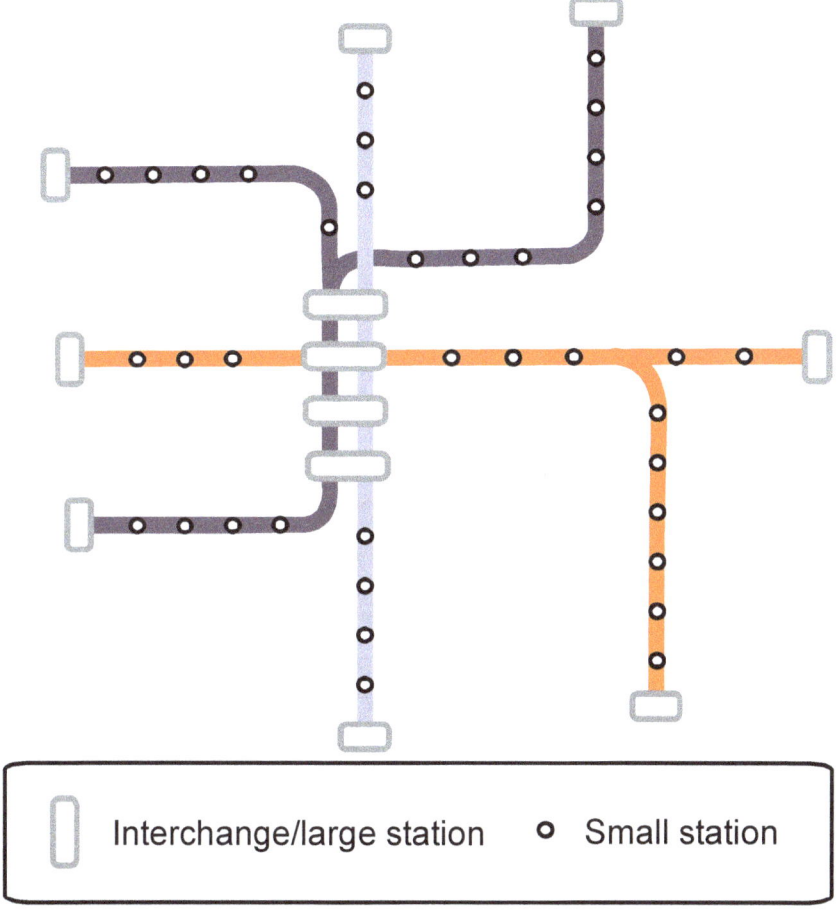

The schematic above shows trains moving from a central point through to the edges of a city or CBD, and further from the centre the green and the blue lines diverge.

Radial designs are also quite common, and seem to occur without any serious planning. Most medium size cities in countries with rail networks will have this kind of rail system, because there will be a major rail line into the city, and then a couple of others linking a few nearby towns, giving rise to the radial structure.

Ring Designs

A ring design is where the rail system has a ring around the centre of the city. A ring railroad may pass several other rail lines, and connect them all together. The ring line does not pass through the centre of the city, but around the periphery. Ring rail lines are uncommon, and seem to be difficult to build in practice.

The schematic below shows what a ring railroad might look like.

Figure 8.19 A Ring Rail Line

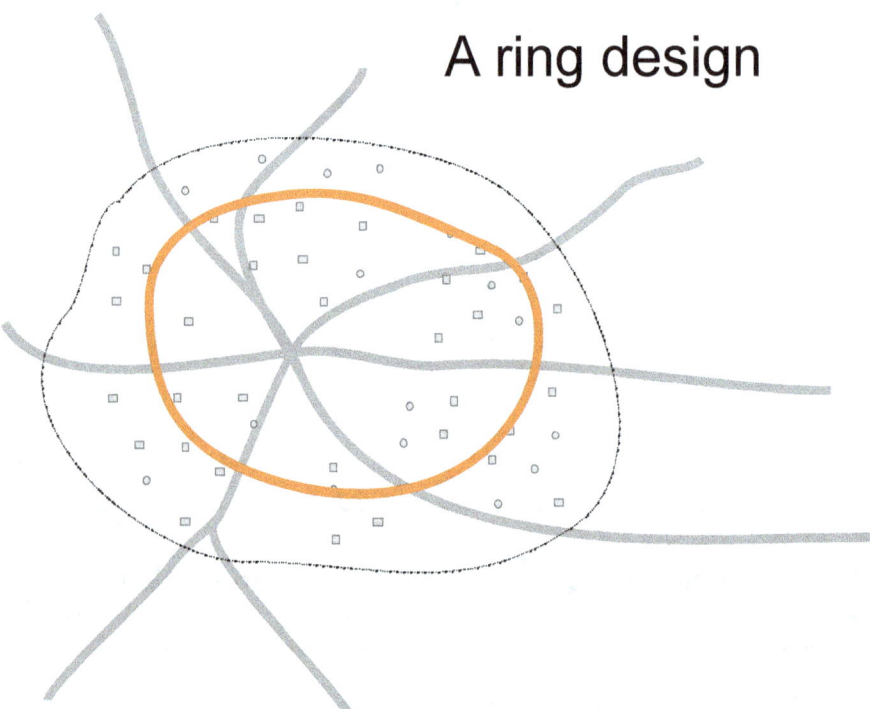

Ring rail lines seem to be often proposed as a new type of rail transport project, and in Australia there have been many suggestions to build these in one place or another. However, they are hard to economically justify, despite seeming to make very good sense to build. Buses seem to be able to maintain transport connections between different lines, and using buses is far more common than building a ring railroad.

The main problem is that ring railroads need large numbers of people using them to be justifiable, and as the ring does not pass through the centre of the city, getting these passenger numbers is difficult. Moscow metro has a ring railroad, but Moscow is the largest city in Europe, and has very large numbers of people using the system each day. Beijing also has a ring metro, and this was one of the first lines constructed. The general rule seems to be that only a very large city can justify having a ring railroad.

Rail Systems and Connections to HSR

HSR lines are very expensive to construct, and so there is a strong desire on the part of government to minimise the cost. One way of doing this is to construct the rail line so that it avoids the centre of the city, and another public transport connection is needed to provide passengers with a way to get into the centre of the city.

The schematic below shows the "normal" configuration of an HSR line, and where it terminates in the centre of a city. It terminates at an interchange between line A and B, and so passengers can make their way from the HSR system onto the local rail line.

Figure 8.20 Shared Stations on Two Lines

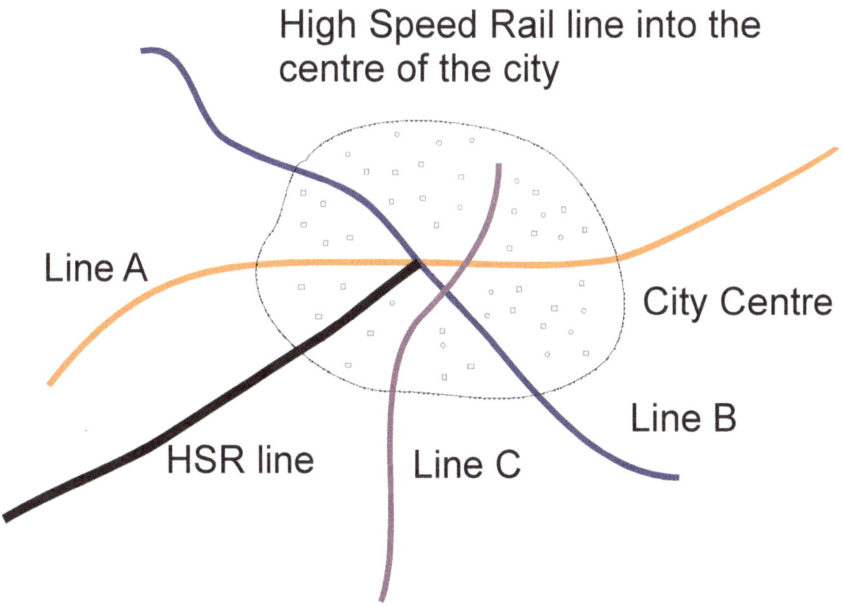

The alternative to this layout is a terminus or HSR station outside of the city. This type of network design is also common, and the HSR station

Kaohsiung in Taiwan is built this way, and does not extend to the centre of the city. This design is shown below

Figure 8.21 Shared Stations on Two Lines

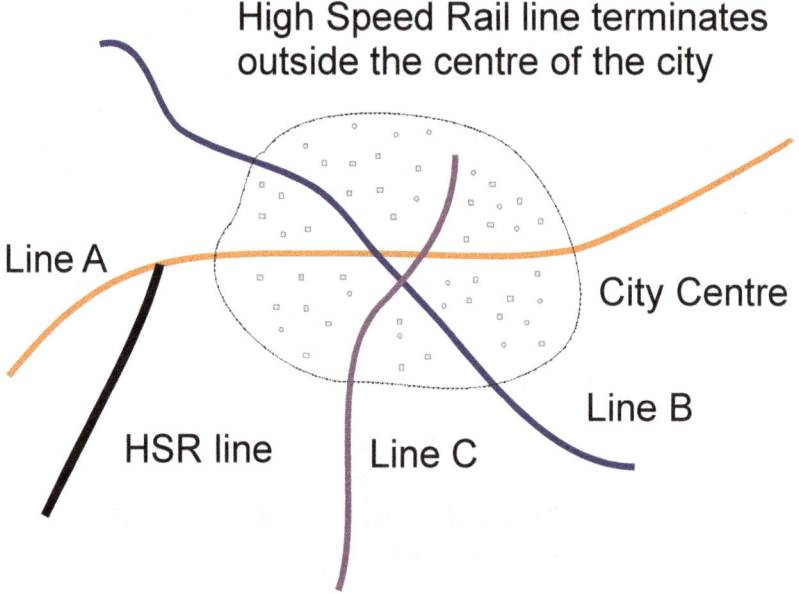

The HSR line does not enter the centre of the city, but terminates early, and then passengers make their way on the local rail line into the centre of the city. This type of design is substantially inferior to one where the HSR line reaches into the centre of the city, but can be dramatically cheaper. This network layout avoids the need to build a large terminal in the centre of cities where land can be very scarce, and difficult to obtain for a large rail terminal. The cost of the land in any major city can be very large, and again land does not need to be acquired to build this system.

REFERENCES

1. Cho-Lam Lau, J. *The Performance of public transport operations, land-use and urban transport planning in Hong Kong*, Cities, Vol 14, No 3, pp 145 – 153, 1997

Chapter 9 The Kinematics of Train Movement and other useful equations

It is important in the planning of any new rail line or extension to calculate the time taken to get from one end of the rail line to another. This information can be used to estimate how many people will use the rail line, or the utility of the rail line to people near the rail line. For freight it is beneficial to know the total trip time. The travel time of any rail service is an important metric that should be understood when assessing any change to a rail system.

Kinematics is the study of the motion of bodies, without any consideration of the forces involved in creating that motion. Whilst most readers may think of kinematics as something that is studied by high school students about small objects being thrown around, this topic is actually very relevant to the movement of trains, as they, strangely enough, are physical bodies, and many of the equations in kinematics can be applied successfully to train movement.

Travel time is a key parameter in the design of any rail system. Railways are very expensive to build, and rail systems are often implemented due to their superior speed. Rail needs to provide substantial benefits to justify its very high construction and maintenance cost, and speed can be one of those. To take one example of this, metro trains moving around a city need to exceed 30 kms/hr to really justify the expense of construction. Buses and other road vehicles may travel between 20 to 30 kms/hr, and trains need to be just a little faster than that. As we will see below, a common speed for metro services is 30 kms/hr.

The same applies for commuter trains, and of course high speed trains. High speed trains particularly, need to move very quickly, and if they are too slow then the service may be poorly patronised.

So travel time is a key piece of information. So how can this be estimated? There are a number of equations that are used for calculating travel times, and these are the standard kinematics equations of motion that can be found in any high school textbook on physics. To write them down again, here they are:

$$Speed = \frac{distance}{time} \qquad (1)$$

$$\text{Time} = \frac{velocity}{acceleration} \quad (2)$$

$$v^2 = u^2 + 2as \quad (3)$$

$$s = ut + \frac{1}{2}at^2 \quad (4)$$

$$v = u + at \quad (5)$$

Another useful equation, derived from equation (3) above, is:

$$s = \frac{v^2}{2a} \quad (6)$$

This equation is used for distances for stopping, and for distances to reach specific speeds when starting from 0 kms/hr.

The terms are:

v = final velocity
u = initial velocity
t = time
a = acceleration
s = distance

So how can we describe the motion of trains along a rail line? The graph below roughly shows how a train moves, and is applicable for trains moving through rail systems in a city, or in a metro line. The acceleration of a train as it leaves a station can be described in terms of speed and distance. As the train accelerates its speed increases, as what this looks like is shown below in graphical form.

Figure 9.1 An Accelerating Train

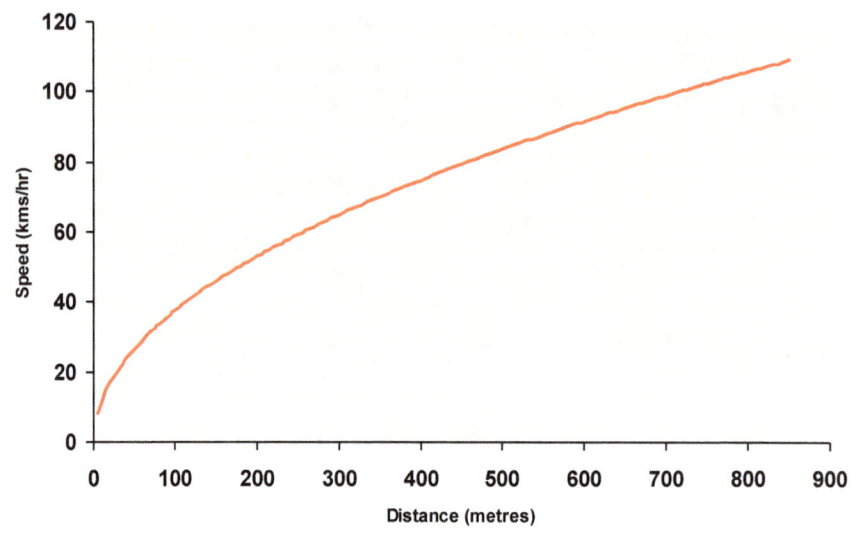

It takes hundreds of metres for a train to reach its top speed, or possibly even more. Cars can accelerate very quickly, and can get to maximum speed much faster. A train is not the same as a car, and accelerates more slowly. High speed trains make takes minutes to reach top speed, and sometimes people underestimate the time it takes for a train to reach top speed.

For closely spaced stations, such as in a metro system, careful consideration is needed of the spacing between stations. As a train takes so long to get up to high speeds, if stations are spaced too closely together then the train will never reach an acceptable speed. Furthermore, should the average speed drop too low, then the public will avoid the system. In practice a spacing of at least 1 km between stations is appropriate for metro stations, or even more, otherwise the average speed will be too low. The average speed is calculated below.

For a train system that needs to stop more frequently than once per kilometre, a light rail or a tram system might be more appropriate. These systems are more suited for frequent stopping. Light rail systems often run at street level, whereas metro systems are usually below ground. As light rail systems are faster and quicker to board, the slower travel speed is not such a problem. Light rail systems, especially where there are many frequent stops, should not be used for moving people long distances, typically more than 10 kms, and sometimes even less, as the travel speed is just too slow. Of course, with all of this, there are exceptions that could justify braking these simple rules. The author has travelled on the Hong Kong tram system on Hong Kong Island, which must be one of the slowest tram systems in the world. It has quite a long length, but to get from one end to the other takes several hours in peak time! It is nonetheless a very heavily used system.

The speed profile for trains operating in a metro style environment (or light rail in some cases) is shown below. Metros can maintain this profile all day, as they do not need to cross roads, or negotiate through complex junctions. Light rail vehicles, especially ones that cross roads, will have difficulty in matching the speed profile below.

Figure 9.2 Modelling Train Movement

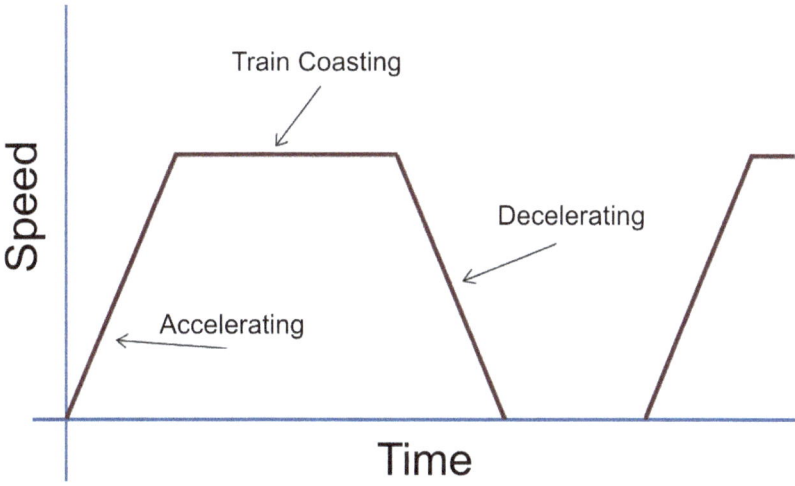

We can use this speed profile to estimate the time taken to move from one end of the rail system to the other. The time a train spends at a station is called the dwell time, and during this time passengers board and alight from the train.

Note that in this book it is assumed that trains accelerate and decelerate at the same rate. In practice this assumption is ok for simple calculations, but for any detailed work perhaps more accurate numbers should be used. The author has had long arguments as to the actual acceleration rate a driver must use, and it is generally agreed that it is easier for the train to decelerate faster than to accelerate. On the other hand, and this is true especially for rail systems without ATO, a driver is penalised if he misses the station, or "overshoots". This happens when he drives too far, and part of the front of the train is beyond the station, and some passengers may not be able to alight from the train. This is an undesirable situation, and one assumes that drivers will be liable to disciplinary action if it happens too often. So drivers will be careful in entering stations, and decelerate more slowly. Overall then, it's likely the acceleration and deceleration of trains will be somewhat similar, close enough for the simple and useful calculations contained in this book.

In actual practice train movements are similar to this speed structure, but not the same. A number of studies have examined the speed profile of trains moving through a rail system. In Sydney a very substantial study was performed on the speed profile of suburban trains, and again, it was found that trains move as per the diagram below. In actual practice trains moving between stations have the speed profile more similar to what is drawn below:

Figure 9.3 Practical and Theoretical Train Movement

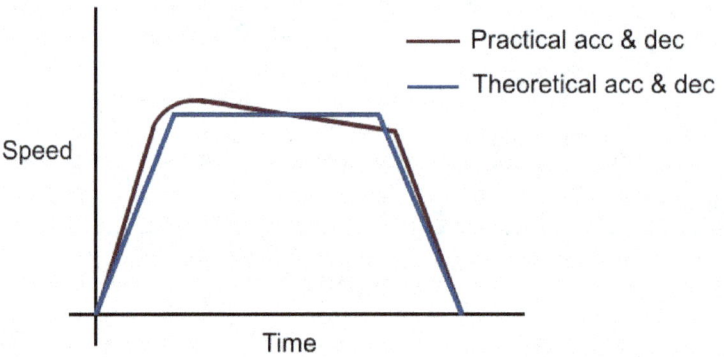

In practice drivers do not need to follow any particular curve or speed profile, they are usually free to choose any speed. However, it has been found that drivers mostly follow the curve drawn above. Some rail systems post signs that advise drivers of the "best speeds" to drive their train at. The best speeds are often chosen on the basis of energy efficiency, although operational considerations (i.e. the timetable) is also very important.

Where trains are moving between distant stations, and not closely spaced stations like the example above, and there are many different speed limits between the two stations, then the speed profile might look like something below:

Figure 9.4 Multiple Speed Limits from Station to Station

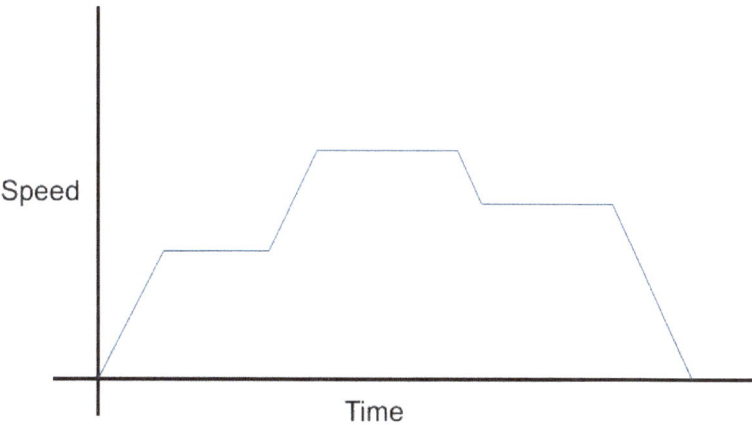

To calculate the travel time would require an analysis of the different parts of the trip, and then add them together. This is relatively straight forward, and easily done.

So let's analyse the movement of trains between stations. The train accelerates, then maintains a constant speed, and then slows down. We can assume that the train accelerates and decelerates at the same rate. The time taken to accelerate to maximum speed is given by:

$$Acceleration\ time = \frac{line\ speed}{acceleration}$$

Or we can put this as:

$$t = \frac{v}{a}$$

The distance covered when accelerating is given by:

Kinematics of Train Movement

$$s = \frac{v^2}{2a}$$

The travel time between one station and another is given by this equation:

$$\text{travel time} = t_{acc} + t_{coasting} + t_{dec}$$

Where:

t_{acc} = acceleration time
$t_{coasting}$ = time spent coasting
t_{dec} = deceleration time

The equation for travel time can then expressed as:

$$\text{travel time} = \frac{v_{max}}{a} + \frac{D_{station} - 2\left(\frac{v_{max}^2}{2a}\right)}{v_{max}} + \frac{v_{max}}{a}$$

This can be simplified to:

$$\text{travel time} = \frac{2v_{max}}{a} + \frac{D_{station}}{v} - \frac{v_{max}}{a}$$

Which becomes:

$$\text{travel time} = \frac{v_{max}}{a} + \frac{D_{station}}{v_{max}}$$

Where:

$D_{station}$ = distance between stations, from the front of both stations
v_{max} = maximum velocity in ms^{-1}

Of course in calculating this formula we must be careful that the train has sufficient time to reach the maximum line speed, and we can test this using the equation below:

$$\frac{v^2}{a} < D_{station} \qquad (7)$$

If this condition is true then we know that the train can reach maximum speed before needing to begin slowing down to stop at the next station.

The speed profile of a train moving through a suburban network is shown below. The train accelerates and decelerates as it leaves and then arrives at stations.

Figure 9.5 Train Moving through Multiple Stations

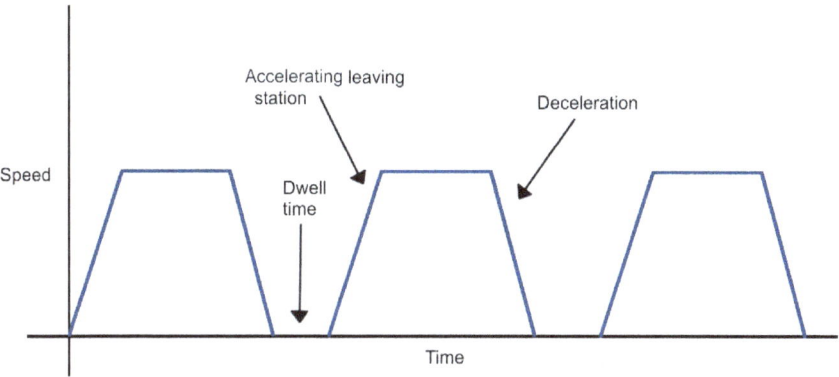

So what speeds can be achieved in practice? The limiting factor, especially for suburban networks or metros can often be the distance between stations, and the graph below shows the maximum speed based on the distance between stations. We assume that the train accelerates evenly and reaches the maximum speed, at which point it then begins to slow down to stop at the next station. To create the average speed between stations in the graph below, the assumption was made that train must spend at least 15 seconds at its top speed before starting to decelerate. Also an acceleration of 0.54 ms^{-2} was used. Dwell times were not factored into the calculation, so in practice average speeds will be a bit lower than what is shown below.

Figure 9.6 Top and Average Speed

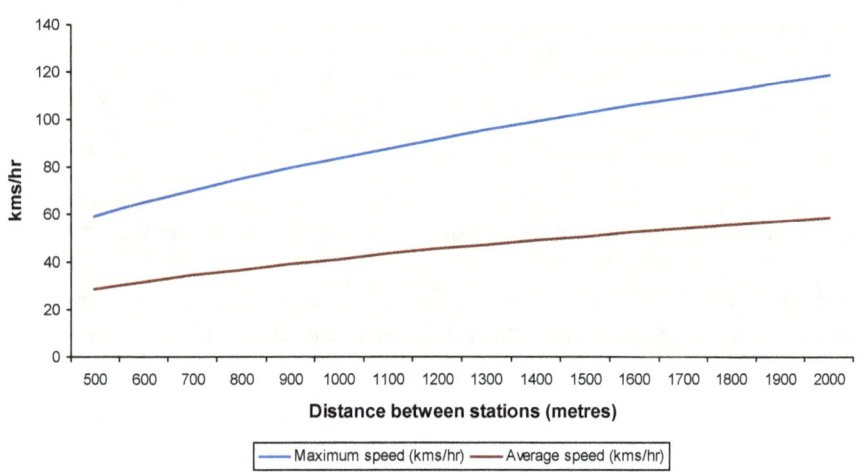

The table that accompanies this graph is:

Distance between stations (metres)	Maximum speed kms/hr	Realistic top speed kms/hr
500	59	29
600	65	32
700	70	34
800	75	37
900	79	39
1000	84	41
1100	88	43
1200	92	45
1300	95	47
1400	99	49
1500	102	51
1600	106	52
1700	109	54
1800	112	56
1900	115	57
2000	118	59

Notice how the average speed increases as the distance between stations increases. Something of a rarely stated rule is that stations for a metro style system should be at least 1000 metres apart.

A more complete explanation of average speeds is provided below. Once again the speed profile is shown below for the movement of trains throughout a suburban network with closely spaced stations.

Figure 9.7 Dwell Time and Maximum Speed

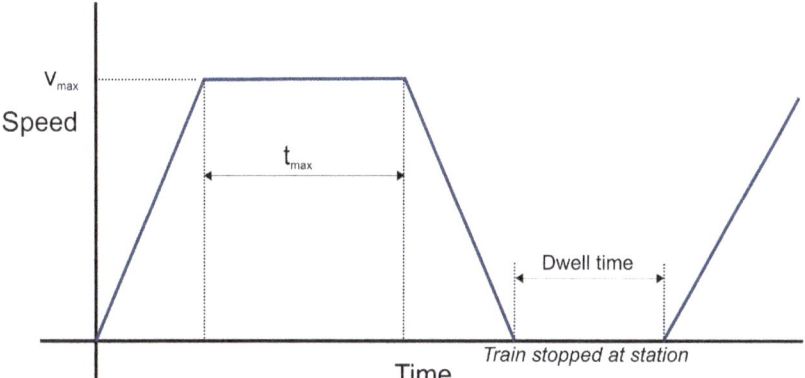

It is possible for a train to accelerate from a station, and then as soon as it has reached its maximum speed, start decelerating, but it is rarely done. Doing so is very wasteful of energy, and in practice very few rail organisations would do so. Drivers will accelerate until a target speed is reached, and then coast, and then start decelerating. The lower the maximum speed, the lower the power consumption. For this reason, and a number of others, trains usually will drive for at least a short period of time at the maximum speed.

We can calculate the maximum speed a train can reach, based on the acceleration and the distance between stations. Using equation (7):

$$v_{max} \leq \sqrt{aD_{station}}$$

This will give us the maximum possible speed between stations. With some simple manipulations we can derive the formula for the maximum speed between stations, including the time trains are coasting. The time t_{max} is essentially the time trains coast between stations.

$$v_{max} = a\left[\sqrt{\frac{D_{station}}{a}} - \frac{t_{max}}{2}\right]$$

The average speed along the rail line is a very important number. This number is often used in rail planning, as there are certain minimum speeds as for trains to travel at, as mentioned earlier.

The average speed of any train is:

$$Average\ speed = \frac{D_{station}}{travel\ time + Dwell}$$

It's important to have some reference on average speeds throughout cities and in transportation systems. Below are some typical values for average speeds, for reference, to compare with when calculating average speeds for new rail lines or other rail transport projects. As with any numbers in this book, the values are indicative only.

Typical Average Speeds		
Location	Service Type	Average travel speed (kms/hr)
Cities	Trams	10
	Buses	10
	Light rail	20
	BRT	30 - 50
	Metros	30 – 45
	Commuter	50 – 80
Countries	Regional	60 – 100
	High speed	> 200

The table below shows some indicative values for acceleration.

Indicative Acceleration and Deceleration Rates

Acceleration	Comment
0.3 ms^{-2}	Typical acceleration for a freight train (and this changes depending of speed)
0.5 ms^{-2}	Acceleration used widely in metros and commuter services
0.8 ms^{-2}	Limit where passengers start to feel some discomfort in braking and acceleration
1.1 ms^{-2}	Limit of acceleration and deceleration of some metro trains
1.3 ms^{-2}	Commonly used acceleration rate in the US and Canada, also the limit of acceleration at which passengers can remain standing
1.4 ms^{-2}	Another common limit for the maximum acceleration and deceleration of metro trains
2.5 ms^{-2}	A common limit for the maximum emergency braking of light rail vehicles

In practice there are many other constraints on how quickly a train can move through a rail system. Congestion of the rail system is something that often slows trains down. Light rail vehicles moving along city streets will slow down for other road traffic, depending on how the rail line is constructed. The equations presented here work best for rail systems that are completely grade separated, and have regular patterns of acceleration and deceleration.

Top speeds are also limited by the geometry of the track. For top speeds around 70-80 kms/hr (50 miles per hour), the distance between stations will have a large effect on average speed. For metro systems especially, the calculations presented above are exceedingly useful. Also monorails, and intermediate capacity systems, and APM, also can make use of these equations. Other rail systems such as HSR, these equations are still relevant but not as important. HSR trains are limited by track geometry in most cases, and need to speed up and slow down at curves.

Freight was not mentioned above. Freight trains movements are a little more difficult to predict. For example, the loads the freight train is carrying will have a large impact upon the acceleration, and maximum speed. The weather conditions, and slipperiness of the top of the rail, is also important.

Freight trains are affected by a large number of parameters, and tops speeds are difficult to calculate.

REFERENCES

1. Halpern, P *Non-collision injuries in public buses: a national survey of a neglected problem*, Emerg Medical Journal 2005 Feb: 22(2): 108-110

Chapter 10 Stabling

Stabling is where trains are stored, often at night, and sometimes during the day when they are not used. Passenger trains are commonly stabled during the day between peak periods. The reader will probably note the similarity between trains and horses, because the same words are used to describe both. Stabling is very important for any operational railway, as trains often need to be stabled, and the location of stabling can dramatically affect how trains are scheduled to move throughout the network.

Stabling facilities need to be distinguished from maintenance and maintenance centres, and they are quite different. Trains are not normally stabled in maintenance centres, as these have limited space, and far more space is needed for stabling of trains than is normally available in maintenance centres. Maintenance centres may be able to store a small number of trains, but ordinarily trains are stored in large stabling yards. It is also common for stabling to be co-located with maintenance centres, 20 or 30 metres away, or trains may need to pass through the stabling to get to the maintenance centre.

Stabling yards are not pretty things, and while rail transport is sexy and good to look at, stabling yards are ugly. Full of tracks, cluttered with trains, and with a very industrial look and feel, many stabling yards are very unsightly. In many cases cities with large stabling yards near the centre of the city have moved them away just to avoid having to look at them, or hide them so that no one can see them. In Melbourne much of the stabling available in the centre of the city has been removed, as it was considered a terrible eyesore. Likewise, for the tram depot in Hong Kong, it is superbly well hidden, and it's not a pretty thing, but it is well hidden. The larger the stabling yard, the worse this problem seems to be.

Given the poor visual appearance of a stabling yard, they are often hidden away as best as possible. This might be achieved by walls, or other structure that hides the yard. Alternatively, the yard may by sandwiched between two other rail lines, so that no one can see it through the other trains. Alternatively, it may be hidden in a place where there are no people to be affected by its poor appearance.

The problem is a little less serious for the various forms of light rail, such as trams, light rail proper, and Automated People Movers (APMs). These smaller trains can be tucked away in places where they cannot be seen, or buildings can be used to house all the vehicles. Larger trains, such as HSR trains, or commuter trains, will be difficult to hide, and the stabling yards will be large. Freight yards are truly enormous, and are extremely difficult to hide. Freight yards are just dreadful, and noisy, and should be put in industrial areas where no one lives nearby.

The picture below is of a tram depot in Brunswick in Melbourne. This photo was taken around lunchtime so the depot is almost empty. Tram depots are a type of stabling, and unusually for rail transport, trams can be stored inside under cover when stabled.

Tram Depot in Melbourne

Stabling yards are often a maintenance problem, and require a lot of maintenance compared to plain track. Where large numbers of trains are stabled, there needs to be a corresponding large amount of infrastructure to accommodate the trains, and this means a high concentration of infrastructure in a stabling yard. The cost of installing stabling can be substantial, especially where the number of trains to be stabled is very large. Given the quantity of infrastructure, there are constant failures of the engineering equipment, such as points and track circuits, so maintenance crews will need to be stationed very close to a stabling yard to ensure any failures are fixed quickly.

A common problem with older railways it seems is that there seems to be stabling all throughout their networks. A reasonable amount of stabling is very desirable, but too much of it can be a problem. Putting stabling everywhere is very attractive for operators of railways, because it provides all sorts of operational flexibility; if a train breaks down then it can be quietly stored in a stabling yard somewhere until it can be moved to a maintenance centre to be repaired. There are many advantages to having stabling everywhere, and operators of rail systems may ask for lots of stabling to be installed, even when there already is quite a lot. From a maintenance and cost perspective it's a real problem, and stabling yards should be installed only where needed.

Stabling needs to be properly designed and installed to allow the most efficient operation of any railway. Stabling is important, and where it is installed in the wrong place, or poorly designed, then operational railways can face some serious problems. Some of the problems with poorly designed or located stabling includes:
- Trains need to be moved large distances to start their runs in the morning, or finish at night in poor places, and again need to be moved
- Stabling can't accommodate all the trains that operate on a line, and only some can be stabled
- Infrastructure in the stabling yard is in poor condition, as the yard is so busy that important maintenance cannot be performed
- The stabling yard is too large for the number of trains stored there, and much of the equipment is not used, and is rusting away
- The stabling yard is in a place that is difficult to access, and far away from where maintenance staff are based
- Entry and exit from the stabling yard is a bottleneck, and the stabling yard cannot put trains into and receive trains from the network quickly enough
- Stabling is not long enough to accommodate the length of trains that are needed

Overall stabling yards are quite important. The author's observation is that a significant percentage of rail transport projects seem to either be about stabling, or involve changes to stabling. It is possible for a rail line to be designed to handle large numbers of trains, but the stabling is inadequate to meet the needs of the rail line.

Much consideration should be given to the placement of stabling yards. Stabling yards may be located where land is available, and this might be well away from where trains start operating and finish for the night. This can create large problems, as trains are moving around all the time, to get back to a place where they can be stabled. Moving trains from poorly placed stabling yards is expensive, staff need to staff early to get trains into position, there are the power costs and wear and tear on the train, and it makes the maintenance window for track smaller, as there are many train movements before the start of train services.

Another common problem is the entrance to and exit from stabling. It is a common problem for the capacity into and out of the stabling to be insufficient. Where this is the case, the stabling yard is limited in how many trains can be managed, regardless of its actual size. Resolving this problem can be difficult, as enlarging the entrance to the stabling can often be a difficult thing to achieve. Land, and the lack of it, can be the problem.

Freight is stabled, but it's a bit different from passenger services. Freight locomotives can be coupled to many different types of freight wagons, and when not being used these need to be stored somewhere. Some freight wagons may be very infrequently used, and spend most of their time sitting in some freight yard somewhere. The long term storage of different freight wagons is not normally called stabling, but rather just storage in the yard. Nonetheless it is a type of stabling. .

For trains with dedicated locomotives, when the train drives into any kind of stabling, or for that matter a terminus, the question arises as to how to get the locomotive out again. Locomotives can move in reverse, and entire trains can be propelled backwards if needed, but it's always better to put a locomotive at the front of the train rather than the rear. It is possible to put a second track next to the first to allow the locomotive to get out from behind the train, and sometimes this is a called a run-around road. EMU's do not have this problem, and can normally be driven from both ends of the train. Turntables were once common, and these are a way of turning locomotives around. In some situations there may be an electric locomotive pulling coaches which are unpowered, and one solution to this problem is to put an electric locomotive at each end of the train. Otherwise, just like diesel locomotives, the locomotive will need to be moved from one end of the train to the other.

As part of the asset management of any railway there needs to be continuous removal of any surplus assets, and stabling is a perfect place to do this. Over time the operational need of the railway changes, and stabling yards are often full of old disused equipment, and so an asset removal program can be useful in removing unwanted equipment. Removing old rusting equipment is often not done, because the equipment costs very little to upkeep when it is not used, but the number of asset items of disused equipment can build up quite quickly. Whilst this book is not really about asset management, it's not really good to let the amount of disused equipment build up to the point where there is more equipment not used than actually used, and this seems to be common, at least in Australia.

So how is a stabling yard described? The key parameters for a stabling yard are:
- The number of tracks (sometimes called roads, even though it a rail track) which can be used to stable trains
- The length of the stabling tracks
- The number of trains that can be stabled. This is normally the number of tracks that can be used for stabling, but sometimes these numbers will be different
- The number of trains that can enter and exit the stabling yard per hour. It is entirely possible for a stabling yard to possess an exit through which it can take hours to get all the trains out
- The expected used capacity of the stabling yard, and this can be a number anywhere between 0 to 100%. It seems normal that for any new stabling that almost all the capacity would be used, but for old ones the percentage used might be close to zero.
- The type of train that can be stabled, electric, diesel, or even steam. Stabling for diesel trains often requires fuel pumps, where trains can be refuelled with diesel. Steam trains require water for the boiler, and often sand, and these need to be available.
- The availability of decanting. Long distance trains have toilets, and the effluent needs to be removed from the train. Old style trains did not store their effluent, but thankfully most all these trains have been removed from service around the world.
- The availability of water to add to any water tanks on trains (used for flushing toilets, drinking water for passengers, etc).

A quick point should be made here; refuelling trains and adding water is not something done only in a maintenance centre. Maintenance is performed at a frequency normally around months, ie, 3 months, and this far too long to add water only at these times. Whilst it may be possible to add water to a train at a maintenance centre, normally this would be done where trains are stabled. There is no reason why a maintenance centre should not have these facilities, but removing effluent from a train needs to be done almost daily, and this is far too frequent to be done at a maintenance centre.

The calculation of the total capacity of the yard is normally pretty easy, but the number of trains that can be moved in and out is a bit harder. Speeds in stabling yards are normally limited, and 25 kms/hr seems to be common, at least in Australia. Capacity into and out of a stabling yard is often limited when there are only two tracks in and out. Where only one track is available into and out of a yard, problems with entry and exit can be even more severe.

Tram depots are an interesting form of stabling, because of the short length of trams, tram depots are often covered. Very large numbers of trams can be stored in one place, because trams are short in length, and are narrower than most trains. As mentioned above, tram depots can be hidden because of their small size.

The photo below is of a turntable, and this is where train locomotives where turned around. Little used now, turntables were once very common. The way a turntable works is that a locomotive is driven onto the turntable, and then the turntable rotates so that the locomotive faces the opposite direction. Turntables are essentially a giant circle, with a movable section of track in the middle. In NSW at least turntables were often hand powered, and railway staff would turn a handle, and in so doing the turntable would spin around slowly.

Locomotive turntable

Most turntables were in stabling yards, so that the carriages or wagons of the steam train would be decoupled from the locomotive, and the steam engine would be turned around, and the reconnected to the carriages, and then move off in the opposite direction from whence it came. Very old staling yards may still have turntables in them, especially where old steam trains are occasionally used for heritage and tourist purposes.

The Tidal Nature of Commuter Services

Recall that commuter services are a special type of rail system, which specialise in moving people to their place of work, particularly on weekdays. The structure of commuter services is relatively standard, passengers are moved from outlying suburbs to a central location, usually where businesses are located. These businesses are often offices, and need office workers to staff them. Shift work is rare with offices, so there is little need for rail services outside of business hours. Office work is mostly day work, Monday to Friday, so many workers are needed during these times.

Commuter services are markedly different from metro style services, which operate throughout the day, and may have a higher service frequency during the day, but do not stop operation. Some of the key differences between a commuter service and a metro style service, or light rail for that matter, are:
- Some stations will close once the peak period has ended
- Trains operating in the peak are very crowded, and those that operate outside the peak are much more lightly loaded, or even almost empty
- The demand for passenger services is towards the centre of the city in the morning, and away from the centre of the city in the afternoon
- Rail services may cease away from peak periods
- There are direct services on a line to a city centre of business district in peak, but away from this passengers need to change trains to get to a city centre

In any city with a significant number of corporations operating in a large business district, there are normally rail services that cater for the employees of these businesses. Rail services start early in the morning, and then run throughout the peak period, and then resume in the afternoon when people want to go home. Commuter services have a reduced service between peak periods, or potentially no service at all. In some cases services only operate at certain times of the day. Alternatively services from the CBD to any extremely large regional centre may continue 24 hours a day, if the demand is there to justify it.

Train movements, especially for commuter and regional services are tidal. What this means is that in the morning trains move from the outskirts of a big city into the middle in the morning, and in the afternoon, when city workers finish work, trains move from the centre of the city to the outskirts or regional centres. So trains start their morning in a rural or regional stabling yard, and then move to some central point, where they are stabled again, waiting for the office workers to complete their day, and then move out again. In this situation there will be two stabling yards at least, one at the end of the line at the regional centre, and then another in centre of the large city. Train movements are tidal because they all move together in a daily pattern, much like a tide.

So how is all of this relevant to stabling? Well as there are more services into the city centre rather than out, trains accumulate in the centre of the city, and then in the afternoon these trains are needed, to move passengers from the CBD out to the suburbs again. This means that there is a requirement for stabling yards in the centre of the city, to accommodate these trains, and them some more stabling yards at the end of several rail lines to accommodate these commuter trains at night. Stabling does not necessarily need to be provided, but where it isn't there will be large numbers of empty train movements, which cost money to make.

Well designed stabling

The ease of use of any stabling yard is another important consideration. Well designed stabling, in addition to having plenty of capacity, located in the correct place, and having the ability to get trains in and out quickly, also needs to be designed so that rail employees can use it efficiently. Drivers need to be able to quickly and efficiently get into and out of trains. There should be toilets and other facilities available. There are many problems with stabling that has either been poorly designed, or has some kind of problem that makes it hard to use. Some of these problems include:

- The lighting is very poor and driver and train staff cannot see where to walk when they are getting in and out of trains
- The ground is uneven and train staff can trip or fall over when walking to or from trains
- Access is difficult into and out of the stabling yard
- The stabling has some environmental factor that impacts upon its function as a stabling yard, such as being located near the ocean and sea spray washes up onto the train
- The stabling yard is located in a high crime area and drivers and train staff get attacked going to and from their trains
- Fencing is inappropriate for the stabling yard
- Toilets are inadequate or too far away

- Other staff amenities are not available

Fencing is quite important for any stabling, as vandals commonly spray paint trains in yards. The experience in Australia has been that the location where trains are stabled needed to have substantial fencing to prevent vandalism, and 2.5 metre high fences are common, with razor wire on top of the fence. This level of security is necessary to prevent a lot of damage to trains.

Different Configurations of Stabling

One of the most important features of any stabling is the entry and exit. Stabling needs to be large enough to accommodate all the trains that are stabled there, but most passenger rail networks have a peak period in the morning, and it is necessary to get trains in and out quickly from the stabling yard onto the running lines. Many different types of entry and exit into a stabling yard exist, but most of them have severe limits on the throughput of trains in and out. The schematics below demonstrate this.

In the layout below the stabling is shown as purple, and the running lines in black. The configuration below is very common, and trains need to move from the running lines to get into the stabling yard. There is only one entrance into and out of the stabling yard, so this is a strong limitation on the number of trains that can enter and exit the stabling yard, notwithstanding the small size of the yard.

Figure 10.1 Single Entry Stabling Yard

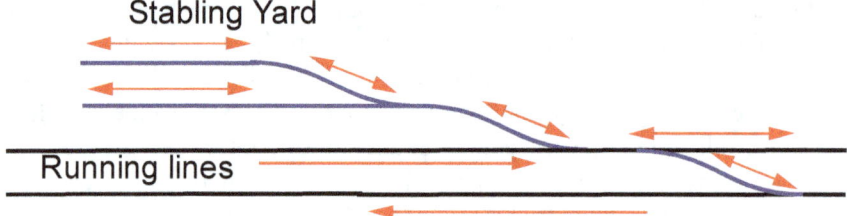

The stabling yard below is larger than the one above, and has two entrances and exits into the yard. Trains will be able to enter and leave more quickly than the one above. Also note that trains leaving the stabling yard to go to the bottom running line will need to cross one of the running lines to get there, and this movement may cause operational problems, and interfere with the passage of other trains. However, despite this, it is clear that this layout is superior to the one above.

Stabling Page 222

Figure 10.2 Multiple Entry Stabling Yard

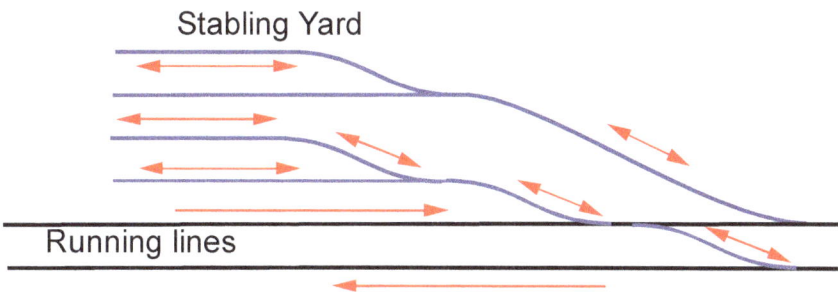

The above layout allows for something called parallel moves, where trains can move in and out of the yard at the same time. This layout is better when large numbers of trains need to be moved in and out of the yard quickly.

The layout below has stabling at the end of the running lines, and they run out and are replaced with a stabling yard. This type of layout can be very efficient, because trains can have direct access to the running lines.

Figure 10.3 Stabling at the End of the Rail Line

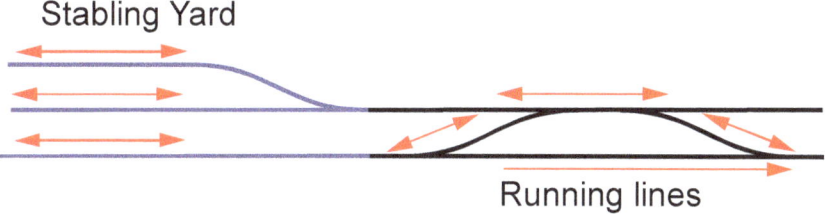

Interestingly a review of the stabling yards in and around Sydney shows that this layout, despite many advantages, is very uncommon. In practice this type of stabling can only be implemented where the rail line ends, and the stabling yard is put at the end of this line. Many rail lines, especially for regional, commuter and intercity services do not end, but continue past the terminus to another destination.

The schematic below shows how stabling is often designed in practice. In the schematic below there is a terminus on the left, where trains arrive and depart from. The terminus is the end of the rail line, and the tracks do not continue any further than this. There is often a high value location just located past the end of the rail terminus, and the railway cannot be built up or continued any further.

Figure 10.4 Terminus and Stabling

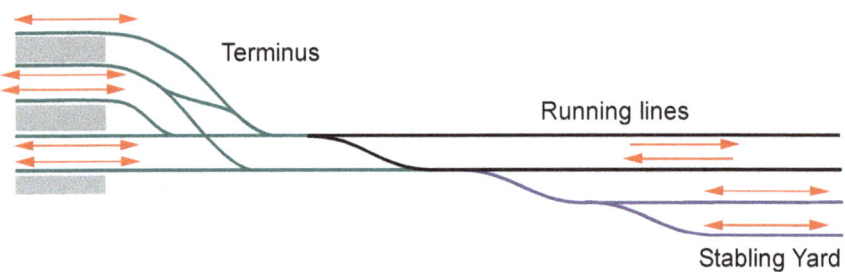

On the right hand side is the stabling, which is located further back away from the terminus. Trains arriving and departing from the terminus will pass alongside the stabling, and the number of tracks will appear, to passengers, to be quite large. This layout is quite common, as it has the advantage that trains, after completing their revenue service, can be moved back into the stabling yard to be stored, and then retrieved when needed. The presence of the stabling increases the effective capacity of the terminus, and more trains can terminate in the terminus. When the terminus becomes full, trains can be moved from the terminus to the stabling yard very quickly. Also, if there is a problem with a train, it can be brought in to the terminus, passengers taken off, and then moved into the stabling yard to await repair. The usefulness of this layout is the key reason why it's so common.

Unfortunately it is a very ugly layout, and aesthetically very unappealing. As the terminus is almost always located next to a city centre, them the stabling yard will also be located on high value land.

In some cases the running lines are so busy that stabling needs to be accessed through a dive, or possibly a flyover. What is shown in the figure below is a dive, but essentially the concept is the same for flyover. Trains need to get from either track into the stabling yard, and there is a desire to avoid an at grade crossing, so the track needs to pass either under or over the running lines.

The layout below shows a dive combined with a stabling yard. The stabling will almost always need to be on one side or the other of the running lines, so one of the lines will need to cross to the other side. In this case it is the lower line that needs to cross to the stabling yard, and it does so through a dive. A dive is a rail tunnel that dips down below the track and then comes up again on the other side.

Figure 10.5 Stabling Accessed through a Dive

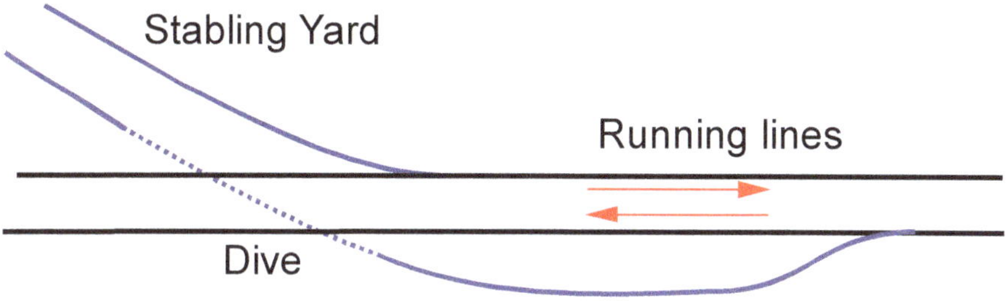

One problem with dives is that they fill up with water. Being the lowest point in the rail system, much of the water from rain and seepage makes its way into a dive. Dives, unless they are in an area that has almost no rain at all, will need a pumping station to remove all the water. Once water makes its way into a tunnel it becomes the responsibility of the railway, and this may mean cleaning and processing the water.

A flyover performs the same function as a dive but goes over the track rather than under. Both require a lot of space and are expensive to build. Once constructed the maintenance cost is quite small. Railways tend to avoid dives and flyovers, given the cost of construction, but they are very effective.

Note that flyovers and dives are used to get rail vehicles into and out of stabling, yards, and maintenance centres more efficiently. They allow trains to pass over or under the running lines without interfering with the movement of trains on the running lines. They are clearly the best way to get trains in and out of stabling yards, but are expensive.

Stabling of Freight

Freight trains need to be stabled like any other train, but freight stabling is a little different to stabling for passenger trains. Some of the differences are:
- Freight trains are very long, often over 1 km, and sometimes over 2 kms, so any stabling for freight will be very long and large
- Freight trains are rarely electric and so this large freight yard will usually have no overhead or electric traction power (although there are exceptions)
- Many freight wagons are only occasionally used, and this often sit in a freight yard waiting to be used, and may be covered in rust. In Australia milk wagons are rarely used, but milk was commonly

transported by rail, so there are many surplus wagons sitting idle in various freight yards
- Freight locomotives will need to refuel, so there will often be refuelling facilities in the yard
- Very large freight yards will sometimes have other freight facilities around them, such as road freight terminals. For large freight yards with a lot of traffic, the combined road rail freight terminals can cover a very large area
- As rail freight often only generates a small profit, any freight yard are often in poor condition and covered with weeds. Coal freight yards are the exception and are almost always in good condition because of the much higher profitability of selling coal (at least in Australia)

The diagram below shows how freight may be stabled. The running lines move around a long freight yard, and the stabling yard can be entered from either end. Note that stabling yards are often more complex than this, and the yard drawn below is a bit simplified.

Figure 10.6 Freight Stabling Yard

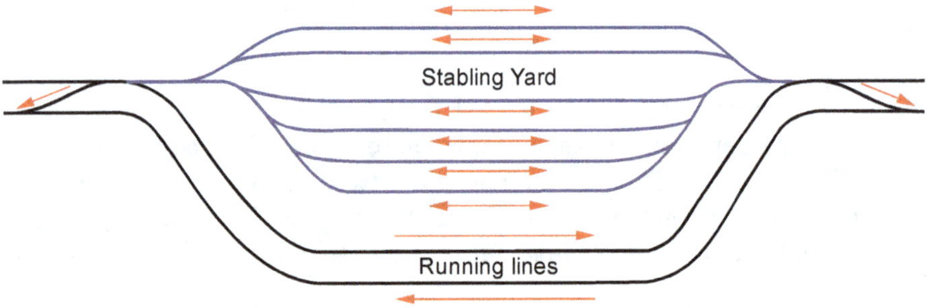

This type of stabling is suitable for long freight trains. The yard show above can be extremely large, and over 1 kilometre long. Also trains can enter from either end, have wagons added or removed, and locomotives added or removed, and then can enter or exit from either end. In many ways this layout is very suitable for freight, particularly for intermodal traffic, or any other freight where freight trains are marshalled.

Stabling Page 226

Different Configurations of Freight Terminals

There are many different possible designs of freight terminals. Freight terminals needs a structure that supports the operation of the freight that is moving in and out. Some freight trains are all unit trains, where the train is not divided, and moves only one product, and it is moved directly from the terminal to destination without storage or stopping. A unit train operates on a loop, and moves slowly around the loop when it is being both loaded and unloaded. The terminal design that is shown below is called a balloon loop, and these are often attached to mine. The train enters the balloon loop, and then moves around the loop, being filled with whatever bulk material is being shipped. Whilst it is possible to combine a balloon loop with intermodal freight, this combination does not seem to exist in Australia.

Figure 10.7 A Balloon Loop

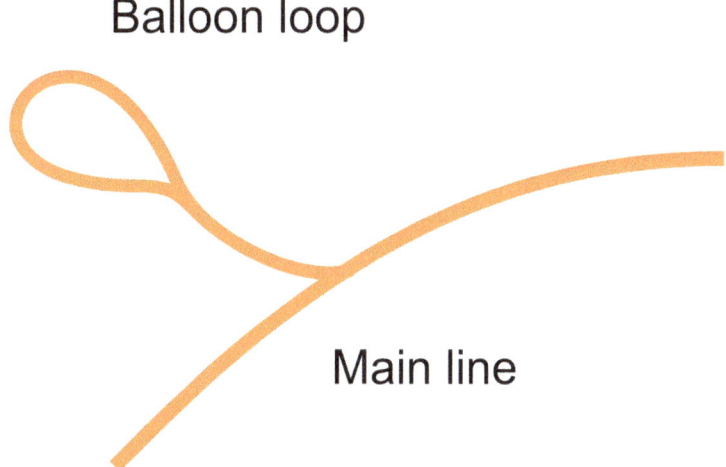

The great advantage of a balloon loop is that the train moving through it does not need to be divided and/or shunted, it can slowly move around the loop and receive its cargo. This type of configuration is more efficient than a pure siding. Trains that use a balloon loop may not need to have wagons added or removed, and will travel empty to the balloon loop, and then full when taking the bulk materials from the balloon loop to where they need to go, often a port but not necessarily so.

Below is a freight terminal that is more suited for intermodal freight. This terminal is relatively small, and intermodal terminals can be very much bigger than this. This terminal allows trains to enter, and then one or other of the freight roads would allow loading and unloading. As the terminal is structured as a passing loop, locomotives can be moved from one end of the train to the other.

Figure 10.8 A Simple Freight Terminal

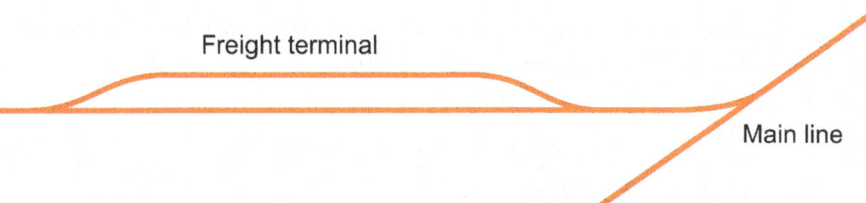

Another common configuration with freight yards is to put a diamond crossover in the middle. The freight yard is essentially split into two halves, with the crossover allowing movement between the two halves. The purpose of the crossover is to allow trains from any one road in the left freight yard to get to any road in the B yard, and vice versa. This type of configuration allows for the efficient storage and management of freight trains.

Figure 10.9 Freight Yard with a Diamond Crossover

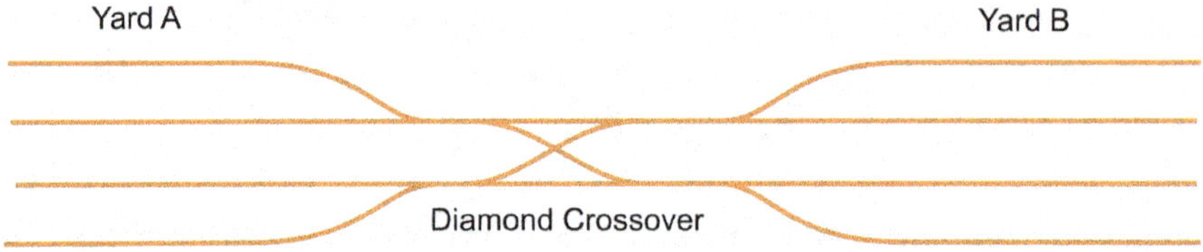

Chapter 11 Types of Transport Projects

There are a surprisingly large number of different possible rail projects. The most well known is the construction of a new line, and this type of project requires a lot of planning to plan and build. There are however many other types of projects that can be done, and the variety and scale of all these different projects is quite striking.

Many projects for rail systems are related to improvements to the rail system. Any system needs to be constantly maintained and updated, and many of the different types of projects listed focus on doing this. As system requirements change, there is a need to implement projects to update the system.

So some of the rail transport projects are:

1/ New line construction

A new rail line is a common rail transport project. This is typically what people think of when talking of rail network design. A new rail line usually consists of:
- New stations
- New track connecting these stations
- Facilities in and around these stations, such as bus interchanges and commuter car parks
- Stabling for trains
- New trains

Often new rail lines are built to specific rollingstock types. A rail system in one city may have several lines where rollingstock cannot be used on any other line. New rail lines may or may not integrate into the existing system.

The construction of a new rail line is an exciting thing, and considerable interest is usually generated in the media before the announcement and completion of the rail line. The opening ceremony for the new rail line is a time of great anticipation.

2/ Construction of an extension to an existing line

Existing lines are often extended, increasing the length of the line. It would be rare for the extension of the rail line to not use the same rollingstock as the original part of the rail line. Often a rail line can be easily extended to reach a major centre or destination, and a project is launched to create this connection. Care must be exercised in building any extensions, as the line can become very long, and metro trains may not be suitable for the longer extended line.

Extensions to existing rail lines are "easy" projects, as many of the choices are clear for the design of the new rail line. Much of the equipment installed in the rail line will need to be compatible with the existing equipment, and even better if the equipment is the same. Station construction should be standard, as should the rollingstock. Estimation of the number of passengers is easy, through comparison of the existing stations to the new ones.

3/ Upgrade of an existing line to take longer trains, or larger trains

Rail lines are constructed based on estimates of passenger numbers. Obviously, no one knows how many people will use the rail line until it has been built. Sometimes, and it does happen, that the rail line once constructed is a fantastic success, and the system cannot cope with the volume of passenger traffic. This is particularly the case for some smaller medium capacity metros, which have limited capacity. A series of projects are needed to increase capacity, and this often involves extending platform lengths. Once all the platforms are extended then longer trains can be purchased, and this increases capacity.

Alternatively, train sizes may be increased. This type of project seems to be more uncommon, for passenger systems at least, but is common for freight systems. Intermodal rail systems can be described as either single or double stacked, and re-designing rail systems to allow for larger trains and higher loading gauges can allow for double stacking. In many cases this can increase the efficiency of the rail system.

In some cases it is desirable to increase the structure and loading gauge, as new trains are purchased that need it. For example, tilt trains require an increased loading gauge for the same interior space, as the tilting action of the train means that the kinematic envelope is larger. A project to increase the loading gauge will allow these trains to use part of the network where tilting was previously impossible.

4/ Increases to maximum speeds

Speed increases result in a more efficient railway. The number of trains required to maintain a timetable decreases when average speed increases, as well as the number of passengers increases as they can now more quickly reach their destinations. Some of the common ways of achieving this are:
- Increasing the radius of vertical or horizontal curves
- Resignalling to reduce headways, or fix some capacity problem
- Increasing the strength of track components or bridges
- Expanding the structure or loading gauge, this may allow an increase in average speeds
- Widening tunnels

Increases to maximum speeds are a very good thing for any rail system, and can have a very beneficial effect on the efficiency and attractiveness of the rail system. Speed increases to a rail system can have large economic benefits, and these can be calculated quite accurately, which can make creation of the business case for the change easy.

5/ Remodelling a junction

Junctions are important to move trains from one set of tracks to another. Many junctions were designed more than 50 years ago, or in some cases over 100 years ago. The need for which the junction was designed may have significantly changed, and the junction can be remodelled to better suit modern train movements and paths. Junctions can be very complex, and a pathway through a junction may not be installed or available.

Junction remodellings are actually a very common transport project. They can allow better capacity, on-time-running, and more efficient use of infrastructure. A further benefit is that once a junction is remodelled, it is usually upgraded with new equipment. Junctions are often located near major stations, and a remodelling of a junction may allow the use of new platforms that have recently been built.

One problem with this type of transport project is that a junction remodelling is a technically very complex project. The risks associated with this type of project can be high.

6/ Resignalling

A resignalling is a type of project where older signalling equipment is removed and replaced with newer equipment. This type of project has been mentioned in some of the other types of transport projects, and this type of project is often combined with others. Alternatively, these projects can be implemented independently.

Some of the benefits of resignallings includes lower maintenance costs, better safety, lower headways, and so higher capacity, and remote control of signalling. Particularly the improvement of reducing headways can have a powerful effect on the utility of the system, as a lower headway can mean more trains, improved service, and greater capacity. Resignallings are very popular in the rail world at the time of writing of this book, and many projects are being implemented to improve headways.

Whilst the improvement to headways is one of the main and key drivers to resignallings, it is not the only one. Older signalling equipment could be very expensive to maintain, and newer signalling equipment is often cheaper to install and maintain. This is particularly the case for rail freight systems, where the newer signalling equipment is dramatically cheaper per kilometre than many older style systems. In many cases these systems are installed for cost reasons, rather than for the reduction in headway.

7/ Introduction of the newer computer assisted signalling systems, such as ATP

There has been a great upsurge in the number of projects implementing some sort of computer assisted control of trains around the world. Automatic Train Protection (ATP) to summarise very quickly; there are two main benefits to an ATP system, and this is better safety, and better interoperability between the signalling systems in different countries.

ATP stands for Automatic Train Protection, and is a system of speed control of passenger trains. More advanced ATP systems offer improvements in the capacity of rail lines, or for a reduction in the headway. ATP systems are popular in rail systems where large numbers of passengers are placing the rail system under pressure, and there is a need to increase the number of services.

There are other types of computer based systems, and one of these is ATO, or Automatic Train Operation. This system allows trains to be driven by a computer, which can make the acceleration and deceleration of the train more even and consistent. Also the need for a driver disappears, and this can result in a substantial cost saving.

8/ Upgrade of lines to accept heavier trains

Since rail was invented there has been a trend towards greater and greater axle loads. This allows greater efficiency on the use of freight wagons, as one wagon can now move more material. This trend is continuing, and axle loads of over 25 tonnes are now common. One problem with doing this is the damage that this causes to the infrastructure, especially the rails, ballast and sleepers. Also many bridges are not capable of taking this type of heavy load.

All of these systems and engineering items can be upgraded to accept heavier axle loads. The rail can be made larger, as can the sleepers. The ballast can be changed to a higher grade, or just made deeper and fresher (ie, without the quantity of fines or debris). Bridges can be strengthened, and allow greater axle loads. These things all help, and with effort almost any rail line can accept up to 40 tonnes per axle or even higher.

9/ Removal or upgrade of level crossings

Level crossings are probably the highest risk area for safety for almost all rail systems. Level crossings are a constant source of safety risk, as road and rail vehicles mix. Perhaps over 25% of all fatal rail accidents occurred at level crossings for the time period 2000 – 2009 for the industrialised world.

The removal of a level crossing can occur through many different means, and these include:
- Replacing the level crossing with a bridge
- Closing the level crossing to traffic
- Closing the roads that leads to the level crossing

Level crossings have varying levels of protection to road traffic. Simple level crossings have no bells or booms to tell car drivers of approaching trains. The installation of lights and bells, either with or without booms, has been shown to dramatically improve safety at level crossings. Upgrades to level crossings can dramatically improve the safety of level crossings, but increase the maintenance cost of the crossing.

Level crossings can be designed so that the driver of any road vehicle approaching the level crossing needs to enter it on a curve. This has been shown to "wake" drivers, and so they can be more alert when approaching a remote level crossing with few trains per day. This also is a rail transport project.

Many railways have a system to rank the risk related to level crossings. This system can be used to assess the benefit of removing the level crossing. It is often possible to estimate the number of lives saved per hundred or thousand years from any level crossing project.

10/ New station construction, or remodelling existing stations

Stations can be constructed onto existing lines. As cities and regions have population increases, there can be a need to build additional stations. The spacing between stations may be such that more stations can be built between, and this can be a cheap and effective way of allowing passengers access to rail systems is to build more access points. Care must be exercised in deploying this strategy because too many stations will result in a reduction in average travel times.

Alternatively, existing stations may be upgraded to accept larger trains or a greater number of people. Stations which are over 100 years old were often built to accommodate small numbers of passengers, and upgrades to these stations are common. This can include larger or more entrances and exits, widening platforms, or removing obstructions such as structural columns.

Another common upgrade for a station is the installation of facilities to assist people with disabilities. Lifts can be installed at stations to allow access for people who are mobility impaired. Escalators can also be installed, as an alternative to stairs, to assist people getting to and from platforms.

11/ Building new freight terminals, or upgrades

Freight terminals are the equivalent of stations for freight trains. Terminals are critical to the efficient movement of freight on a rail system, and a poorly designed terminal can slow the movement of freight substantially. Where a new freight terminal is needed, it can be built from a greenfield site. For a new terminal, determination of the capacity of the terminal is a critical calculation.

Existing terminals are also frequently upgraded. This can include building more storage area, adding more services such as the cleaning of intermodal containers, or building more sidings where trains can be stored or stabled. Where a rail line is converted to double stacked container traffic, then changes may be needed to any freight terminal. All of these upgrades are common, and can add substantial value and efficiency to the freight terminal.

Another common upgrade to a freight terminal is lengthening the maximum length of train that can use the terminal. This also can add to the efficiency of the terminal.

12/ Infrastructure upgrades (such as converting to 25 kV)

There are many possible upgrades for infrastructure. As rail technology advances more infrastructure options are possible, and these can be installed. Many of these upgrades reduce the cost of maintaining the infrastructure, and number of people. A large rail network may take many years to install even one of these new infrastructure systems, but once installed the benefits are significant. Maintaining a cost effective rail network often requires the installation of the best equipment, much of which is new and was only recently designed.

Some of the possible infrastructure upgrades are:
- Replacement of timber sleepers with concrete
- Upgrade of the voltage of the overhead power lines to 25 kV AC
- Replacement of rail with larger rails that can take higher loads and have longer lifetimes
- Connection of railway power supplies to stations
- Installation of concrete bearers under points
- Replacement of old style hydraulic lifts with more modern MRL lifts
- Conversion of overhead transmission lines to underground power cables
- Replacement of old bridges with new concrete ones, especially older wooden bridges
- Consolidation of signal boxes
- Installation of condition monitoring

There is always something more a railway can upgrade, and at any one time, for a large rail system there might be several of these projects ongoing at any one time.

13/ Construction of additional stabling, or changes to stabling

Trains are stabled in stabling yards. Stabling can be a significant constraint on the number of trains that are moved throughout the network. If the train can't be stored, then it can be used for moving passengers. For this reason stabling is a critical part of providing train services.

Stabling yards are places of high intensity of infrastructure. Stabling yards often have large numbers of signalling equipment, as well as other equipment that is unique to the stabling yard. They are also very problematic for maintenance, as trains are constantly moving in and out of them, and so it is difficult for maintenance teams to get access. The equipment of some stabling yards could be described as being in awful condition.

The management of stabling yards requires for any railway requires significant thought and consideration of asset management and the needs of the rail system. Where changes are identified, then these need to be implemented through a project. Stabling is often located in the wrong place, or is too small, or in rare cases, too large. Stabling needs to be updated from time to time for any operational railway.

Projects involving stabling can be any of the following:
- Building more stabling to allow storage of more trains
- Rebuilding the stabling with more modern infrastructure
- Re-designing the stabling to allow for different movements of trains in different directions
- Creating a new stabling yard to replace an older yard in a different place
- Creating more access into and out of the stabling yard
- Removing the stabling yard altogether

14/ Modification or construction of freight loops and passing lines

Freight trains usually move at different speeds to passenger trains. A slow moving train ahead of a fast moving one will force the later faster train to slow down. This is an undesirable situation and passing loops can be constructed to help alleviate this problem. A passing loop, or refuge, is a place where freight trains can stand until the faster moving passenger train passes. Passing loops are a cost effective way of improving the movement of rail traffic in a mixed system.

This type of project can often be constructed to one side of the railway line, and then tranche of work can connect the completed passing loop to the main line.

Some projects also involve the extension of passing loops. Where train lengths have increased, then passing loops also need to be extended. This is also a common type of rail project.

15/ Construction of freight corridors

Freight corridors are a dedicated rail corridor, exclusively for freight, that pass through built up or busy areas. The construction of rail freight corridors can be a substantial win for any rail freight company that uses the corridor. The movement of rail freight can increase substantially, and the cost to move this freight drops.

The need to build rail freight corridors is easy to identify, but difficult to achieve in practice. The corridor must be free of problems such as level crossings, and not mixed with passenger traffic. Also local residents may not be too excited about the increase in rail freight. The path of the freight corridor through a city or other difficult area may be problematic to find, and even more difficult to resume and build over.

Freight corridors may be single or double tracked, but where possible the capacity of the trains should be as large as possible. This means double stacking, long trains, and if at all possible, high speeds.

16/ Conversion of existing lines to HSR lines

The construction of any HSR line is a difficult and expensive goal. One solution is to convert an existing line to an HSR one, and whilst this type of HSR system may be a bit slower than a custom built HSR line, it is only a fraction of the price. Ordinarily most lines are not designed to accommodate trains moving at greater than 200 kms/hr, and allowing them to do so requires some work. This typically means reducing curves, both horizontal and vertical, and improving tunnel clearances. It can also mean building more tracks to accommodate slower moving traffic.

Conversions to HSR lines can continue for many years. One line might be slowly converted, starting from one end or at the worst bottleneck, and then improving the line over time.

17/ Remodelling of disused freight lines to passenger lines

The large quantity of old freight lines in some countries has meant that some of them have fallen from use and been abandoned. Where this has occurred, then there is an opportunity to use the rail corridor for something else. In some cases the old rail freight lines are converted to hiking or bike trails, but the rail corridor may be converted into a passenger line. These types of projects often are created in unison with extensive redevelopment of the local area.

In many cases old freight lines are converted to light rail. Rail freight lines often do not pass through high density areas, at least when they are freight lines, so there is often not enough passenger traffic to justify a full metro system. This is particularly the case for freight lines in major cities.

Where a light rail system is built through a old freight terminal or port, when combined with construction of high quality residential property, the area can be dramatically transformed. This type of project can be extremely successful in rejuvenating an old part of a city.

18/ Construction of additional platforms

In some cases stations may need to be increased in size. This is especially the case where large numbers of additional services are added to a timetable. Some older stations need to be upgraded to accommodate the additional services. In some cases it may be appropriate to add platforms to already large stations.

Where platforms are added to stations, then needs to be some space next to the station to build the platform. The construction of additional platforms need additional space next to the station, and this is not always available. This type of project will depend a little on luck and opportunity.

19/ Duplication or quadruplication of existing lines

Duplication of a rail line occurs where a single line section of track has a second track added. Many older rail lines in Australia are still single track, and the addition of a second track can greatly increase capacity. Many operational problems largely disappear when a second track is built for a single line section.

Another variation on this theme is to quadruplicate and existing two track section. This is sometimes done where there is a need to be high speed traffic past local or slow moving services. Quadruplication of a rail line takes a lot of land, and time, but the increase in average speeds of rail services can be spectacular. These projects are a little uncommon, which is perhaps a little unfair given how effective they can be in the right situation.

20/ Closing rail lines

Sadly, in some cases, it is necessary to close a rail line. This is something to be avoided if at all possible, but sometimes this needs to be done. This can be the case for old freight lines in towns now deserted, or to mines now closed. Another possibility is that passenger services were so poorly used that it didn't make any sense for the rail line to remain open.

Some rail lines should be replaced with bus services, and the entire line closed. When this happens then it can be a sad occasion for all involved. The remediation of the old rail line can be a costly and expensive process, especially where there are lots of chemical spills or old machinery lying around the rail line. In many cases old rail lines may have asbestos in buildings and may need to be carefully removed without any risk to anyone doing the removal.

In some cases old stations may be retained as historical sites, or as museums. These may be maintained by volunteers from the local community.

REFERENCES

1. Ang-Olson, J. & Mahendra, A. *Cost Benefit Analysis of Converting a Lane for Bus Rapid Transit – Phase II Evaluation and Methodology*, National Cooperative Highway Research Program, Research Results Digest 352.

2. Texas Department of Transportation *Austin San Antonio Commuter Rail Study*, 1999

3. Gauthier, J. Montreal Commuter Train System, *Investments in new Infrastructures, International Rail Forum*, Valence Espagne, Nov 2007

4. Yang, Q. *How to Improve the Efficiency of Railway Freight Transport in the Urban Area?*, Service Operations and Logistics, and Infomatics, 2008

Chapter 12 The Process of Designing a Rail Network

Rail network design occurs within the overall process of transport planning within an area. Transport plans are developed over many years, and subject to great scrutiny. Once the objectives of a long term transport plan have been identified, it is possible to start with the process of designing a rail network.

It is important to understand the different pieces of the planning puzzle, to know where rail network design fits in. This chapter explains where the different pieces fit. Any good transport plan specifically states the problems it is trying to solve, and how the plan was rated and assessed. The overall goals of a transport plan are very helpful in providing information for what should guide rail network design. So let's talk about the problem statement.

A Clear Problem Statement

A good problem statement should clearly state the problem in a few sentences, without specifying a solution. It needs to succinct and clear. The problem statement also needs to specify who the problem is relevant to, and the scope of the problem. One might ponder if there is always a enough of a problem to create a sensible problem statement in every city, but there is. Nothing is ever perfect, and an improvement is always possible to any system.

It can be very helpful in selecting the key goals of a master plan by examining the motivations behind the creation of a master plan, or reviewing transport solutions in an area. If a master plan is being created, then people will probably have a reason that motivates them. No one really needs a transport master plan. Not having one won't bring on starvation. What is this reason? Some possible motivations could be:

- A general desire on the part of the populace to improve the rail system
- Specific strategic goals that are pressing that must be met
- Detailed analysis of an existing network has identified a series of problems, which need to be resolved
- Other countries, with similar cities, environments, or countries, have implemented a number of projects with great success

- Analysis and reporting on the performance of a countries' network indicates that there are problem areas that really should be addressed
- A city is hopelessly congested and a rail system is needed to reduce the congestion
- A strong desire to reduce emissions
- A strong desire to create a cheap form of public transport that poor citizens can access
- A standard rail system has been implemented many times before, with great success, and more is wanted
- The cost of operating the rail system is too great for the political organisation to maintain
- A big new event needs a high level of public transport
- Socio-economic factors that are very significant
- The desire to acquire the prestige from having a world class rail system
- A strong desire to link the centre of cities with regional areas

Every one of the motivations above could be linked to a specific city or country where this was the primary motivating factor in developing a master plan, and projects following it. Rightly or wrongly, the author has identified the following list of motivations behind several rail systems, but their identities have been excluded from the book to avoid offending anyone. The status and prestige from owning a world class rail system often seems to be a powerful motivating factor.

Once we understand what motivates people then we can begin to build a clear problem statement. With the problem statement built, it is then possible to construct the master and any medium term plans.

Building Plans

A problem statement is a short statement, which can fit onto one page. In contrast, plans and projects are, as documents, very long and contain a lot of information. Building from the problem statement, we move on to building a series of plans, and subsequent to this, a series of projects to make all this happen. Once again, there should be clear linkages between all of the plans and the problem statement that has been developped.

The outcomes of transport planning can be roughly divided into four broad categories:

- A master plan, specifying transport solutions for the next 20 or 30 years in a specific area, city, or country
- Medium term plans, which provide more detail and outline changes that will be made in 5 to 15 years
- Large projects that will substantially change the character of one part of the area as defined in the master plan
- Smaller projects that are completed to support a larger project or master plan. These are numerous and lower in cost than a large project.

The master plan and any medium term plans should have strong links to any land planning in an area or region. As rail transport has the capacity to dramatically change the use of an area, there needs to be a consideration of land use at many if not in all levels of the planning process.

The Master Plan

Production of a master plan is one of the most exciting aspects of any transport planning. The creation of maps, and plans, discussing strategy into the night, can be very rewarding for the rail transport planner. Many plans are possible, but only one will be chosen, so it is necessary to get this right. A transport plan gives people certainty and direction, and allows them to direct their efforts into creating a fantastic rail system.

A transport master plan sets out the broad direction for transport in either a city or a country, or possibly between countries. It's a long term statement of the transport needs of the area, with a simple statement of the intended solution, and the type of transport system. A transport master plan will usually have a 10 or 20 year time frame, or maybe even longer. A transport master plan will rarely be over a 1,2 or even a 5 year time frame, as that is too short. Master plans are often created when large changes are needed to the transport infrastructure; where a stable and well-functioning system is in place a master plan may be created but they tend not to be as dynamic or as interesting as a plan with lots of large engineering projects and excitement.

A good transport master plan will identify many key needs for an area, and provide a broad statement of the solution. Reasons should also be provided for why a particular solution was chosen. A really good transport master plan will also attempt to look into the future and predict future needs and how they will be addressed. One possible structure for a transport master plan is as follows:

1/ A statement of the people or area covered by the master plan
2/ A review of the current transport solutions provided, and a description of the transport challenges that exist
3/ Where possible, clear goal or goals should be stated for adressing transport needs, built of course from the problem statement. The better and clearer the goals, the better the transport master plan.
4/ A review of the strategic implications, and the implications for the overall country or region, should also be made
5/ An attempt to predict the future and to estimate and transport needs into the future
6/ A discussion of a number of different solutions, identifying the advantages and disadvantages of each and how the transport solution will address the need
7/ Key challenges that will be faced in implementing the master plan, and some statement as to how they might be overcome (finance especially)

One of the most important outcomes of a transport plan is focus and orientation of future transport projects. It's best if the main focus of the master plan is clearly identified, if not, then an intelligent reader will discern the major focus of the There are many competing needs for any city or country, and a transport plan needs to identify which of these are more important. Otherwise it is not clear which objective has priority over any other. Some of the objectives of any transport planning and improvements are:
- Moving people around quickly and efficiently
- Cost reduction for existing transport systems
- Reduction in maintenance requirements for transport systems
- Improvement in the productivity of the economy, by reducing travel times or allowing more public transport
- Environmental, ie, reducing emissions
- Strategic considerations, which can be numerous
- Reducing the cost and improving the movement of freight
- Improving the amenity of people living in the country or the city
- Improving the image of the city or country
- Supporting the bid for a major public event, such as the Olympics or world expo
- Political objectives, which are varied

So it is not clear at all which objectives are important, or have priority over others. This decision needs to be made at a very early stage, otherwise any transport planning will be ad hoc and messy. It is possible for a country to address many of these objectives at the same time, but addressing all is not possible, or even desirable. Choices need to be made.

One again remember that there should be strong links between the master transport plan for a city or region, and the land use plan. A city or region needs to identify where all the different component parts are to be located, and how this is to be supported. The creation of new residential districts should also drive the need to more transport systems, and possibly new rail systems. A well-developed land use plan is key to the successful development of a city or region.

Medium Term Plans

Once a master transport plan has been created, then a series of plans should be created for more specific issues. If the master transport plan is comprehensive enough, and the needs of transport planning are not too great, then a single master plan without any smaller plans may suffice. However, in most cases a series of smaller more details plans are required.

A common division between the plans might be:
- Plans for trams and light rail systems
- Plans for metro systems
- Plans for any freight systems
- Plans for smaller specific rail systems, such as a tourist railway, or a monorail
- Plans for the construction or management of any high speed rail system
- Plans for any intermediate capacity metros, not connected to any other system
- Plans for other types of transport

It would normally make sense to split transport planning on the basis of the different rail types, but in some cases it may also make sense to have medium term plans on the basis of specific regions or parts of countries.

A medium term specific plan should ideally contain:
- A short history of the rail system being discussed
- Strengths and weaknesses of the system being discussed
- Key opportunities
- A review of the potential options for the system, and these could contain both expansion or contraction of the system

- A decision on what to do, with clear links back to the master plan, if possible
- A summary of how and why decisions were made
- A list of projects, and funding required, to complete the medium term plan
- Details of key linkages with other medium term plans
- Details of these projects, and this may include architect's drawings, details of alignments of train lines, detailed passenger estimates and interchange information
- A final vision for the fully implemented system is provided

Once again we see the key role of the plan in shaping and identifying key projects, which will then make the approval of these projects easier in the future. Master and medium plans that provide no guidance as to which projects to choose, fail in their role as major transport plans.

Some rail systems may be too minor to be discussed extensively in the master plan. For example, some cities still have small tram systems left over from the 1930's, and these small systems are too inconsequential to be included into a large master plan. This is quite normal.

Feasibility Studies

Feasibility studies are used to manage the planning of individual projects. A feasibility study is used to manage the approval of one off projects that are not part of any major transport plan. These arise as citizens observe that particular projects could be beneficial to a city or region, and the costs and possibility of completing the project need to be reviewed.

As with other parts of the transport planning process, the output of the process is a document/report. Feasibility studies sometimes have a bad name, as they can sometimes be seen as a way of delaying building something or spending money whilst the study is conducted. Also feasibility studies cost only a tiny fraction of the total cost of a project, and sometimes are seen as a way of governments proving they are doing something which is actually fairly minor.

A feasibility study is almost always focused on a single project, and only rarely may look at multiple projects. The project does not need to be clearly defined, this is one of the advantages of a feasibility study, as it can cope with vague or goals and aims that are not clear. As the feasibility study progresses, goals and targets will hopefully become more clear.

A good feasibility study needs to provide a methodology with which a project is assessed. Most studies use cost benefit, although there is not real reason why this is the assessment method that should always be used. Other assessment systems could simply include the number of passengers moved, without focusing on costs. A clear methodology is also needed on assessing passenger numbers, costs, different possible projects, and risks for each option.

Unlike other transport planning documents, a conclusion is needed. The study needs to recommend at least one course of action, from a field of many. Some of the possible conclusions of the project include:
- Do not proceed with the project
- More study is needed to determine the value of the project
- The project should proceed
- The project will only be needed should certain conditions be met
- The project, whilst not viable under the terms and conditions as presented in the original scope of the project, may be viable if the government were to extend various taxation concessions, or subsidies to the project

One of the major downsides of a feasibility study is that they are often conducted in isolation from any other transport planning in the city or region. As a result, they may struggle to identify the benefits of completing the project, unless the project is clearly so beneficial that it should proceed regardless of any master transport plan. The author's experience of feasibility studies is mixed, as they mostly involve assessing "nice to have's", without any real context provided as to the overall needs of the city or region. Many feasibility studies recommend that projects not proceed.

Rail Transport Planning and Projects

A project is a body or work with clear goals and a pre-determined end date. Projects are the primary mechanism for implementing any kind of significant change within a transport system. Projects, and their management, have been the focus of business change and management for many years, and the implementation of successful projects is one of the keys to a successful business.

Projects are not transport plans, although they contain project plans which detail which tasks are completed when. Projects are how things get done. There is a specialised body of project managers around the world whose key skills are the management of projects, achieving the best possible outcome for the minimum cost. Courses are available at university level that allow engineers and others to develop key project skills to manage large projects. A new graduate may start with a small project, or assist on a larger one, and after many years experience be allowed to manage a very large project.

Once a project is identified and approved then it can be budgeted, resourced, and scheduled for completion. Projects require large numbers of qualified staff, and as a project progresses then the project team can swell to hundreds of people. Once completed then the project team is disbanded, which for some can be quite a sad and tearful event. Many of the project team move on to the next project.

Large rail projects are very substantial projects that require large budgets, and the work of thousands of people. Often costing hundreds of millions or billions of US dollars, very large projects can dramatically change the character of areas or regions. The quality of rail transport planning in an area is often judged against the quality of large projects, and the success or failure of any master plan.

Once again, as mentioned before, rail projects should be completed as part of a major plan. Projects, especially large ones, should not exist in isolation. Large projects should be identified well in advance, and their announcement should not come as a surprise to anyone. Large projects are the key ingredient to any major rail plan.

In general, transport plans should not contain only one project. It is possible to think of a number of instances where this has been the case, especially in small cities of 1 to 2 million people, but in general one project is not really a plan. A good transport plan will contain a series of plans, which complement each other and build to create a large and efficient transport system.

Smaller rail projects can be very numerous. Unlike major rail projects, which are often conceived at government level, smaller rail projects often originate from the railway already in operation. A particularly small rail project may only be a few million dollars and be finished in a few months. A master transport plan may require dozens of smaller projects to be completed, and yet they may not be identified in the master transport plan, or even a medium term plan. The need for this type of project may only be identified from a careful consideration of the larger transport plans.

It is often not possible to identify all the different smaller projects needed to complete a large master plan. There are many details that were just simply not considered when the master plan was compiled. This should not be a problem, as many of the details can be worked out later. Once the master plan and major projects are reviewed, smaller necessary projects can be identified and scheduled for completion.

Station upgrades are a common project completed as smaller projects. Other smaller projects are the installation of small numbers of points or signals, or changes to passenger display systems. Alternatively, some of the smaller projects can grow to be quite large, and what started as a smaller project may be indistinguishable from a large project.

Approval of Projects

Once a project has been identified then it needs approval. Many countries have detailed approval processes for large capital projects, and rail transport projects would need to follow those. Common activities in seeking approval are:
- Consultation with key stakeholders
- Financial appraisal
- Environmental assessment
- Economic cost benefit
- Business cases
- Risk assessments

Most government departments will have detailed procedures for the creation of economic assessments, and business cases. This will need to be followed. For any rail planner it is useful to know the processes for seeking approval for capital funding, otherwise a very sensible and rational project may be rejected and not approved.

A document is produced as part of the approval process for projects that contains much information concerning the project. This document is often called a business case, but may have other names depending on the country where it is being written. In this document is all of the information that is needed to make a decision on approving the project. It must be noted that at this stage that a lot of the decisions on a project have yet to be made, and

this document may be lacking in a lot of detail. This is usual, and does not mean that the document should be rejected. In particular, the document should have:
- Details of the project
- Why it is being done
- How much it costs
- Key assumptions
- A clear statement of the benefit
- How this project links in to any master or medium term plans
- Financial aspects of the project, returns, timing of funding, etc
- Any safety concerns
- Any environmental concerns
- Significant risks
- Sensitivity analysis
- Cost benefit analysis, or an economic appraisal

Approval for projects is often much easier when long or medium term plans have been created and they require certain objectives to be completed, and the project assists in meeting those objectives. Otherwise a project may be very difficult to get approved, especially if it could be seen as contradicting or working against one or more goals or the long term plan.

A sensitivity analysis is an analysis where some of the key assumptions are modified to see what the final benefits of the project would be. The essential idea is to determine if the entire justification for a project is dependent on one assumption, which is weak, such as final passenger numbers. The best projects are ones where the benefits are broadly based, and the failure to achieve one goal is not serious because many other goals are likely to be achieved. A poor project is one where the entire benefit of the project is undone if one assumption is proved not correct.

In more modern times there has been a trend towards very complex and extensive environment assessment processes. Whilst 50 years ago environment assessment was a small part of any process, now, in Australia at least, environment assessment is a key part of the approval of any major rail project. Environmental assessments can be very lengthy and expensive to complete, and require large volumes of paperwork to complete, or to even to begin the process for approval. The complexity and length of the environmental approval process seems to have spawned an industry of people who only job it is to know how to create and submit environmental assessments.

Whilst the term environmental assessment is used a lot for this kind of planning process, it is a little of a misnomer. In Australia environmental assessment often seems to mainly involve the noise of any new railway line, and the amenity and conditions around it. The colour of the railway line and facilities seems to be relevant, and the assessment of things like global warming gasses not so important. The impact on local flora and fauna is also important, and also needs to be considered. Overall the creation of this type of submission has become an important part of the planning process for any rail project, and needs to be taken seriously.

Another issues that should be considered in the planning process is the relationship with other governments in the jurisdiction where the rail project is being planned. For example, most local council and governments will have some sort of plan about what they are planning to do with an area, and any transport plan or project may interfere with those goals. A new project may be helpful to the local government, and they may be willing to contribute to the financial cost of the project to help ensure that it is completed. Getting a local council on side can mean access to more resources, and more plant and equipment, and should be attempted at least in the planning of any project.

Land Use

There is a very strong connection between transport planning and the use of land in a region or area. The construction of a significant rail project can entirely change the character of an area. Likewise, the purpose of land can be entirely changed through rail transport projects. Rail projects can have a larger impact than other forms of public transportation, such as buses, which tend to have a much lower impact upon the surrounding area.

The high cost and visibility of rail projects, and the ability of rail lines to move vast numbers of people, means that rail projects can be a very effective way of achieving the desired use of for land. A good city plan will identify the different uses for land, and link this back to the transport master plan.

In large cities much of the railway may be underground. Building rail lines underground can be an expedient way of avoiding large scale demolition of city blocks, but can be very expensive. To help reduce costs it is helpful to not build the station underground, but dig down to where the station needs to be, and then build it. A consequence of this is that there is now a new building sitting over the top of the station, which can be developed and used to produce income.

The development of land around stations is sometimes referred to as Transport Orientated Development (TOD). The purpose of TOD is to improve the value of the surrounding area to a rail project. Apartments, businesses, shops, banks, are provided next to or on top of the station. This makes the station a much more attractive place for people to go, and pass through, as people can work and eat in the vicinity of the station. Rail systems generally need lots of people to make them viable, and providing such facilities can significantly increase the number of people passing through the station.

In addition to the additional passenger income, some railways are large landowners, and the rents from the properties that are owned are considerable. In big cities the value of the rents and the properties developed may allow the railway to be profitable. Hong Kong MTR has been very active in promoting this kind of development.

There is often land available for a transport project. Sites change hands, or old disused stations can be redesigned and put back into use with a new rail project. Reusing this type of old facility can be a very effective way of reducing the costs. It can also be a good way of rehabilitating an old industrial area, where factories and other industries used to be located, but is now sitting empty.

REFERENCES

1. Cho-Lam Lau, J. *The Performance of public transport operations, land-use and urban transport planning in Hong Kong*, Cities, Vol 14, No 3, pp 145 – 153, 1997

2. Nugent, M. & Schuppan, R. *The Metropolitan Rail Planning Trilemma*, Conference on Railway Engineering, Perth Sept 2008

3. Nielsen, G. *Network Planning and Design for Public Transport Success – and some Pitfalls, Association of European Transport and Contributors*, 2006

4. Sakanishi, A. *Commuting Patterns in the Osaka Metropolitan Area: A GIS-Based Analysis of Commuter Rail Passengers*, RURDS Vol 18, No 1, March 2006

5. Nielsen, G. *Network Design for Public Transport Success – Theory and Examples*. Thredbo Conference Proceedings, No 10, 2009

6. Dodson, J. et al *The Principles of Public Transport Network Planning: A review of emerging literature with select examples*, Urban Research Program Griffith University, Issues Paper 15, March 2011

Chapter 13 Measuring Success and KPIs for Rail Systems

As part of any major project, an assessment is needed of the success of failure of the system, or the project. A project review phase is common in many large projects, and some measure of success is needed. The public, government, construction companies, and the rail industry in general want to know if a project of rail system has been successful. Often a description of the success or failure of any system can be very short but succinct, and the answer to this question can range from highly successful to disastrous.

As with any assessment of any large system, measurement of key operating parameters is the best way to make a decision on the worth of the system. Using these numbers it is possible to construct a picture of the success or failure of a system, based on commonly used measures. As the measures are common, many varying systems can be compared this way, and this also ensures fairness in any comparisons. The most important or commonly used of those measures are listed below.

It is possible for a rail system to be built that is very successful, where most projects were also successful, but a small subset of projects were not. Alternatively one project may be a success but overall a large rail system may not be. A set of metrics are presented below that provide guidance on when to describe a project as successful and when not to.

Of course, any changes to a rail system need to be completed before these metrics can be measured and calculated. Some particularly poor projects may never be completed, and in these cases there is no need for calculating metrics. Rail projects that are cancelled or dramatically delayed, or where people are killed in the construction, are clearly failures. Some of the problems that can occur with large rail projects include:
- It isn't completed
- There are extremely large cost overruns
- The company that managed or built the project became insolvent, causing major disruption or embarrassment
- There was an accident during construction with loss of life
- The initial target date was not achieved by several years
- Widespread corruption resulted in the construction of a rail line riddled with flaws, engineering problems, or structural defects

- The project, when completed, is unrecognisable from what was originally proposed
- The rail line, or part of it, is destroyed by some natural disaster or major accident
- The quality of construction is so poor that the rail line cannot be used in a form for which it was originally intended

Where any of the above occurs, it is pretty clear that the project is not really a success. Having said that, a really good rail project should not be abandoned because of some major setback, and whilst it is unfortunate when any of the above happen, some projects should still be completed. Where no major disaster occurs, then making an assessment of a project is more calculated and mathematical.

Most railways use a common set of measures to gauge performance and the success of any rail project. The values provided below are intended to only be a guide, and it is easy to find railways whose values do not fall within the ranges given below. Some very general indicative values are provided, and these numbers are only meant to be used as a rough guideline, and not as a hard rule where rail systems that do not meet it are a major flop.

So, some of the more commonly used parameters are:

- **Passengers moved per day or per year**

A very common measure is the number of passenger trips made on the rail system. Of course no typical measures of success or failure are provided here, as rail systems can be designed for large or small numbers of passengers. Usually a rail system will count the number of passengers, and for significant milestones have an announcement that reflects the degree of success. Common milestones are 100 million passengers, or a billion passengers, cumulative since the creation of the rail system, and per year. For smaller systems, a smaller target may be more appropriate.

Any rail system can be successful where it is used by large numbers of people. Packed trains, large numbers of passengers using a system, busy stations, make a rail system look and feel successful. Where a rail system is extensively used, it tends to be very integrated into the local urban environment, and its use becomes natural and automatic.

Any rail line that moves tens of thousands of passengers per day is likely to be successful. A metro line should move at least 50 thousand a day to be properly said to be successful, preferably much more than this. Again, this may depend on the expected outcomes of any rail project.

- **Loading factor**

A closely related success factor to the number of passengers moved is the loading factor of trains. The loading factor is a ratio of total number of passengers travelled to the capacity of the rollingstock. This measure is commonly used in the aviation industry, and is often the difference between a profitable and unprofitable airline. It can also be applied to rail vehicles and systems, and the formula below can be used:

$$Loading\ factor = \frac{passenger\ kilometres\ per\ day}{seat\ kilometres\ per\ day}$$

Passenger kilometres are calculated from adding all the distances for different trips passengers complete on a given day. Seat kilometres is the number of kilometres that the total of all seats travels in one day. This metric is useful for rail systems which are based on seats, and where passengers mostly sit, which is a large percentage of all rail systems. Some rail systems, such as metros, have very limited seating, so the loading factor is based on a different formula.

The formula for loading factor for rail systems where passengers stand is:

$$Loading\ factor = \frac{passenger\ kilometres\ per\ day}{capacity\ (spaces)\ kilometres\ per\ day}$$

The loading factor will depend on the rated capacity. This is a choice, as some railways will rate the capacity for people standing on a metro as higher than others. Typical values for capacity for a flat area with no seating range from about 4 to 6 people per square metre, so the total capacity will be based on this number.

A typical value for loading of seated trains is 34%.

- **On time running**

On-time-running, sometimes abbreviated to OTR, is one of the most important KPI's for a railway. OTR is critical for any railway, but expectations can be different for different types of railways. Below is a table of "normal" OTR figures for different types of railways. The lower this figure is, the more poorly performing the railway is:

Railway Type	OTR (minima)
Metro	98%
Light rail	80%, depending on the amount of separate right of way
Trams	80%, depending on the amount of separate right of way
Long distance regional trains	86%
Commuter, separated from freight	96%
High speed rail, separated	99.5%
High speed rail, combined with other services	96%

In practice OTR can vary enormously, depending on the length of the line, the presence of freight trains, or congestion on the line. The expectations for a metro are far higher for OTR, as this type of system is normally underground and does not share tracks with any other trains. The higher performance of metros for OTR is one reason why they have become so popular.

Also note that the OTR figures for light rail and trams are very low. In practice for a rail system that runs down the middle of crowded city streets to provide for a timetable, and keep to it. Whilst on Sunday mornings and other times when streets are not crowded, trams will run to time, at busy times getting trams on time is almost impossible.

OTR is usually calculated from the following formula:

$$OTR = \frac{\text{No of trains late on a given day}}{\text{Total trains}} \times 100\%$$

So when is a train late? A common measure for lateness is to compare the timetabled arrival time with actual, and if the difference is greater than 3 or 5 minutes then the train is late. Of course there needs to be a timetable for a train to be judged late. Frequency based rail systems will need to have a scheduled arrival time for trains to be judged on time or late.

The choice of a definition for the number of minutes late is an important one. Increasing the definition, from 3 to 4 minutes, will result in less trains be reported late. In practice a definition of anywhere between 2 to 10 minutes is acceptable, with 3, 5 or 10 minutes being common.

The target for an OTR for any rail system needs to be based on past experience with the railway in that area. There are often local factors that will either increase or decrease OTR that need to be considered.

OTR is difficult to calculate before a rail line is constructed. OTR can be estimated from complex simulations, with varying degrees of accuracy. The final OTR of some rail systems can be determined best when the rail system is completed.

- **Capacity**

The capacity of a rail line is an extremely important measure. The capacity of a line is usually measured in thousands of people per hour, or *pph*. The *pph* measure is for people moving in one direction, so the total capacity of the line in both directions is double. Typical values for the capacity of a line are listed below, and as with all the typical values in this book, should be used with some caution:

Railway Type	Typical capacity values
Metro	30,000 to 60,000 pph
Light rail	3,000 to 5,000 pph
Trams	1,000 to 2,000 pph
Long distance regional trains	6,000 to 8,000 pph
Commuter	6,000 to 10,000
High speed rail	2,000 to 5,000 pph

The capacity of a rail line should be specified before construction of any new rail line, or transport project. This figure should always be calculated before a rail line or system is constructed.

In terms of the success or failure of a rail system, the capacity of a rail system should be considered along with many other variables. For example, where the capacity of a rail system is 10,000 people per hour, and only 1,000 of that is used, then the rail system is probably chronically underused. It is possible to plan a rail system for large increases in patronage, and expect low usage up front, and in some cases this is appropriate to do this, especially with HSR systems. Capacity of a rail line comes with a cost, and large capacity systems are mostly much more expensive than ones with lower capacity. One problem in rail network design is when a system is created where the capacity is insufficient for the passenger loads, and so the system is overcrowded.

- **Headway (or frequency)**

Recall that the headway is the time in minutes between successive trains on a rail line, moving in one direction. The headway is actually the minimum possible time that is needed to separate trains, that can be achieved consistently, where the trains are travelling at a speed consistent with reaching its destination in a minimum time. The frequency per hour is the inverse of the headway. The units of frequency are trains per hour. The relationship between both is given by the formula below:

$$Frequency = \frac{60}{Headway}$$

The headway can be determined quite accurately before construction begins of the project. Indicative values are provided below:

Railway Type	Typical minimum headways
Metro	2 to 5 minutes
Light rail	2 to 5 minutes
Trams	Very low
Long distance regional trains	5 to 10 minutes

Commuter	5 minutes
High speed rail	10 minutes

Headways can be determined very accurately from analysing the signalling design before construction of any rail project. Reducing headways increases the cost per kilometre for construction. Headways should not be reduced to the absolute minimum, unless there is a very pressing reason for so doing (such as a high demand for passengers). Increasing headways can also reduce the maintenance cost considerably, and headways for rail freight systems can be very high, to minimize cost. The headway for a thinly used freight line may be as much as 1 hour, or even higher.

For fully grade separated rail systems, there is a high degree of control over the headway, and what is proposed for a headway in the design should achieved without fuss. For rail systems where rights of way are shared with other road vehicles, design headways may not be achieved. In some cases, with tram systems, the headway may be poor because of road congestion. In this case it is possible that the desired headway is unachievable, which may have far-reaching consequences.

It is also possible that the headway was designed at too high a level, for cost or other reasons, and the railway is under political pressure because not enough trains can be moved through the system. This can particularly be a problem for rail systems that share tracks with freight, and where the headway is often high because of the mixed traffic. In some very unusual cases, problems with headway may be severe.

- **Average speed**

The average speed is a very important metric for any railway. The higher the speed, the more likely it is that the line will be used. Slow moving rail services will struggle to attract passengers, but fast moving ones will attract large numbers. The reality is that slow moving rail service are very unattractive to the public, and so there is little point building a system that provide such a poor service. Many rail systems across the world have this problem, especially where journeys include long transit times.

Typical Average Speeds		
Location	Service Type	Average travel speed Kms/hr
Cities	Trams	10
	Buses	10
	Light rail	20
	BRT	30 - 50
	Metros	30 – 45
	Commuter	50 – 80
Countries	Regional	60 – 100
	High speed	> 200

Whilst it is possible to calculate average speeds, the calculation can change once any rail project is finished, as the number of people using the rail line can change the average speed. More passengers boarding and alighting will make the dwell time longer, and slow trains down. Notwithstanding this, metros that have average speeds lower than 30 kms/hr will be poorly patronised, in comparison to the number of people in the surrounding area. Low average speeds should be avoided, regardless of the number of people using the system. Commuter services slower than 50 kms/hr again will struggle to attract passengers.

Average speed calculations are also somewhat difficult for light rail systems, especially ones that share roads with vehicle traffic. The final speed will depend on how the road traffic behaves with the train around, and some differences are possible with the average speed calculation.

In many cases the quality of the design of the rail system will be decisive in determining the average travel speed. A well designed rail system will allow passengers to move around it quickly.

- **Cost per kilometre (construction)**

The cost per kilometre is an important measure. The cost needs to be kept low as countries need to provide infrastructure to their citizens for the lowest possible cost. Often the final price for the new infrastructure will only be known once the project has been completed. The table below contains some indicative values for total cost per route kilometre.

Costs and how to manage them is discussed extensively in the chapter 29. However, some indicative values are provided below to allow comparisons.

Comparative costs (2012)	
Rail system	**Indicative Cost (US dollars)**
Trams	5 to 10 million per km
Light rail, mostly sharing roads	10 – 20 million per km
Light rail, fully grade separated	40 -60 million per km
Metros	100 million per km
Intercity rail, mostly through long tunnels	200 million per km
High speed rail, flat land, elevated tracks	10 – 20 million per km
High speed rail, mountains	50 million per km
Light rail/intermediate capacity metro, fully automated	100 – 140 million per km
Bus Rapid transit	12 – 15 million per km

Sometimes high value projects should be completed because the return to the country or city is very high. Alternatively, often costs for a rail project are high because of some problem with the project management. An outsider looking in may have difficulty in determining, for a very expensive project, what actually happened to cause costs to be so high.

In many cases rail projects are completed cheaply because of effective long term planning. A city or country may set aside land in sensible and strategic places, and so when construction begins costs are easily kept low. Alternatively, a government may have invested in rail systems and technology, so that they understand how to build a cheap railway. There are many factors that can change the cost associated with a rail system.

When reviewing rail systems and their creation, industry professionals are impressed by projects that are completed quickly and cheaply.

- **% recovery of running costs**

It is important for railways to attempt to recover as much of their operational costs as possible. In practice only a few railways can attempt to breakeven, and these are usually either metros or tourist railways. It is best that any railway attempts to recover as much of their costs as possible.

The percentage of costs that are recovered is an important figure. For many railways, at least 40% of total costs should be recovered, including everything, such as rents and advertising revenue. In some rare cases, especially where the total subsidy is small compared to the government's revenue, going below this figure may be acceptable. This is especially the case for wealthy cities with small rail systems, where the total subsidy is not great compared to the wealth of the city.

Once again the total running costs can only be determined once the railway has been in operation for a number of years. Estimates of the cost of operation of any railway are just estimates until all projects are completed, or a substantial part of the rail system is in operation. The ability of any railway to predict future costs will vary considerably, with some railways better at this than others.

- **Cost per kilometre (running costs)**

The cost per kilometre can be interpreted one of two ways, and these are:
- the cost per seat kilometre for moving passengers 1 kilometre
- the cost per kilometre for maintenance per each track kilometre

Indicative values are provided below for the cost of providing the service for both measures.

Comparative costs – seat kilometre	
Description	Indicative Cost (US dollars 2012)
Cheap	$.05 per seat kilometre
Expensive	$.5 per seat kilometre

The costs above are for all costs, rollingstock, fixed infrastructure, operating the trains, included in the total cost of providing the service.

Below are very rough costs per kilometre for maintenance of fixed infrastructure. The cost is expressed as a yearly figure, for providing the number of track kilometres in the network.

Comparative costs – track kilometre (per year)	
Description	Indicative Cost (US dollars 2012)
Freight system	$50,000 per km
Low cost	$100,000 per km
Mixed use, medium cost	$250,000 per km
High cost	$500,000 per km
Very high intensity	$2,000,000 per km

It is possible for any rail project to trade construction and capital cost for operating cost. More money can be spent to make infrastructure easier to maintain, and this is discussed in a chapter below.

Metros typically have very high maintenance costs per track kilometre. The intense use of the rail system, the fact that most of metros are built underground, and the large number of passengers and stations, will increase the maintenance costs dramatically. As metros move very large numbers of people, this may be entirely acceptable, and the costs may be covered by selling large numbers of tickets. Also note that metros have a very low number of kilometres, so the total maintenance cost may be low when the number of passengers may be high.

The running and maintenance costs are relevant because, with more money and capital cost, the maintenance cost can be reduced. For example, for commuter and regional railways, the construction of level crossings is much lower than for bridges, so the capital cost can be kept low if very few bridges are built. One problem with level crossings is they are very expensive to maintain, as they are a point of safety risk for a railway. A low construction cost can be achieved, but the cost to the owner of the railway may be high because of the long term need to maintain expensive and costly assets.

- **Power consumed per seat or passenger kilometre**

This measure is an important one, for a variety of reasons. It is important because global warming is a serious issue, and the reduction of emissions, through reduced power consumption, is a worthy cause. Just as important, well designed and operated railways require only small amounts of power for moving people, and power consumption is a very good measure of the design and efficiency of a railway.

It should be mentioned that this measure can only be applied to rail systems that use electric traction. Rail systems that rely on diesel should not be measured on this KPI, but rather on the one below for the amount of CO_2 emitted per passenger.

Power consumption can often be changed favourably by moving large numbers of passengers. Many of the measures regarding power consumption are calculated on a per passenger basis, although not the one presented below, and so large numbers of passengers will make the KPI much more favourable. Even a poorly designed railway can achieve good power consumption values if passengers extensively use the system.

One of the best measures of power consumption is kilowatts per seat kilometre. To calculate this, the number of seat kilometres is divided by the number of passenger kilometres. This measure is complicated when making comparisons for metros, as most people are standing. As metros have very few seats, the best measure of power consumption is kilowatts per passenger kilometre. This value is usually calculated by adding up all the train trips, calculating their trip length, and then dividing the power consumed by the total train seat kilometres. Indicative values are provided below:

Power per seat kilometre	
Description	Indicative Power Use
Lower	.025 kilowatts per seat kilometre
Higher	0.055 kilowatts per seat kilometre

The power consumed per passenger kilometre, as indicative values, is shown below:

Power per passenger kilometre	
Description	Indicative Power Use
Lower	.05 kilowatts per passenger kilometre
Higher	0.15 kilowatts per passenger kilometre

A lower number is much better for power consumption. Once built, it is very difficult to change the power consumption of a rail line or system.

- **Carbon dioxide emitted per seat kilometre**

The carbon dioxide emitted per seat kilometre, or passenger kilometre for metros and any other system where passengers stand, is a useful measure for comparing different rail systems and different transport modes. The final calculation is however very dependent on the source of the electricity that supplies the rail system. The CO_2 output of electricity generation in a country is determined by the way the electricity is produced, with high emitting generation technologies pushing up the amount of CO_2 produced. Coal is particularly bad, although there are different types of coal and there is a large range of possible emitting rates. Nuclear is rated as producing no CO_2, as is hydroelectricity.

The carbon dioxide emitted is strongly related to the amount of electricity consumed. Some railways use diesel trains, and so the CO_2 emitted will be strongly dependent on the quality of the fuel. More diesel trains in service will normally mean higher emissions, unless the electricity in that area or region produces large amounts of carbon dioxide per kilowatt hour.

For an all electric railway, there are limits on what can be done to improve carbon emissions. There are some measures that can be put in place but options can be quite limited. However, mostly, any railway will be dependent on the energy production method. For any country, this is normally quite fixed, and rarely changes. Over years the mix of energy in many countries has changed, so that the emissions per kilowatt has fallen, and this has improved the statistics for the carbon dioxide emitted per passenger kilometre.

The calculation for carbon dioxide emitted is much simpler for diesel than for electric trains, as the standard conversion used is 26.5 grams of CO_2 per litre of diesel fuel. This conversion is mandated by various European Union documents relating to transportation.

The emitted CO_2 is useful for comparison purposes, but in practice a railway is often quite constrained as to what can be done to change the rate at which carbon dioxide is emitted. One possibility is to build a gas turbine for use for railway electricity production, or to procure electricity from a different source. One of the main uses of this figure is for comparison to other transport modes, such as buses, ferries, or private road vehicles. These modes of transport often produce far higher emissions that rail transport. Comparisons are often useful when a rail project is completed, and there has been a large saving in emissions after the project has been concluded and passengers are using the service.

- **Cost per kilometre for operating rollingstock**

Rollingstock is a major cost for any rail operation. Its purchase, or replacement, is often the largest single cost facing a rail system. Rollingstock only lasts 20 to 30 years in most cases, and needs to be replaced with a high degree of frequency. The need to replace rollingstock over this time interval can drive costs for a railway much higher.

Many design problems with a rail system manifest themselves in the cost of operating the rollingstock. A common problem with many rail systems is that the geometry is unfavourable, or even worse, platforms are at different heights. These problems make the cost of rollingstock expensive, and maintenance will be higher. For example, where platforms are at different heights, specialised equipment can be installed on trains to allow passengers to be able to board and alight from these platforms, but the cost is high, and there are maintenance costs associated with that. A better way is to make all the platforms the same height, reducing maintenance costs.

The best design for any railway is to have long non-articulated carriages, the longer the better. Some carriages are over 27 metres long, and these are generally more cost effective to operate. Also, wider carriages are also more efficient, but allowing for such a wide and large train will require increased expenditure on wider tunnels and structure gauge. It is possible for a rail system to exchange capital cost, reducing it, but increasing the cost of rollingstock maintenance.

So to properly compare any rail system, it is important to have all the important metrics. Where construction costs were low, it is possible that compromises were made that had the effect of increasing the maintenance cost of rollingstock. In any fair and frank evaluation of a rail system, this needs to be considered.

To calculate the cost for maintaining rollingstock, this is normally calculated per carriage, and per set. The cost of depreciation, quite large for almost all rollingstock, may or may not be included. As it is such a large cost, where it is included, this should be mentioned. The cost is normally calculated in these terms:

$$Cost\ per\ carriage\ kilometre = \frac{total\ yearly\ costs}{total\ carriage\ kilometres}$$

REFERENCES

1. AMTRACK, Office of the Inspector General, *Amtrak's Infrastructure Maintenance Program, Evalution Report E-09-05*, September 2009

2. Union Internationale des Chemins de Fer, *Lasting Infrastructure Cost Benchmarking (LICB), Summary Report December 2006*

3. DG-TREN, *Final Report BOB Railway Case – Benchmarking Passenger Transport in Railways*, Aug 2003

4. Chun-Hwan, K. Transportation Revolution: The Korean High-speed Railway, Japan Railway & Transport Review 40, March 2005

5. Smith, A. et al *The role of international benchmarking in developing rail infrastructure efficiency estimates*, Utilities Policy 18 (2010) 86 - 93

6. Texas Department of Transportation *Austin San Antonio Commuter Rail Study*, 1999

7. Metro de Porto *Annual Report 2011*, http://www.metrodoporto.pt/en/

8. Transport for London *Rail and Underground Annual Benchmarking Report* June 2012

9. Flyvbjerg, B et al *Comparison of Capital Costs per Route-Kilometre in Urban Rail*, European Journal of Transport and Infrastructure Research, Feb 2008

10. Washington Metropolitan Area Transit Authority *2010 Performance Report*, http://www.wmata.com/about_metro/public_rr.cfm

11. Efron N, & Read, N *Analysing International Tunnel Costs*, Worcester Polytechnic Institute, Feb 2012

Chapter 14 Keeping Costs Down

Introduction

Rail transport projects can be very expensive and many countries struggle to find the funds to build rail projects. Money is almost always quite limited, so obviously it's important to keep the costs as low as possible. Whilst a lot has been said on the need to do this, relatively little is said about how to achieve it. Collected in this chapter are the many ways that have been mentioned in various conferences papers, journals, and other documents for keeping costs low. It is not an exhaustive list, but even so there are a lot of potential factors that need to be considered in reducing cost. Included in the references in the back of this book are the papers where cost reduction is discussed, and how it was achieved. One final comment is that, through good management, costs can really be cut substantially, by at least a factor of four, or perhaps even more.

The rail industry is notorious for cost overruns in projects. This seems to be very common, both in Australia and in the UK. There have been papers written on project cost overruns, so common are they. In this chapter, no specific examples are given, but the reader can rest assured than in every case there is a project and a story attached to each example. Many of the simple rules provided below were learnt at substantial pain and expense, but the specifics of the project clearly won't be included as this would be embarrassing to the project or railway involved.

Strategies to Reduce Costs

Building rail and roads at the same time

Building two projects, for different transport modes, at the same time can be a very good way of reducing costs. A rail system can be built down the centre of a highway, and if built at the same time then part of the cost of construction, especially the earthworks, is split between two projects and not one. The earthworks are often one of the biggest costs, and if split between two projects, then the project cost can be split. Another benefit is that a highway is very wide, and if there is room for a rail system then it will be along the ground next to the road. There will be no need for tunnels or even for viaducts. Another benefit, for very large highways, fencing is not needed next to the rail line as there fences for the highway , and the size of the highway are sufficient to keep people out of the rail corridor.

Light rail

Light rail as a system is designed to reduce cost. The ability of light rail vehicles to travel across roads allows for the use of stretches of land that could not be used for metros or commuter trains. Light rail vehicles can even travel for long distances in the middle of roads. A light rail system constructed at grade with roads, such as a tram system, can be very inexpensive, as complicated infrastructure is not needed. Once again, the need for tunnelling is avoided, and this dramatically reduces cost. Light rail has a slower average travel speed than heavy rail, and cannot move as many people, so the lower cost results in a compromise of performance.

Good project management

The quality of the project management is a large determinant of the successful management of any project. Examples abound of poorly managed projects, and the consequences can be quite large where rail projects are managed poorly. Some of the key factors to success of projects include:

- A well defined scope of works, where it is clear what work should be done
- Responsibilities for the project and relevant tasks are clearly defined
- The best possible people are recruited
- Appropriate controls are in place for costs, and the monitoring of activities of the project team
- Staff have sufficient power and control over their respective parts of the project
- Cost estimates are accurate
- Appropriate risk management strategies are in place
- Stakeholders are managed effectively, and kept informed as appropriate
- Changes to the scope of the project are managed appropriately

One of the best ways to ensure projects are managed effectively is to hire the best project managers. Some project managers are very effective, and can complete projects very efficiently, whereas others are not quite as effective.

Another common problem with projects is the initial estimated cost of the project is too low. It is only natural that people want projects to be approved, and sometimes allow themselves to be convinced that projects are less costly than they actually are. In this case the project manager faces an almost impossible task, as the budget for the project is too low, and there is no chance of finishing the project for the price provided. This situation can be very stressful for the project manager and all involved with the project.

Another common problem is that the scope of the project tends to grow over time. As the project progresses, people identify possible changes that generally are beneficial to society or the government, but are expensive. This process is often referred to as "scope creep", and is one of the greatest threats to a project. A good project manager will attempt to provide a clear process for managing scope changes, and seeking additional money when changes are suggested. One of the more important points to managing this process is to clearly define the initial scope of the project, and then changes to the project are clear. People who want changes will often argue that their particular change is already part of the project, and that the additional cost for the change should be born by the project. A good project manager will know what is included or not in the original scope of the project.

Reserving land before the rail line is constructed

The cost of tunnelling is very high, and avoiding tunnelling is an important way to reduce costs. If a city or region has planned effectively, and if a rail project needs additional land, then buying this land and then demolishing the buildings can be very expensive, or politically impossible. Tunnelling is approx five times more expensive per kilometre than building rail lines above ground, so there is a strong incentive to build rail lines above ground. The maintenance costs of an underground rail line can also be very high.

Where land has been reserved, then this can have a powerful effect on the costs of rail projects. This method of reducing costs is one of the most effective of all the strategies mentioned in this book. There is little that can be done once land is given away, and/or something is built on it.

Gold plating

Gold plating is a term commonly used in Australia to describe over-engineering assets, to a level which is beyond what is needed. It is important and cost effective for any project to have the minimum level of assets required to complete the project. Engineers often want the best possible assets, which usually means the most expensive equipment, and lots of it. This type of attitude can quickly make the project very expensive, and costs can quickly get out of control. The electrical power system, or fire equipment in tunnels are often like this, and can be over designed.

Another problem can be specifying too many assets. This problem occasionally arises with rail systems, as most rail engineering systems cannot be duplicated. Communications and power systems can be duplicated, and again care must be taken that designers do not to "get carried away" and build one or more additional systems that aren't needed. A good level of system analysis is important here, and effectively determining the appropriate level of assets is quite important.

Using established technology

Engineers are often tempted to customise or modify existing designs, and create custom solutions. This provides the opportunity for them to fully exercise their design skills, and this can be very exciting and professionally rewarding. The use of standard designs or existing technology is a powerful and effective way of reducing costs. This is particularly the case for rollingstock, where the major rail companies have attempted to standardise on standard train designs to reduce cost.

A custom design requires substantial design and engineering resources to create. Designers need to draw up new designs, cost them, seek approval for their use, and then build them. Once constructed testing will be required, and further changes needed to improve upon the initial design. Depending on the country where the designs will be used, different testing regimes are needed. An equipment item that may impact upon passenger safety may need extensive testing before being allowed to be used. All of these steps need to be completed, and take time. They are also not cheap, and the cost of any new design can be very high.

One of the arguments put forward for creating new designs is that the railway will then be able to sell the design to someone else. This is difficult to do in practice, and most railways are not in the business of selling technology. How would this contract be managed, who in the railway has the experience in commercialising intellectual property? Railways are not really the right business to do this, but it is possible for a railway to commercialise a design, but it's difficult.

Using a custom or non-standard design is a decision that should not be taken lightly. There are some situations where a non-standard design is needed, and this should be identified. This is particularly so where the railway has some special or unusual needs that most other rail businesses do not have. Regardless no one single railway will need several custom designed systems, at most one or two are needed.

As a rough guide, non-standard engineering systems can cost anywhere from double to six times the price of an off-the-shelf system. For large engineering purchases and projects, this increase in cost can be very large.

Using standard technology often is not as convenient as designing new equipment. Standard equipment can often be difficult to use in many situations, and any deviation from the environment in which it was designed may be difficult to accommodate. One of the challenges of any project management, and of the construction of a new rail project, is to assess how useful a standard design is, and it is can be used successfully. Minor changes can often be accommodated, but large scale changes are mostly impossibly expensive. There may be substantial resistance from any existing operational railway from accepting standard technology, and many argument may be put forward as to why the technology cannot be used. Again, a detailed understanding of the workings of the technology is needed to make of proper assessment of these claims.

Using standard designs

Off the shelf equipment items can be assembled into larger systems. For example, stations are composed of many constituent parts, and many or all of these should be standard. The combination of these standard off the shelf items is itself a design, and this needs to be considered and thought through.

Standard designs should be capable of being modified to be used in a variety of different situations. A non-standard design is one that can only be used in one specific instance, and a rail system made up of non-standard designs will be an expensive one. A standard design avoids the need to design the same item over and over again. Standard designs are common for stations, and many railways will have standard designs for stations. Other engineering disciplines also have standard designs, and overall in the rail industry these are common. One of the key benefits of a standard design is that much of the risk assessment, and safety modelling has been considered and accounted for.

Underground stations need to be modelled for what happens with a fire, and each simulation or modelling exercise can be very expensive. Using a standard design, which can allow for small changes in the design, means that the modelling needs only to be done once. Modelling is also often done for passenger flows, to get people in and out of the station quickly. Once again, a standard design should ensure that this modelling only needs to be performed once.

A standard design can be created afresh, and many large existing rail systems have these. Standard designs are available for many different types of rail technology, but it is also possible to develop a new standard design that no one else uses. Acquiring a standard design from another railway can be an effective way of reducing costs, if one can be obtained. The development of a standard design can be a very effective way to reduce costs, and much thought should go into what that design contains. Some countries are better than others in the quality of their standard design.

Managing consultants

Consultants are a very common thing in the rail industry. Most industrialised countries have a large pool of consultants who can provide advice on a diverse range of rail related topics, and wider non-rail related topics. On some topics consultants have a lot of knowledge, and can be very helpful, and in others they have limited experience. Certainly in Australia rail employees often view consultants negatively.

Consultants can assist with rail projects in providing design and project management resources where the local railway is lacking in those skills. This can be very helpful, where managed effectively. One needs to remember that consultants have a high hourly rate, and the resources required to maintain the skill set of a group of people in one particular area can be high, so they charge a lot of money. Consultants need to keep a steady flow of work coming in, otherwise they could be out of work. What can happen on a major project is that too much control over the project specification is given to consultants, who then are tempted to increase their part of the project. A cynic might say that they are serving their own interests in increasing the scope of the project, but a more charitable view is that they want to do the best possible job in their area, and naturally over specify the design because they want to do the best possible job. Either way, small parts of projects can swell very quickly, and grow to have a budget 10 times or even more compared to the original budget. This challenging situation needs to be carefully managed, and needs to be detected before the project budget grows too large.

Perhaps the best way to manage consultants is to provide clear boundaries of the scope of the task, and to know ahead of time how much this task will cost and what is required. Value engineering can be a useful tool here, and this part of engineering is concerned with valuing the function of things, and estimating how much things should cost. Regardless of if value engineering is used or not, simply giving consultants "carte blanche" is an efficient way to spend money. Project managers should know ahead of time how much things cost and what the project gets for its money.

Tunnel design

Tunnel design can dramatically shape the cost of an underground tunnelled project. The key to reducing the cost of any tunnel construction is to minimise the excavated volume, to make it as low as possible. Tunnel design is a specialist area, but in general avoiding the use of tunnels, or keeping the cross-sectional area as low as possible are the keys to success.

Managing or preventing corruption

Corruption is a problem that exists in certain countries, especially in the third world. Some countries are better than others, but some countries almost nothing can be built or government approval received without engaging in some form of corruption. In the Asia Pacific region, Australia, New Zealand and Singapore are almost corruption free. China, India and Indonesia have a lot of corruption, and getting projects finished can be near impossible. The payment of government officials for approvals can make any project expensive. In addition, many first world countries have criminalised the payment of brides to officials in third world countries, and company officials that engage in the practice in the employment of a country based in a first world country can risk being jailed at home.

Providing advice on managing corruption is beyond the scope of this book. It's a really tough area, so good luck!

Managing legacy systems

Older rail systems may have legacy systems installed. These are often signalling systems, such as old ATP systems, or can be something else, such as a communications system. These old systems were often designed long ago, and are often unique. Changes to this type of system can be extremely difficult, as the people who knew the underlying design principles behind its construction are long since dead from old age. Extensions or changes to this system may require the project team to relearn how the design works, which can be a time consuming and painstaking process. There may be many details that a design team will not understand, and need to rediscover.

Modifications to an existing legacy system can make rail projects prohibitively expensive. Often the only sensible choice is to avoid modifying the older system entirely, and building a new system side by side with the older. This situation requires very careful and high quality management to resolve, and the input of the older more experienced technical staff can be invaluable in finding cost effective ways to make changes to these system. Sometimes the entire system will need to be replaced, and changes are simply impossible.

Managing Heritage Buildings and Installations

In many countries older buildings have legal protection from being altered or demolished. In Australia this is quite common, although many of the buildings are relatively new in comparison to other countries, and would not be considered to be old enough to be preserved in Europe. Alternations to heritage buildings are costly, and can often only be done with original materials using the same craftsmanship as was originally used when the building was first constructed.

Managing heritage buildings is very difficult. The cost associated with making changes to maintaining the building can be very high, and heritage buildings are often left empty because they are too expensive to maintain. Sydney is full of old heritage buildings that now cannot be used. In some cases these buildings can be converted to a use that does not compromise the structure and history of the building, and shops sometimes operate from these buildings.

In most cases avoiding heritage buildings altogether is probably the best strategy for any rail project. Where this is not possible, then some clever thinking may be able to identify a use for the building that is not inconsistent with the history of the building. This is particularly the case with old railway stations, which may be usable in their existing form when care is taken with any new designs using the existing buildings.

In some rare cases it may be possible to demolish the heritage building, but retain parts of the building for historical reasons. There are a small number of such cases in Sydney of building where the inside was demolished, but the outer skin of the building retained. This kind of solution is at best a poor solution, but for the exasperated rail project manager may be the only solution.

A particular problem exists with heritage stations. Many of these are still in use today, and the design standards of today are quite different to those of 100 years ago. Stations built from those times had funny access points, and structures and columns in funny places. Passengers cannot move as easily in older stations, and they do not conform to fire and safety standards.

Once changes are made to an old station, especially one that is heritage listed, then there will be pressure to convert the station to have modern fire and life safety equipment. Remember that old stations need heritage materials, so the combination of the two changes can get enormously ridiculously expensive. Changing a heritage station is something that should be done with enormous care, as costs can quickly get out of control. Again, perhaps the best way to manage the situation is to avoid any changes to heritage stations at all, and leave them as they are, if possible.

Digging deep rail tunnels

Deep rail tunnels are very expensive. Cut and cover is a construction system that is significantly cheaper than blasting or tunnelling, and should be used wherever possible. The deeper a tunnel is, the less likely that cut and cover will be feasible as a construction system. The problem with cut and cover is that the sides of the trench can be unstable, and need to be reinforced if the cut and cover trench is too deep. The use of cut and cover will also depend on the stability of the ground, or how much it moves when the trench is dug.

Tunnels deep underground will need to be tunnelled, possibly with something called a tunnel boring machine (TBM). The cost of tunnelling using this system does not change significantly depending on the depth of tunnelling, assuming that there are no other problems with groundwater. The cost of building stations however changes substantially. Deeper stations require more excavated space, as the distance between the platforms and surface becomes greater. Building stations more than 70 metres underground is the current limit of what is considered reasonable.

Very deep stations will require much more infrastructure to allow passengers to get to the surface. This will include escalators and lifts, which for a deep station are much more expensive and difficult to install. The ventilation systems will need to be much more advanced, as air will need to be transported deep underground, for a large open space. Substations supplying the power will also be larger. In short, building a deep underground station is highly inadvisable, unless there is simply no other alternative.

Tunnels beneath the waterline (and building on floodplains)

Tunnels can be built lower than sea level or below the water table. This is unusual, but sometimes happens, especially when building metros in cities next to the ocean, or for rail lines that go under the ocean, such as the cross channel tunnel. Water seeps in to the tunnel, and it needs to be removed, otherwise the tunnel will flood. Tunnelling in ground underwater is an expensive business, and a commonly used strategy is to pressurize the tunnel with air so that no water can seep into the tunnel.

Pressurisation of a tunnel requires airlocks to maintain the pressure. Workers inside the pressurised area have the same problems as deep sea divers, and can get the "bends" if they move too quickly from the pressurised area to normal pressure air. Again, as with deep stations and tunnels, tunnelling below sea level or below the water table is something that should only be done if there is absolutely no alternative.

Sometimes it is desirable to build a railway line underground in an area that routinely floods. In this case provision must be made to ensure that when a flood occurs that water can be prevented from entering the tunnels, or pumped out fast enough to remove it. Again this involves additional cost, and it is preferable to not build underground in a place that can be flooded so easily. This was one of the factors that led to the government in Bangkok to build an elevated system rather than a metro system, as Bangkok does from time to time have large floods.

Archaeology and artefacts

Building metros in very old cities can result in the discovery of numerous artefacts and objects of tremendous historical significance. Whilst this is normally not a problem in Asia, either because most of the cities are new, or because generally less importance is placed on these types of discoveries, but in very old cities in the Middle East and Europe this can present a great problem. Once tunnelling begins many discoveries can be made, and particularly important find may result in tunnelling stopping altogether. The Marmaray rail project in Istanbul is a very interesting example of how significant this problem can become. During tunnelling the Harbour of

Eleutherios was rediscovered, including several galleys in relatively good condition. This substantially delayed the project and very substantially added to the cost of the project.

Transport planners will not know that there are artefacts there until the tunnel is actually being dug. As such it is a bit difficult to plan for their presence, and even more difficult to manage. One possible strategy is to convert part of a station located in a area of high historical value into a museum, and turn a problem into a well-liked feature of the station.

Performance based specifications

There are essentially two ways of specifying a contract; with detailed specific requirements, or specifying the needs or overall goals of the project, and allowing the contractor more authority to achieve the goals of the project rather than detailed requirements. It seems that it is generally agreed that performance based requirements are better, as these allow the contractor more scope to achieve what the project needs. In practice it's not that clear, as there are benefits to clear specifications to contractors building infrastructure.

Each project will have a specification or group of specifications that describe what is required. A project specification may be created before or after approval of the project, but before is generally better. The specification is a detailed listing of the engineering and performance requirements of the project. The development of a specification for any rail project can be a significant cost.

A common mistake in writing a project specification is to over specify the requirements. For example, if a train needs to move 2500 people standing up, and 200 seated, and have 5 doors, then providing detailed specifications on the positioning of windows, doors, and seats might add little value. Whilst it might seem sensible to specify the size of seats, specifying a non standard size, or something that can't be easily accommodated, means the entire train will need to be redesigned. The purpose of the specification is to obtain a train, not have a seat 377.3 mm wide or other very particular size, and this needs to be remembered. Specifications should be converted into a form where the final function of the system is required, and not specific dimensions, except where necessary.

Furthermore, specifying a function provides the opportunity for innovation. Generating a clear description of the need of a design, and fewer details, can allow competent designers the scope to produce truly innovative and creative designs, that are effective and low cost. Innovation needs to be encouraged, and over specifying projects can kill any chance of innovation.

The two areas where clearly performance based specifications are better and more cost efficient are the construction of rollingstock and the digging of tunnels. In both of these areas there are large specialised companies who have substantial experience in the construction of equipment or infrastructure. Rollingstock companies, such as Bombardier, have a wealth of experience in designing trains, and almost definitely know more about it than a small metro with a couple of lines. Providing them with excessively detailed requirements for new rollingstock will only add to the cost, when they are perfectly capable of building the rollingstock required to a performance specification.

The same applies for tunnelling. Tunnelling is a specialised area, with engineers spending entire careers building one tunnel after another. Tunnelling is dangerous, and tunnel collapses can kill construction workers. A railway or government planning department is unlikely to know as much about tunnelling as a specialised company, and providing clear goals to the design company will allow them to select the best possible design, which will probably be something that the railway or planning department would not be able to think of or design.

Alternatively, for many other parts of a railway line, providing clear specifications can help the project be built quicker. Allowing a project too much flexibility will result in project managers needing to research different options, and that will add cost and time to the project. Clear specifications can be invaluable in setting the right goals for a construction company, especially if the task is not particularly complex or technically difficult, such as building a station.

Care of course must always be exercised in not over specifying things that are not needed, or providing too much detail. To provide a silly example, a railway should not specify the metallurgy of handrails for passengers, or the crystalline structure of the metal used in the handrails, it is too much detail, and it is enough to provide a material that meets a standard on materials for station design. It is important in writing contracts that the right level of detail is provided, not too much, and not too little.

Geotechnical problems

Geotechnical problems are mostly relevant to rail projects that require tunnels. Good quality rocks around tunnels can make tunnelling a lot easier. It is preferable to tunnel through high quality rock, to reduce construction time and reduce cost.

The geology of the ground varies widely from area to area. There are many different types of rocks, and tunnelling can be made either easier or harder by the quality of the rocks through which the tunnels travel. Good quality rocks and soil is dry, hard, but not too hard, and maintains its shape once tunnelled. Poor quality geology can include sand, full of seawater, which moves around during tunnelling, and does not maintain any shape at all. The cost of tunnelling can be changed dramatically based on the quality of the geology.

Part of any tunnelling project is to determine the quality of the rocks through which tunnels will go. Unfortunately, it is not possible to fully survey all the rocks where the tunnel will be as it's underground and difficult to access. It is important to drill test bores to determine, as best as can be done, the quality of the geology where a tunnel might be.

Areas of very poor soil and rock condition should be avoided. These are often places which are full of water and the rocks there are unstable and do not maintain any type of shape.

Concrete viaducts

A viaduct is an elevated pathway for the train to travel. It can also be a series of small bridges or arches, providing a continuous running surface for trains. Viaducts are very common in some parts of the world, and are used extensively in the Bangkok Skytrain as well as the metro in Singapore.

Crowded cities often have no room for additional railways at ground level. The choice is to either build underground in a tunnel, or to build a viaduct above the city. Either option is acceptable, but generally tunnelling is preferred over building elevated railways. Elevated railways are often considered to be visually intrusive, and ugly, and tunnelling is much preferred. Elevated railways cost approx. one fifth of the cost of tunnelled track per kilometre. Elevated railways represent a good compromise between cost and utility of the rail system.

Elevated railways are also used for high speed rail lines. The problem with running high speed rail systems along the ground is that if any animals or people are hit by the train then there is a potential for a derailment. Whilst in Europe and in Japan there are very few animals, in places like Australia there are large animals everywhere, which can even derail trains moving at much lower speeds than 200 kms/hr. In this case an elevated railway is not one of many choices, but the only possible choice.

Contract management

Professional contract management is one very important part of success of any project. Contract provisions need to identify all important requirements of a project, identify clearly who is responsible for what, and provide clear statements on what needs to be delivered. Vague specifications, which sadly seem to be common, allow many different possible interpretations, and a construction company may build one thing and the government building the rail system thinks that they are getting something different. Once a contract is signed, changes can only be made with the payment of the appropriate compensation, and if the provisions of the contract are vague, there may be a lot of changes.

Changing the scope of a contract is called a variation, although other names are also used. The management of variations, and the payments required for them, is a critical part of contract management. Many construction companies take the view that every possible variation will be claimed for, and ask for exorbitant amounts of money for each one. One of the most important roles for contract managers to make sure this process does not get out of control, and preventing the government paying far more than what was originally promised. Messy and poorly written contracts can be a spectacular failure.

REFERENCES

1. Clendon, J. & Skilton, J. *Axle Counters – The New Zealand Experience*, The Institution of Railway Signal Engineers Inc Australasian Section Incorporated, March 2010

2. Zhang, C. & Li, L. Zhang, D. & Zhang, S. *Types and Characteristics of Safety Accidents Induced by Metro Construction*, 2009 International Conference on Information Management, Innovation Management and Industrial Engineering, 209

3. Kemp, R. *T618 – Traction Energy Metrics*, Rail Safety and Standards Board, Interfleet Technology, Dec 2007

4. Taipei Rapid Transit Corporation *2013 Annual Report*, http://english.metro.taipei/ct.asp?xItem=1056448&ctNode=70219&mp=122036

5. Zoeteman, A. *Life cycle cost analysis for managing rail infrastructure*, European Journal of Infrastructure and Transport Research, EJTIR, 1, no. 4, (2001), pp 391 - 413

6. Smith, A. et al *The role of international benchmarking in developing rail infrastructure efficiency estimates*, Utilities Policy 18 (2010) 86 - 93

7. Lu I.F. *Construction Project Management and Insurance Program for Taiwan High Speed Rail Project* Leadership and Management in Engineering Jan 2011

8. Flyvbjerg, B et al *Comparison of Capital Costs per Route-Kilometre in Urban Rail*, European Journal of Transport and Infrastructure Research, Feb 2008

9. Victorian Auditor General *Maintaining Victoria's Rail Infrastructure Assets*, May 2007

10. Efron N, & Read, N *Analysing International Tunnel Costs*, Worcester Polytechnic Institute, Feb 2012

11. Wagner, H. *The Governance of Cost in Tunnel Design and Construction*, 1 Congresso Brasilero de Tuneis e Estruturas Subterraneas Seminario Internacional South American Tunnelling

12. Andersson, M. *Marginal cost of railway infrastructure wear and tear for freight and passenger trains in Sweden*, European Transport no 48, (2011): 3 – 23

Index

Articulation, 13
at grade. *See* Grade separation
Automatic Train Operation, 232
Automatic Train Protection, 232
Ballast, 57, 58
    Fines, 62
Balloon loop, 226
Bangkok Skytrain, 27
bi-level. *See* Double decker
Boardings, 2
Broad gauge, 7
Bus Rapid Transit, 3
Cape gauge, 7
Capping layer, 58
Codeshare, 41
Commuter rail, 34
Concourse, 133
Contact band. *See* wear band
Control system, 92
Crossover, 107
Cut and cover, 288
Diamond crossover, 107, 227
Diesel multiple units, 40
Dispatcher. *See* Signaller
Dive, 224
Double decker, 14
Double slip, 108
Dwell time, 30, 34, 202
Dynamic gauging, 152
Electric multiple units, 39
Flying junction, 13
Flyover, 224
Formation, 58
Freight corridors, 237
Freight terminal, 234
Grade separation, 12, 184
Halts, 5
Heavy haul, 12
Horse crossing, 92
In-cab signalling, 67
Interchange stations, 129
Kinematic envelope, 151
Light metro, 26
Loading factor, 265
Loading gauge, 151, 230
Loop, 178
Maintenance centres, 213
Metro, 29
    Rubber tyred, 57
Mixed system, 6
Movement authority, 67
Moving walk, 130
Narrow gauge, 7
On-time-running, 265
Overhead wiring, 76
Pantograph, 7
Pantograph well, 156
Parallel moves, 222
Passenger information systems, 36
Passing loops, 236
Pedestrian crossing, 91
Pendulum line, 181
People per hour, 267
Platform length, 118
Platform screen doors, 131
Portal, 82
Pumping station, 224
Quadruplication, 239
Rail
    Tram, 61
Rail cruise, 46
Regional rail, 38
Ring network, 195
Rollingstock
    Pantograph, 76
Route length, 3
Running direction, 104
Russian gauge, 7
Shuttle, 100, 187

Signaller, 69
Signalling
　Route signalling, 70
　Speed signalling, 69
Single slip, 107
Sleeper carriage, 46
Sleepers, 58
Smart cards, 137
Stabling, 3, 213
Standard gauge, 7
Station
　Interchange, 118
Stations
　Concourse, 140
　Halt, 122
　Island platform, 121
　Paid area, 133
　Side platform, 120
　Spanish solution, 134
　Vending machine, 121
Stopping pattern, 36
structure gauge, 151
Structure gauge, 151
Terminus, 118, 176

Tickets
　Proof of payment, 137
Track
　Dual gauge, 65
Track length, 3
Traction power, 75
　AC, 7
　DC, 7
　Third rail, 76
Trams
　Powerhouse, 6
Tram-train system, 13
Transport Orientated
　Development, 255
Tunnels
　Ventilation, 84
Turnback, 177
Turntables, 216
Unit train, 226
Unit trains, 179
Unwired. *See* Traction Power
Viaduct, 292
Wayfinding, 136
Wear band, 59

www.ingramcontent.com/pod-product-compliance
Lightning Source LLC
Chambersburg PA
CBHW071859290426
44110CB00013B/1204